500

OF
STI
YOU

4/

500

OF THE MOST IMPORTANT STRESS-BUSTING TIPS YOU'LL EVER NEED

BANISH STRESS FOREVER AND GET A LIFE THAT WORKS

SUZANNAH OLIVIER

CICO BOOKS

London

First published in Great Britain by
Cico Books
32 Great Sutton Street
London EC1V 0NB
(020) 7253 7960

10 9 8 7 6 5 4 3 2 1

A CIP catalogue record for this book is available from the British Library

ISBN 1 903116 48 1

Designed by Paul Wood

Printed and bound by
Creative Print and Design, Wales

PUBLISHER'S NOTE
Always consult a doctor before undertaking any of the advice, exercise plans or supplements suggested in this book. While every attempt has been made to ensure the medical information in this book is entirely safe and up to date at the time of publication, the Publishers accept no responsibility for consequences of the advice given herein. If any doubt as to the nature of your condition, consult a qualified medical practitioner.

While every attempt has been made to ensure the information in this book is entirely correct and up to date at the time of publication, the publishers accept no responsibility for changes in prices, stockist arrangements and locations.

Suzannah Olivier MSc., Dip ION is a lecturer, author and nutritionist. She writes regularly for *The Times* and national magazines, appears on television and radio, and runs workshops on stress management and nutrition. Her previous books include *What Should I Feed My Baby* (Weidenfeld & Nicolson), *The Breast Cancer Prevention and Recovery Diet* (Penguin), *The Detox Manual*, *Banish Bloating*, *Allergy Solutions*, *Maximising Energy*, *Natural Hormone Balance*, *Eating for a Perfect Pregnancy* (all published by Simon & Schuster) and *The Stress Protection Plan* (Collins & Brown).

CONTENTS

INTRODUCTION

This book is intended to be a really practical tool. It is crammed full of ideas and inspirations for each reader to take and mould to their own needs. When we find ourselves in stressful situations, it is usually not the case that a fairy godmother will come along and wave a magic wand – even though we might dream of this. But we can make our own magic with strategies to find realistic solutions.

Simplified decision making and small daily actions can build up in effect enabling you to achieve big changes in your life, redefining the quality of your relationships, both at home and work as well as your health, emotions, and finances.

Ours is a unique moment in history which, on the one hand, offers us endless opportunities while simultaneously overloading us with too much to do. The only way to win respite is to seek it for ourselves. We need inner resources, life management skills, physical health and emotional balance to benefit from the opportunities we are offered and to get the best from our individual world – without paying the toll of tiredness, anxiety and self-esteem problems and other stresses that life can impose on us – if we allow it.

When we leave formal education, we are armed with certain skills and, possibly, the certificates to prove that we have achieved those skills. But there are no courses or qualifications for a well-rounded person, who can deal with the vagaries of life and who will not feel like they want to implode every time they get themselves into a difficult situation or are overwhelmed with too much to do in life. Instead we are left to find out how to manage the stresses of our world as we go along.

However, stress is not inherently bad and there is such a thing as positive stress. The short-term effects of stress help us to strive and achieve our goals by enhancing creativity. We can use positive stress to propel ourselves forwards without letting the negative effects of stress wear us down.

Sometimes it is tempting to think, 'If only I was slim, had a million in the bank, lived in a better neighbourhood, had an understanding partner, didn't have to do everything for everyone else, all my problems would be solved and I wouldn't feel so stressed'. At other times we might think, 'I couldn't possibly do that!', 'I'm not interesting enough', 'What if it goes wrong?' This book is all about giving you the resources to stop repeating such mantras to yourself and to help you find the tools you need to reach your goal of de-stressing and balancing your life. Use this book as a guide to accessing your innate wisdom to find your own solutions from within.

In many ways, this book is a highly personal one for me. As I re-read the tips and techniques compiled here I realize that I have personally used the majority of them myself – through illness, house moving, job changes, divorce, retraining, self-esteem and mood problems. By studying and researching these methods throughout my life I have absorbed these principles into my very being, and learned and grown stronger from them. I am thrilled to be able to share them with you.

HOW TO USE THIS BOOK

YOUR ROUTE MAP

This book is divided into five main categories – Home, Work and Money, Health, Emotions and Relationships. Within each category, the various subdivisions are listed alphabetically. You will immediately know which ones are important for you when you glance at the contents listing, and some of the headings will instantly strike a chord.

You may find that only two or three sections from each main category apply to you, in which case you will be able to focus on those issues in a pretty straightforward way. However, if you find that all the topics which are of interest are grouped under one category, say Health or Home, then this is a pretty strong hint that this is where you need to concentrate your mental resources. If one area of your life is the focus of your stress, say Work and Money, you may find that other areas of you life, say Health or Relationships, suffer as a result.

We feel at our best when all the elements of our lives are working harmoniously. Achieving a balance between work and home, money and relationships and health and emotions is a valuable goal. We all know someone, either personally or in public life, who seems to give 101 per cent to one area of their life at the expense of another, and who might appear to thrive on this formula, but for the majority of us this will almost inevitably lead to meltdown in the areas to which we are not paying sufficient attention.

Watch out for moments of multiple or 'compound' stress. You know that if you are getting married, while expecting a baby, moving house because you need more space and experiencing a change in your finances because of your expanding family – all at the same time – that you are going to be feeling a range of stressful effects.

If you find that you are looking at the contents list and that many of them seem pertinent to you, you may be tempted just to shut the book and have a stiff drink. But do not feel overwhelmed by this (or read the section Overwhelmed? on page 162!). Choose the subject that speaks to you most strongly. You will find that if you start on Order out of Chaos (page 29), for example, you may not need to look up the sections on Arguing and Bickering (page 11) or Planning and Prioritizing (page 34).

If you find the individual tips helpful and would like to know more, you can dig deeper by turning to the Appendices starting on page 219. These explore, in more depth, some of the techniques that have helped many thousands of people before you and which you too can use to change your life.

It is a good idea to buy a spiral-bound notebook, and keep it readily available, so that you can make immediate use of any tips or exercises. When you read about an exercise – do it! Put the book down and work through your thoughts and solutions. This stops the advice in this book being theoretical and turns it into a practical tool.

Don't be tempted to do everything all in one go. You know that making resolutions to turn your whole life around overnight rarely work. Making small and consistent changes to your attitudes, routines and diet, creating new habits based on solid foundations, is the way forward. Each tip takes no longer than three minutes to read. Tackle them systematically, one bullet point at a time, get each one more or less right, and then move on to the next one. This way you will be able to focus on practical issues no matter how stressed you feel. And by rewarding yourself with small successes and victories, which accumulate one after another, you begin to feel in control, less stressed and really good about yourself and your life.

CHAPTER 1

HOME

Home is where the heart is – or at least it should be. If your heart sinks as you walk in the door because it is not the cocooning nest you think it ought to be or if you find yourself going out more than you want to – then it is time to do something about it.

The daily routine of your home life and the people who live with you all affect your stress levels. If everything is running smoothly then it frees up mental and physical energy for other, more pressing, aspects of your life – like enjoying yourself! Conversely even minor mishaps at home, such as a child's messy room or a lost bill, can build up stress, which then impacts on work life, relationships and even health. Turning your home into a pleasing refuge and a safe emotional haven will only enhance your life.

ARGUING AND BICKERING

While arguments can act as a safety valve, if handled carelessly they can create an atmosphere in a home which is counterproductive. There are different styles of arguing that develop between two people. Some will niggle and bicker all the time, while others build up resentments until they have major blow-outs that come infrequently but with huge ferocity. Understanding how you argue with someone with whom you live helps to shorten their impact on daily life. The reason that this item is listed under the Home section is because we rarely argue and bicker in quite the same way at our work place. At work we have a different, often hierarchical, set-up and we tend to be more reserved about letting loose with our true thoughts. Frustrations at work are usually dealt with in a different way (see Office Politics page 57).

Top Tips

■ Minor frictions and tensions build up if not dealt with. A great sense of relief can be achieved just by admitting there is a problem.

■ Disagreements are not the same thing as arguing. It is perfectly normal to disagree with someone, but it is how you deal with those disagreements that makes the difference. Aim for a constructive outcome by listening to the other person, talking things through and making an action plan together by, if necessary, systematically writing down the pros and cons of the situation and of the various solutions. If the solution is a division of labour refer to Delegating on page 35.

- Listen – really listen – to the other person. Not just to what they are saying, but how they are saying it. If your complaint is that the other person does not listen to you, the first step to remedy this is for you to listen to them. If they are still not really listening then maybe work needs to be done on Communication Skills (see page 181).

- Get things into perspective. Other people's habits and niggles are just that, they might wear you down, but they ought not. Adjust your thinking to 'This is irritating' rather than 'This is driving me crazy'. If you think it is driving you crazy, it will do precisely that and you will pay the price in terms of stress. Anyone who has had a major trauma such as illness or a car accident will inevitably say that it has taught them one thing – that the things we worry about on a daily basis are, in the general scheme of things, not worth the energy and adrenaline we put into them.

- Beware of using arguing to undermine the other person's confidence – and don't let it happen to you. If you find you are getting nasty and going for the jugular, this is a bad habit. Remember to make arguing constructive. If one of your family spills something, avoid saying 'You are stupid' or 'You are clumsy'. Take your comments out of the personal and offer solutions. Instead say 'That was a clumsy thing to do, next time use a tray'.

- Laughter solves rows. Find a common line of humour without belittling the situation – make sure you are laughing with the other person rather than at them.

More Hints

- If there is a pattern of bickering at home, aim to decipher it. Are you bickering with your kids, parents, partner, flatmate? Identify the flashpoints: the washing up, muddy boots in the hall, bedtime routine, money. By understanding the patterns, you can do something about them.

- Never go to bed, or say goodbye to someone for the day, with bad feelings. Make it a priority to make it up first, or at least make a 'date' to talk things through.

- Avoid interrupting the other person or finishing their sentences for them. Let them have their say and then hopefully you can have yours.

- Some people avoid letting their children hear them argue at all costs in the belief that this makes them feel vulnerable. It certainly can do if the arguing is destructive. However, if children see that arguing is not destructive, that it is a way of resolving disagreements, that a constructive way forward comes out of it and that everyone kisses and makes up afterwards, then they can learn to argue, or more appropriately to have disagreements, in a constructive way. This is a skill they will take with them into adult life.

- Remember to say sorry to kids after a row with them, as you would with an adult. Often adults will not think about doing this, but this is the training ground for adults of tomorrow and if they learn that saying sorry is OK then they will be better for it.

■ Avoid mind-reading. Because he says 'I don't want to go out tonight', he is not necessarily saying 'I don't like you any more' and if she is saying 'You are not pulling your weight around here', she is not really saying 'You are always lazy'.

Holistic Help

■ If you have had a row – do something thoughtful if you have not had time to make it up. A nice e-mail, a bunch of flowers, a cinema ticket are all ways to say 'I care'.

■ **Bach Flower Remedies** for people who find themselves arguing all the time include: *Chicory* if you enjoy arguments and are domineering and fussy; *Impatiens* if you are impatient, irritable and find fault with others; *Vervain* if you enjoy argument and debate and are strong willed; and *Vine* if you are dictatorial, strong willed and lack sympathy for others.

■ Meditate and the answer to a particular disagreement can appear with surprising ease (see Meditation on page 224).

DIARIES, LISTS AND FILING

We all have diaries, make lists and have a filing system but if yours are not effective and do not work for you then you might just as well not have them. Time spent systemizing these will be time well spent.

Top Tips

■ You will probably have your favourite type of diary, but consider the following. The most efficient is probably one with a week at a glance on one side to list appointments and essential deadlines. The page facing is a blank page, for important memory jogs for that week and to-do lists. As each item is completed, get into the habit of crossing it off and you can easily see which items then need to be carried over to the next week.

■ Avoid loose bits of paper cluttering up your life – if it is an important thing to do – put it in your diary. Alternatively, have a spiral-bound ideas note pad always to hand and keep a running log of ideas, lists and collected phone numbers. Pull out the sheets as you deal with the tasks and they become redundant.

■ Back up your computer discs. Back up your computer discs. Back up your computer discs. I cannot say this enough.

More Hints

■ Keep just one diary for personal and work appointments otherwise there is a risk that you will forget to look at one.

■ Keep an extra copy of all important documents, including your address book, in case of loss.

- Bulging folders of redundant papers clog up a filing system and make it unworkable. For instance, clip your bank statements together by year, or by tax year. Weed out guarantees for long-discarded equipment, and bring your children's health records up to date with a master list attached to all important documents such as vaccinations or prescriptions. If sorting out your filing system seems too horrendous to contemplate, just do one folder each day, three or four times a week, until you are through it. This can become quite a satisfying task to work on. Have one large filing cabinet for historic stuff that you can't throw out (such as old tax forms and receipts) and one that is current, for things like bank statements.

- If you are one of the growing army of freelance or self-employed people working from home, keep your work and personal files separate. Keep a dozen clear wallets, labelled January to December (or April to March) into which you put your receipts for each month. These can then easily be entered into a ledger or computer spreadsheet, or passed on to your accountant.

Holistic Help

- Attractive filing boxes and diaries always help to make the job more pleasant.
- If you have trouble getting down to the nitty gritty of getting your paperwork organized, spend some time visualizing what you are going to do and how you are going to do it (how you will order it, what you will keep, what you will throw out). After this, doing the job itself is almost academic and it becomes easy to complete the task.

DOWNSIZING YOUR HOME

There are many reasons why you might need to move to a smaller home. It could be because you are relocating for work or school purposes and properties cost more in the area you are moving to meaning you can afford less space. You might be separating from your partner. You might feel that your home is too big for you and you want to simplify your life. You could be retiring or have left your job. Once the decision has been made to downsize, you need strategies to avoid feeling overwhelmed by the practicalities. If you are moving for unhappy reasons, the stress is likely to be greater.

This section focuses on downsizing homes but if you are reducing other areas of your life, you could look at other sections such as Budgeting (page 53), Unemployment (page 68) and Spend, Spend, Spend (page 55).

Top Tips

- If you are upset at the idea of giving up all that you perceive you value, focus on the idea that sometimes in life we have to take a step back to take two steps forward. I would like to offer a personal anecdote. I could not afford to keep my house after serious illness and divorce and moved to a much smaller property in a much cheaper area so that I could manage to go back to studying. The studying led to a successful new career. I now find myself, only a few years later, way ahead of where I was originally (in terms of happiness and home). Nobody has a crystal ball, but if you stay positive about the move you can probably make more out of it than if you feel badly about it all the time.

- Look forwards, not backwards. The trick is to not hanker for what might have been, but to say to yourself 'Next!' That one little word can change your whole attitude to life.

- A newly coined term, the Boomerang Generation, refers to adults who return to live with their parents after many years. The most frequent cause is divorce accompanied by financial problems. A recent census found that 17 per cent of people over the age of 65 had an adult son or daughter move back in with them. The only way to deal with this situation is to recognize sources of potential strain and to discuss them, hopefully planning for the change in advance.

These are the most likely sources of stress: one parent may suggest that an adult child move back in but the other parent may not be equally welcoming, especially if they see this time as time for themselves. It may be a burden on parental finances. The returnee may expect more in the way of 'services' such as meals and laundry than the parents are willing to provide. The adult child may bring with them all sorts of stresses, such as depression, relating to any marriage break up or job loss they may have been through, and the parents may not be able to deal with this. The person moving in may bring with them a grandchild or two and the grandparents may not be used to the hurly-burly of the permanent presence of children. The parents may treat their adult offspring like a child and want to know where they are at all times and set curfews for returning home in the evening.

More Hints

- List all the benefits that this move will have for you. You are ditching that neighbour from hell; you are near a really good library and can start to read all the latest novels; you don't have a spare room for guests any more but will have a nook for your computer so you can finally write that novel; and so on. (See Mind Mapping page 226.)

- Instead of trying to cram all your old belongings into your new smaller home, why not be radical and sell the lot and reinvest the proceeds in new, good quality, modern classics? After all, a mattress should be changed every ten years, and a well-designed work-desk might be your best option.

- A smaller home might benefit from a unified approach to decoration. Keep one theme and colour scheme throughout. An attractive setting will make you feel great.

Holistic Help

- On your first day in your new home, make a point of buying two or three large bunches of flowers to brighten up your day.

GOAL SETTING

Having goals to work towards is all about having hope for the future. Are you doing what you want to do with your life? If the answer is no, this could be a significant source of stress in your life.

Top Tips

- Identifying what you want to do is the first step. Goals can be small as well as big, and sometimes the small ones are easier to focus on initially and make you confident enough and motivated to go for bigger ones if you wish to. There can be as much satisfaction in sorting out a dusty, junk-filled cupboard, if that's your goal, as there is at finishing your first novel.

- If you have no idea what your goals are, but generally feel dissatisfied, do the following:

  – Jot down the important areas of your life you want to change.

  – In order to not be overwhelmed, identify which is the most pressing or motivating aspect for you to work on.

  – If this does not come easily, do two things. Place a number from 1 to 10 next to each goal and see how the list then looks. For the top three make further lists of the pros and cons for each one and this should finally sort out your priorities. If you are still unsure, sleep on it for a night or two. It is amazing how things sort themselves out with 'Eureka!' moments as it all starts to crystallize in your mind.

- Taking one goal and dividing it into easy-to-attain chunks is a good idea. Whatever you want to achieve, set smaller goal posts along the way. That way, instead of focusing on a big leap of faith, a long time away, you can tangibly feel each milestone before you even get there.

- How you express your aims can mean the difference between failure and success. If you are always expressing your needs in the negative, this will only serve to tell you what you don't want. 'I wish I wasn't fat', 'I hate my job', 'I don't want to go on holiday there'. Express the same desires in the positive, and in the particular, and you instantly have a goal.'I would like to be 75 kg', 'I will train to be a ballet dancer', 'I want to go to Timbuktu'.

- The only way to realize your goals is to take action. You can dream forever, but only by doing something will you succeed. Create a detailed action plan – now!

- To create an action plan, pick your goal and express it specifically and in a positive frame (not 'I would like to' or 'I want', but 'I will' or 'I am'). Then write down ten specific actions that would get you nearer to your aim ('pick up the phone and make a call' or 'write a précis of my book'). Don't think too hard about these steps, just be inspired and write down anything that comes to mind – you can add further thoughts and edit it later. Put those actions in a logical order. Now write down everything you can think of that will help you (I have a good telephone personality, I have some good contacts). Finally write down everything you can think of that might hinder you ('I don't have a telephone', 'I don't yet know anyone in the business'). If you wish, you can use mind mapping techniques (see page 226) for this. By writing things down they become clearer. Now think of ways of overcoming the obstacles and acting upon the positive points. You have an action plan.

- Do not fear failure. Getting imperfect results when you work on something is just a way of learning lessons. Next time you will be wiser and more targeted in your approach.
- Don't feel pressurized into goal setting just because everyone else is. If you are content and your life is balanced you may be happy at the moment to jog along. But you may still have some dreams that inspire you…
- If you can't get going with your goal setting because of apathy, see Lethargy and Apathy, page 156.

More Hints
- Be consistent in your actions, but remember that flexibility is a great aid to achieving your goals (see Mindset/Flexibility page 159). For instance if fitness is your goal, consistency means doing something towards it regularly — say swimming at least four times a week for half an hour. But flexibility means that if you injure your shoulder and you need to rest it for a couple of weeks, you take up brisk walking until your shoulder is mended. Or flexibility may mean that in the winter months when you are de-motivated to go swimming that you go to the gym, instead of just giving up.
- Don't procrastinate. People usually put things off for a number of reasons: they don't expect to enjoy the task, they lack confidence in their ability to complete it, they think the job can be finished more quickly than it can. Combat procrastination by focusing on the pleasure of completion, reward yourself with a treat such as a nice meal, or an evening out.
- The goals you think of can be for yourself, your family or others you are involved with. However, remember that while you have control over your own goals, other peoples' may not accord with yours which means you may be disappointed. Listen to what it is that they want and need and resolve to help them towards their dreams.
- Ask yourself: 'How will I know when I have achieved my goal?' Define exactly what your goal is. See, smell, feel and hear what it means. By visualizing it in an unambiguous way it will be more tangible.

Holistic Help
- When goal setting, dream your dreams and enjoy the full extent of your fantasies – there is nothing wrong with reaching for the stars if you want to.

HOME GYM

The reason I am focusing on the home gym is that for most people this is the cheapest and most practical option for keeping fit. There are countless sport facilities in most areas and if you are already keen on keeping fit then you will know about these. You can probably choose from health clubs, swimming pools, tennis courts and running tracks which are near to your home or work. But for people who are not exercising regularly, home is the easiest place to start.

Exercise is one of the most important ways we have of de-stressing our lives. It actually clears excess stress hormones out of the body and triggers feel-good brain chemicals called endorphins, which is why a brisk walk will make you feel so much better after an argument or after a tough day. These endorphins allow us to literally self-medicate against feeling tired, stressed and depressed. Exercise has also been shown to improve our immune resistance and to reduce our susceptibility to stress-related diseases.

But staying motivated is the key to being consistent with an exercise regime, and we all know people with unused exercise bikes stashed in their lofts. It helps if the exercise does not cost the earth, does not involve a commute and you enjoy it. Here are some suggestions for exercise routines you can easily do from home.

Top Tips

■ The biggest hindrance to exercising is making the time in a busy schedule. It always seems that there is something more important to do. If you really want to commit to helping relieve the stress in your life by increasing your fitness, you need to make a plan of when you are going to exercise. One or two of the following are likely to work for you.

– Get your exercise out of the way first thing so that for the rest of the day you can forget about it.

– Use your commute to work for exercise. Factor-in walking or cycling some of the way to work. Remember to wear a pair of comfortable trainers or weatherproof footwear – depending on the need – Manhattan-style (where a brisk walk to work is a tradition).

– If unwinding is your problem, make a point of exercising at the end of your working day, but not if you are going to cop out when you finally get to the time you were intending to exercise. Late afternoon to early evening (4–6pm) is around the time that our muscles reach their performance peak.

– If watching the telly while you exercise means you will stick to your regime, check the TV schedule the night before to pick out an interesting half-hour programme during which you can strut your stuff.

- If you enjoy your chosen form of exercise, you are more likely to persevere. Most of us enjoy music and moving to music works on many levels. Not only do you improve your metabolism and get your heartbeat rate up, but you also improve co-ordination. All you need is a tape or CD deck and music you enjoy. Close the door, hang-up a do-not-disturb sign, and go for it.

- All the expensive home-gym equipment in the world is unlikely to beat a work-out on an inexpensive mini-trampoline (which can be hidden under the bed or behind a wardrobe) for stamina, combined with some well-planned yoga poses and stretches for suppleness. Resistance training improves strength and muscle tone and can be achieved with large, exercise-quality elastic bands for strength and a couple of large food tins for weights.

- Skipping is great aerobic exercise and you can pack a skipping rope to take anywhere with you – though there are limitations to when you can do this if you have downstairs-neighbours!

More Hints

- If you think you will work out three times a week, the chances are that it will end up being once or twice, so to really achieve three to four times a week, plan to work out five or six times a week.

- Alter your plans for winter and summer. Different seasons usually mean different exercise routines. It is a shame to run on a treadmill in a gym when you can get outdoors on a magnificent spring day, and it is less likely that you will venture out when the gloom descends in November.

- Following through on the theme of exercising from home (and being free and immediately available), there is nothing like a good fast half-hour walk to clear the cobwebs and to get your heart rate up a bit. Or if walking is too staid for you, how about roller-blading?

- Do invest in some video tapes. They work – but only if you use them. Switch them around and use three or four different tapes during the week to stop yourself getting bored.

Holistic Help

- Take a yin-yang balanced approach to your exercise – find a balance between aerobic exercise, such as fast walking sufficient to build up a sweat but not making you so breathless that you can't hold a conversation, and anaerobic exercise, such as weight training sufficient to sculpt and define muscles. Find a balance between fast and exciting and smooth and calm.

- Hydration is vital to fully benefit from exercise. Keep a bottle of water handy to sip from as you need it, and drink a large glass of water just before and just after exercise.

- Exercising on a full stomach is not a good thing for digestion, but then exercising on an empty stomach can set off migraines and low blood sugar attacks. Just before you exercise eat a small complex carbohydrate snack such as a banana sandwich or a couple of oatcakes spread with nut butter. You enjoy a larger meal at least half an hour after exercising.

■ While exercise is obviously beneficial for us, especially when stressed out, it does cause a degree of wear and tear on body tissues as well as on ligaments and joints. A daily antioxidant supplement which includes vitamins A, C and E as well as selenium and zinc helps to protect body tissues and reduce inflammation of joints. If the supplement also has bioflavanoids and beta-carotene so much the better.

HOUSEWORK

Housework is not my favourite activity! If there is a short-cut I'll take it. Some people enjoy housework and get a kick out of polishing the photo frames or cleaning out the oven and find it soothing and satisfying when a job is well done – it almost has a meditative quality for them. The following tips are for those of us who don't enjoy it quite so much, and tend to let it build up, and drag us down.

Top Tips

■ If you want to minimize cleaning, try to have fewer places where dirt builds up or is more evident. Hard flooring such as wood, tile or stone always wins out over carpet. White and light coloured fabrics are only for masochists (unless they can be thrown in the washing machine and definitely won't shrink) and darker neutrals such as taupe and mole work well with light walls, or go for brights.

■ Pare down your possessions. If you have one treasured item highlighted on a sideboard, you can soon see when the dust builds up, and wipe it down, but it is much more disheartening when that treasured item is surrounded by countless other less-valued objects and they stop you from having the energy to clean the area.

■ Instead of perpetually nagging your family members or flatmates to do their bit, have a calm sit-down meeting with all of you present and bash out an agreement while being determined to stay calm. (See Delegating page 35.)

More Hints

■ There is no point in just moving dust around, which is what most vacuum cleaners do, as does dusting. Most vacuum cleaners spit out two-thirds of what they take in! If you are buying a new cleaner, buy a model guaranteed to keep in the dust it collects (some of the special allergy vacuums are best) and always wet-dust instead of dry-dusting to really pick up the dirt.

■ It is much easier to let the dust build up a bit if you make a point of spring-cleaning twice a year (technically spring- and autumn-cleaning). At the same time you can make a point of clearing your clutter (see Order Out of Chaos, page 29).

■ If you can afford it, you might consider finding some home help. One way to help with the decision is to make an evaluation of your own time. If you figure out that an investment in some help for a few hours a week frees you up to be more financially productive, or less stressed, it could well be worth it. Go by word of mouth if you can, otherwise the stress of managing someone who is no good at the job might make the exercise counterproductive.

- A local teenager will probably be happy to earn a bit of pocket money by helping with the ironing and car cleaning – all time-intensive jobs.

- If you are about to get a new pet, consider a short-haired breed to minimize the dirt and dust.

Holistic Help

- The effect of housework on health and fitness has been studied and it has been found that we don't need to go to the gym after all. If you really put some old-fashioned elbow grease into the job, you can find that you get-fit-as-you-shine-as-you-clean! It makes sense obviously – our grandparents did not have the time-saving devices we enjoy today and as we have become more sedentary we have become less fit. The housewives of the early-to-mid twentieth century apparently did the equivalent of running a marathon once a week!

- Beware the effects of cleaning chemicals on your health. Because our homes are almost hermetically sealed environments these days we are typically breathing in a cocktail of around 400 chemicals. Levels of pollutants in the average home are around ten times higher than outside. This toxic load is another stress for the body to cope with. Instead of using sprays, aerosols, room fresheners and anti-bacterial wipes, use old fashioned cleaning techniques which use brushes and scourers along with soap, water, borax, bleach, white vinegar for cutting grease and moulds, baking soda for kitchen and bathroom surfaces and tea tree oil and grapefruit seed extract as natural anti-bacterials. For a list of products which are free of various harmful chemicals see the list compiled on the Greenpeace website www.greenpeace.org

- For more info read *Talking Dirty with The Queen of Clean* and *Talking Dirty Laundry with The Queen of Clean* by Linda Cobb (Simon & Schuster).

KIDS-ZONE

Nothing transforms a home faster than kids. Depending on your viewpoint they fill a home with laughter, movement and colour OR noise, mess and disorganization – and more often than not it is both of these scenarios at the same time.

Children are only children for a very short time and it is essential to appreciate them. You can never go back in time to recapture these precious moments. But children can also be mini-dictators if we let them.

Remember it is their home as well – not your home in which they are guests (unless of course they are visiting you for a while). Teaching them to respect their own, and other people's homes, comes from your lead.

Top Tips

- Respect your children and they will respect you. Discuss situations with them and explain your viewpoint. Ask them why they are insisting on something – if you hear them out at least they will view you as being fair – if you decide to decline. Explain why – lack of money, value for money, health or safety reasons and so on.

- Work out the flashpoints, typically homework, bedtime, mealtimes, supermarket check-outs. Establish rules that you agree on together (this is dependent on age but can start quite young – say two years old). Prioritize safety and respect for others, and allow flexibility for special occasions – let them eat their party bag sweets! Once the rules are established you have a reference point. But remember that the rules govern you, as well as the children, and you also must stick to them.

- Re-evaluate these rules from time to time. Rules might be: bedtime is 7:30pm sharp, but 8.00pm at weekends, and a parent will always read a story. A piece of fruit (or a fruit- or vegetable-based dish) will be eaten with each meal, followed by a small treat if at least half the main meal has been eaten.

- Children respond much better to rewards than to threats. (Rewards are not the same as bribes.) This does not take away the value of well-placed punishments, such as withdrawing a visit to a friend's house, but to always threaten ends up sounding hollow and unmotivating. Use a star system to reward good deeds – with a mini-prize (say a comic, some home made cookies or some sunflower seeds to plant in a pot) after ten stars and a maxi-prize (say a trip to the cinema) after 30 stars.

- Remember that you are the adult and you have the right to say no – firmly and without shouting. When you say no, mean it and do not waver. Once children learn that 'no' means 'no', and not 'maybe' or 'yes, if you bug me enough', they will realize that 'pester power' has limited effect.

- Avoid giving the children the answers to questions all the time. Teach them resourcefulness and the ability to find answers. You can do this by asking the questions back to them (with little hints) so that they can find the conclusions and by teaching them – depending on age – to find the answers for themselves in reference books. If they are young, you may need to find the answer together. This simple habit instils in them the life-long ability to be curious about life and to find solutions.

More Hints

- Find a friend who will trade child-minding with you during supermarket shops. If you avoid trailing the kids around the supermarket, you avoid, at a stroke, the worst that 'pester power' can deliver.

- Explain to children what advertising, aimed at children, is all about and why they don't need to fall for it.

- When I do my 'agony aunt' columns for children's health, the most frequent questions are about getting children to eat well at mealtimes. Avoid anxiety about food and your children will not pick up the vibes that they can manipulate you with food. Lead by example and eat as a family, and avoid having acres of junk food in the cupboards. Differentiate between them genuinely disliking a food and just being difficult. If they see that the pressure they are bringing to bear does not lead to capitulation where you offer them anything just to get them to eat, they will get on with eating like the rest of the family. Don't avoid giving them child-appeal meals once or twice a week, but don't let it become a routine. Children will always eat if they are hungry enough. I am not suggesting starving them, just don't be panicked if they miss one meal here and there.

■ Parents who are away at work for much of the time often feel guilty about the amount of time they manage to spend with their children. Achieving balance in this area can be difficult for some (see Work/Home Balance page 72). Divorced parents who do not live full time with their children also often have the same set of problems. This phenomenon has created a whole new concept of spending 'quality time' with the children. This idea can lead to time that is often highly structured, and frankly often focused on the parents' needs rather than the children's. Children, by and large, don't really want quality time, indeed they have no concept of it. What they want is close time with their parents. Trust, understanding, love and warmth are what children respond to, need and want. You can go to all the amusement parks in the world but time spent curled up on the sofa or going for a walk and just talking about 'stuff' will be just as well, if not better, spent.

■ If your toddler is less than loveable on more occasions than you would expect and you are struggling, read *New Toddler Taming: A Parents Guide to the First Four Years* by Dr Christopher Green (Vermilion).

Holistic Help

■ Explain to children the advantages of good nutrition in terms they can understand – more energy for sports, strong bones to grow tall, better brains to figure out stuff. They are never too young to understand the advantages of eating fruits and vegetables (which can be every bit as cool as colour laden sweets and desserts) and to understand the importance of complex carbohydrates such as wholemeal bread and porridge (for energy) and protein such as eggs, fish, pulses and chicken (for growth). They can also understand that a little chocolate or sugar is fine, but loads of sugary foods, such as some breakfast cereals, squashes or colas, can make them hyper and tired in the long run. (See Nutrition page 230.)

■ Children need some quiet time during the day and don't need to be constantly wound up like springs with activities. Quiet time is good for unwinding, getting ready for rest times and is a time for introspection when they learn to be resourceful and to amuse themselves.

■ Teach children, and yourself for that matter, the three Rs: respect for yourself; respect for others; and responsibility for all your actions.

LIFE IS FOR LIVING

Shirley Conran said, memorably, 'Life is too short to stuff a mushroom' – that was in the 1970s when stuffed mushrooms were fashionable fare. And how right she was. One of the reasons we descend into stressful chaos in our lives is because we try to do it all – and in the end do nothing particularly well. (Prioritizing is discussed on page 36.) If you worry about not dusting the mantelpiece or producing gourmet meals, here are some ways to avoid life's trivial anxieties.

Top Tips

■ While organization will help your life, don't become a slave to it. If it is perfect weather, forget about the list you made for today – get out in the park or to the countryside for the day. You can guarantee that if you postpone it until tomorrow it will rain!

■ Life is for living, it is not a dress rehearsal. You don't often get second chances. If you really want to take up an opportunity that presents itself – do it. Do your best to reorganize your schedule – the only thing you really can't do is to be irresponsible and completely let people down (though you might be able to defer).

■ Unless you really enjoy it, don't bother with complicated day-long recipes for dinner parties. Learn how to achieve attractive throw-it-together meals from easy-to-cook healthy ingredients. Quickly-made, delicious meals such as cous cous salads, shell-fish platters (fruits de mer), one-pot stews and really good shop-bought ice creams will save you time and stress. Baked meat and vegetable dishes are other great time savers. Life is indeed too short to stuff mushrooms.

■ If, at the end of your soirées, your kitchen looks like a bomb has hit it, then you've got it all wrong – chuck out the ten pans you are using, buy a wok and make life simple.

■ Cooking is also a form of entertainment where you can talk to your guests as you create – or get them to chop and stir as well.

More Hints

■ Remember to fit in pleasurable, healthy activities like going to the gym or swimming baths. You may notice that dust on the mantelpiece but the chances are that others won't. If you spend all your time on such minutiae, and not on more important things like keeping fit or enjoying yourself, you need to prioritize (see page 34).

■ Life is truly not a competition. Enjoy other people's successes, be proud of your own, and don't feel that others have set the pace and you need to keep up. Go at your own level.

■ Don't put off your ambitions. You don't want to get to the age of 80 saying to yourself 'I wish I'd got round to climbing Mount Everest'. No ambition is too modest and can free you up creatively. If you want to learn square dancing or go to art classes, do it. Activities such as these will bring balance to your life, encourage you to re-focus and diminish daily stresses.

Holistic Help

■ If you are too busy meeting deadlines and find it difficult to loosen up your attitude so that you can enjoy other pastimes invest some time in visualization. Imagine yourself booking the art-class or going for long walks. See what you would see, smell what you would smell, hear what you would hear. Get yourself into a state of enjoyment and relaxation and get inside the feelings of pursuing your chosen activity. You will find it irresistible to actually follow your visualization with real activity.

■ **Bach Flower Remedies** might be useful if you need to improve your spontaneity and appreciation of the opportunities you are presented with. For example, *Clematis* helps with apathy and a lack of vitality. *Gorse* is good when you feel low with feelings of hopelessness and *Rock water* when you are self-critical with fixed ideas and opinions, a perfectionist and intolerant.

MOVING HOME

Moving home is right up there at the top of the list, with bereavement and divorce, as one of the most stressful events you can experience. But there are a number of simple, practical strategies to help us make it easier on ourselves.

Top Tips

■ The reason for moving home is often linked to other major events in our life – marriage, divorce, kids, new jobs – no wonder it is stressful. If one or some of these motives apply to your move, aim to avoid further stressful events until after you have moved.

■ If you are buying or selling a home, the actual process can be a minefield. It is the biggest amount of money that most of us will deal with in our lifetime and this makes it stressful. If you are selling, get all your paperwork organized in advance to reduce the potential for problems later. Appoint a solicitor, get the deeds and leasehold papers, get financial statements for the building and possibly a local authority search. If you are buying, do your homework on the area before committing and sort out your finances ahead of time. These steps will hugely reduce the stress when the time comes to complete the transaction.

■ Keep a positive frame of mind. If you do not get the home you had set your heart on (whether you are buying, renting or being given a local authority place), you must believe that this was not the only place in the world for you and that another will come along.

■ If you are relocating for work purposes, remember that this can bring added strains to the existing stress of a normal house move. If you are going to an area with which you are unfamiliar, your social circle is likely to be depleted which means you will need to build up your network again. The same is true for your family. Your children may feel disorientated for a while and take it out on you. As there are fewer people to fall back on, you can find that you and your partner are thrown together more than usual which can lead to strains in a relationship. You or your partner may also need to find a job and you might not have time for empathy as you are holding down a new position at work. Of course, there will be many new and exciting opportunities which, if you view the move in this light, will easily offset any perceived teething problems.

■ If you can, take time off work when you move home. Hoping to do it over the weekend and then expecting yourself to turn up bright and breezy for work on Monday is bound to be stressful and lower your mental and physical reserves.

■ You might as well accept that living out of boxes, and not being able to find everything you need, for several weeks is going to be an added stress in your life. One possibility is to take a week off work and crack through it all in one go. In any event make sure that when you are packing up that you prioritize a few boxes (and label them accordingly with fluorescent stickers or something else equally visible) with the absolute necessities you will need for the first few weeks.

More Hints

■ Avoid 'chains' if you can – rent in between if you are able.

■ We buy properties emotionally as well as rationally. Before you know it, you are already calling it your home and choosing curtain fabrics. This is obviously all part of the fun and what makes the whole process worth it, but if you go too far down that route be aware that you could be sorely disappointed if it all goes wrong.

■ If this is the first time you are moving on your own because you are leaving the family home or going away to further education, this is a great adventure. Your problems are most likely to be financial, so make sure that you are on top of your outgoings if you are managing your own budget for the first time.

Holistic Help

■ Look upon your move as a positive opportunity to sort through your possessions and weed out what you do not want or need – finally a chance to get through that clutter (see Order out of Chaos page 29).

■ Ahead of the move, make up a couple of essentials boxes which include items like tea and biscuits, bubble bath, a scented candle, a warm and comfortable tracksuit and fluffy towel – whatever items will make you feel good on the day.

MULTI-TASKING

If you find yourself nestling the phone between your shoulder and ear hoping to have an in-depth conversation while you check your e-mails and simultaneously note down items for your shopping list, you might think you are an effective multi-tasker. Yet research tells us that in reality we do not complete jobs effectively and accurately if we aim to do too many things at the same time. Multi-tasking can be pretty stressful. Give your full attention to a job and you will complete it more speedily and accurately, and feel less stressed and calmer at a stroke.

On the other hand there are some activities that do lend themselves to multi-tasking. These are activities you can do when you don't have to fully concentrate on something else, such as travelling on public transport or watching TV.

Top Tips

■ In a busy world, the ability to do several things at once might seem to benefit us, but if you are hoping to think clearly about a given task then you are probably better off 'serial-tasking' – completing one task before you move on to the next. It might seem a little slow at first but the benefits are that you don't have to go over old ground correcting mistakes or get accused by people that you are not really concentrating on your conversations with them. Most importantly, your stress levels are likely to be lower. A surprising amount of calm comes from focusing on one thing at a time.

■ You may need to train those around you when you start serial-tasking. They may be used to interrupting you and getting an immediate reaction, and will have to learn to wait their turn.

More Hints

■ Read an enjoyable book or a newspaper to catch up with current affairs while on the bus or tube.

■ Write thank you notes or jot down ideas for bigger projects while on the bus or tube (don't attempt anything more major or you'll miss your stop).

■ Give yourself a manicure or pedicure, or keep your wardrobe in order by sewing buttons or drooping hems while watching the TV.

■ Enhance your healthy eating plans by chopping vegetables for a dish, or to keep as crudités in the fridge, or make a fruit salad, on a chopping board on your lap while watching the TV, listening to a play on the radio or chatting to a friend who has dropped in for tea.

■ Pick through a folder that needs weeding out or sort out your bag while watching the TV news.

■ Listen to recorded books while travelling long distances in the car (your local library will have plenty to choose from). You could even learn another language by listening to tapes and practising in the car.

■ Write shopping lists or a skeleton outline for a report while waiting in the doctor's or dentist's waiting room (see Mind Mapping page 226).

Holistic Help

- If you want to socialize with a good friend, make it a mutually relaxing time and give each other an Indian head massage, reflexology session or a manicure.

- Have chefing sessions with a friend and experiment with new healthy dishes to add to your repertoire – while having a sociable time. If you have children, you can do this with them as a playtime treat, which also gets their meal ready (slowly!) and educates them about healthy eating – all in one go.

NEST BUILDING

How do you view your home? Is it the nest to which you return at the end of the day with a sense of relief? Is it a place where you enjoy receiving your friends and visitors? Is it a place that enhances your life? Or is it just a place into which you decant the various elements of your life in the hope that it will all somehow sort itself out? If your home does not enhance your life, you might like to take steps to make it a more restful place to soothe your stresses away.

Top Tips

- If, initially, you don't have the time or energy for a complete revamp of your home, make at least one area a haven for relaxation – any room will do, sitting room, bedroom, bathroom or kitchen, as long as you use it very regularly and really enjoy 'living' in it. It is not intended as a parlour only for esteemed guests, but a nest for yourself.

- If you can't envisage doing a whole room, at least create a corner of enjoyment. It could be draping a sofa with an attractive throw, placing a table next to it with an good light or some candles, a small bowl of water with a few flower heads floating in it, and a good book or glossy magazine. This can be enough to create your first retreat and your enjoyment of this space can radiate outwards to other areas of your home.

- If the view from your nest is interrupted by loads of clutter, turn to Order Out of Chaos (page 29) and slowly work through the list. In the meantime, if you are desperate, you could put up a screen to hide, say, a cluttered work area or wardrobe, but be warned that out of sight is out of mind and if you have to look at it you may be more likely to do something about it.

More Hints

- For a gradual approach to making a 'nest' of your home, start by redirecting your thinking towards the idea of creating a retreat. Add small things that will enhance your enjoyment of a space. Scented flowers (changed regularly), framed photos of people you love, something fun to read in the loo, a well placed light on a dimmer switch can all have the desired effect.

- Light is vital for energy and life. Draw curtains and blinds to let the light in. Get rid of dingy net curtains and replace with half-height translucent blinds.

Holistic Help

- Keep your home well aired. Central heating in a hermetically sealed home can make you feel groggy and rob energy. Open a window just a couple of inches at each end of your home to allow air, and energy, to flow through.
- Make colour work for you. Soothing colours are in the neutral or the mauve, blue and green palettes.
- Candlelight is extremely soothing and wonderful for creating a nest-like ambience while at the same time distracting you from any 'stuff' or clutter around you.

ORDER OUT OF CHAOS

Clutter creates a sort of 'visual noise' which keeps the volume turned up all the time, and this can be pretty stressful. Yet it is easy to be surrounded by clutter. It is hardly surprising that many of us do not manage to keep on top of this build-up in our lives as we are deluged with junk mail, magazines and advertising tempting us to buy things. But clutter undoubtedly slows us down making us less effective and unable to enjoy our free moments. Tackling the mountains of 'things-that-might-one-day-be-useful' such as unwanted wedding and birthday presents, photos of people we have long forgotten and the 'to be mended' pile will make you feel as if a weight has been lifted from your chest; you dispense with the lethargy and aimlessness that chaos seems to engender.

You may have no idea how stressful your clutter is – until you get rid of it. If you are keeping the clutter under superficial control you may not be thinking about it but it can still deplete you of energy. Better to get rid of the clutter in the first place. If on the other hand the clutter is controlling you, a sure sign of this is that hunt for an essential piece of paper among three teetering piles, then you will definitely be adding to your stress load. Don't buy into the idea that today's junk is tomorrow's antiques. If you are hanging on to stuff for the future in case it is one day of value you might not be maximizing your mental energy today.

Clutter is all the things you no longer use: such as stacks of old magazines, clothes you might one day slim into, cups and saucepan lids without handles or broken equipment. Things you no longer love: the old tea-set you inherited but don't really like, sale bargains that did not seem such a good idea when you got them home, or collections of objects that were once a passion but that no longer enthrall you (no, I do not mean your spouse!).

Top Tips

- Keeping your mail in order not only gets rid of an immediate source of clutter, but also has the effect of keeping other areas of your life under control and unstressful – your electricity won't get cut off, your ancient aunt won't take umbrage at unanswered letters, and the junk mail doesn't build up. Take ten minutes each morning (get up a little earlier if you have to) to sort through your post and deal with it immediately. Separate out torn envelopes and put them in the bin immediately or in your paper recycling pile and keep the jiffy bags if you need to. If your post is junk mail then bin it, if it's an invitation, check in your diary at once, if the letter needs a reply – do it at once, if you are able, otherwise call, e-mail or write later the same day. Pay any bills immediately, making sure you post them when there's money in the bank (in which case date the envelope to be sent). If you use phone or Internet banking make a note of the dates when the bill should be paid in your diary or whichever system (yellow Post-its on the computer) you use as a memory aid. Pencil time in your diary for larger projects such as filling in a tax return, which may take a whole day or more to work out.

- Define what is junk. Broken objects that you can't or won't mend, items you hate to look at and clothes that don't fit, all qualify as junk and need to be got rid of.

- Decide which items you really value and deal with them, either by fixing the broken things or finding a good place for them instead of being irritated by their placement each time you pass by.

- Get four strong boxes. Give each one a label: Junk For The Tip; Charity Shop; Repairs/Alterations; Things To Sort Out. Every time you come across an item that fits one of these descriptions chuck it in there. When the box is full, cart it off or sort it out as a priority. In your Things To Sort Out box you could also put items that you are in two minds about and if you miss them after a few months reinstate them in your home. Keep the boxes on the go all the time, though hopefully after the first deluge there won't be quite so much to deal with.

More Hints

- Your bag or briefcase may be another source of clutter – into which you distil your whole life. Take one day a week to go rigorously through your bag and clear out the detritus that builds up.

- Sort through your wallet regularly. At a time in my life when I was feeling quite poor, a friend of mine saw me take my wallet out which was bulging with receipts, lists, cheque stubs and train tickets and commented that she was not surprised I was feeling the pinch. 'How do you expect money to flow into your wallet if it has to get by all that junk', she said. I have been better off since then, and wonder if de-junking my wallet had the desired effect or if it is just a coincidence. I do know that her vivid visual observation continues to work as a reminder to keep my wallet tidy.

- Aim, at the end of the day, to always leave your desk tidy. While you may not be able to get through all the work, organize projects by subject matter and leave them tidily-stacked for the next day.

- Photos, cuttings and mementoes are a constant source of clutter. If you know in your heart that you are never going to get round to pasting them all in albums do the following: invest in lots of foolscap wallet-style folders with fold over flaps. Date the first one with today's date with a thick marker pen. Place in it all your precious mementoes. Decide then and there which things you wish to keep and get rid of the less than wonderful children's drawings and repetitive photos. Into the wallet put in, as they crop up, all photos, precious letters from friends, school reports and children's drawings. When it is full up secure it with a large rubber band and put the finish date on it. Start the next folder. You will probably end up with two or three folders per year which you can stash in a large box tidied away somewhere.

- If you can't persuade your teenagers to clear up their rooms don't let that be another stress. Make three important rules they adhere to: 1. They always keep their door shut so you don't have to look at their mess. 2. They are responsible for picking up dirty clothes and bed linen and putting them out for laundry on a given day of the week. 3. They don't come complaining to you when they can't find something. If they break these rules, the penalty is that they have to clear up their rooms!

- Glance around you and observe – notice the clutter magnets in your home. Areas where clutter tends to build up include: window ledges, counter tops and open shelves, behind closet doors, by exit doors. Being aware of this will help you to stop dumping things in the first place.

- Have you noticed how other people's mess can be more stressful than your own, especially if you have to live or work around it? If your partner/flatmate/co-worker is guilty of leaving too much stuff around for a sane life, you may have to have a gentle word. Explain how it is affecting you and why it is difficult for you to live or work with. Offer constructive solutions such as you helping out, setting aside an hour a week to work on it, buying boxes or setting aside a couple of drawers and labelling them accordingly. It might be that other people are simply unaware of how awkward you find it, but you also have to be ready for their criteria to be different to yours. Do your best not to be critical or judgmental, but constructive. Outline the benefits to them (finding things, time management, making you happy!).

- If you are lucky enough to be the owner of an attic, spare room, dry cellar or shed, don't make the cardinal mistake of chucking in everything and hoping for the best. Invest time in adding shelving – warehouse style – and stack everything you need but don't use very often (tool boxes, ladders, ski equipment). If you are going to use storage bags then use clear ones you can see through, or make sure you label them really well. Arrange your stuff so that you can see the item you need at a glance.

- Clearing up efficiently is a skill. Many of us are highly inefficient at shuffling objects from one place to another and not really being consistent about how we operate. On the other hand, efficient people can act like human tornadoes when dealing with clutter. As they clear up one item and take it to its destination, they immediately pick up another item that needs clearing, and move it to its intended place, and so on – in doing this they sort of create a chain-link of moving and restoring items to their correct place. They do not dither or consider, they just get on with it automatically, conserving energy and being efficient at the same time.

■ For more, in-depth advice read *Clearing The Clutter* by Mary Lambert (Cico Books).

Holistic Help

■ You may find it useful to employ the services of a reliable Feng Shui expert to give you advice on how to best maximize the energy flows in your home by ordering your chaos. Feng shui is an Eastern theory of energy flow around dwellings (homes, gardens and work places). By keeping areas clutter free and aligning objects in particular areas, it is said that you can bring balance and calm to your life, enhance certain aspects of your life (such as health, love and wealth) and clear out negative atmospheres. Many people find it a fascinating discipline, and at the very least lends itself to creating calm and co-ordinated spaces in which to live and work.

■ Poorly chosen colour and lighting can seem to add to uncontrolled clutter. Clashing colours or designs and harsh lighting (say from a single overhead bulb or strip lighting) do nothing but emphasize chaos. Calm colours such as neutrals or the blue palette, or well co-ordinated bright colours can enhance the sense of order. You only have to pick up a Sunday newspaper magazine supplement and look at their home decorating spreads to see how colour can work to bring things together in the home. Play around with lighting to highlight the attractive features of your rooms. By using pools of light from lamps, you can highlight certain objects or detract the eye from cluttered areas by focusing on something else. You could also use uplighters, or light dimmer switches.

KITCHEN

■ Go through your cupboards and get rid of all kitchen equipment you have not used for two years. You don't need four strainers and if you haven't used the ice cream maker in the last two years you probably aren't going to.

■ Go through your food cupboard and systematically chuck out all items past their sell-by date, and all the impulse purchases that have not translated into meals yet.

■ It is common to have a drawer where items that have no other home are dumped – take away menus, screwdrivers, pencils, notepads, broken handles to be fixed and so on. Clear this out and put pencils in a jar, a notepad mounted on the wall next to the phone and put menus in a plastic folder.

■ A healthy fridge, with lots of stress-busting nutrients, will contain at least a third vegetables and fruit.

■ A cluttered notice-board diminishes the usefulness of the information, or the pertinence of any joke pinned to it, so sort this out.

- Mend broken lids, handles and drawers – or get someone to do this for you.
- Clear out odds and ends of unwanted and broken cutlery and china.

HALL

- Halls are notoriously bad for becoming a dumping ground. If you want to have a coat rack, umbrella stand, outdoor shoe spot and small table for the post that is fine if it is uncluttered. But boxes of things on their way to the dump, bags left unpacked from the supermarket, sports kit that is only used once a week and other items that build up will only make you feel bad each time you walk in the door.
- If you have several members of your household, the build-up of coats, and other kit, can become overwhelming. If each person has their own coat peg, then it is up to them to decide what they want to keep on it, but they can't hijack everyone else's coat pegs.
- If you always leave stuff on the stairs to take up or down when you are passing by, clear it away and use the opportunity of moving the items to get some exercise.

LIVING ROOMS

- As your living room and dining area are the most likely to be seen by visitors take some time to see these areas as they see them when they first walk in. Are they welcoming or an assault course? Make a plan if the latter applies.
- Dining tables are notoriously guilty of attracting items that don't have a home elsewhere. (Or are the owners guilty of dumping things there?) If your table is a mess, consign newspapers to a magazine rack or bin old ones, sweep the kids' toys up into boxes in their rooms, put their homework projects into neat folders to be put away and taken out as needed and do the same for your pile of correspondence. Firmly put a bowl of fruit and some flowers on the table to remind everyone to stop the clutter building up again, and perhaps lay out a jigsaw puzzle that everyone can contribute to each time they go by.
- CDs, videos and cassettes all need a proper home. Invest in some stacking racks, turn over a drawer or two in a dresser to store them or use a crate.
- If you've been meaning to put up those bookshelves for ages, now is the time to do so.
- Trailing wires for TVs and sound systems can be dangerous and are unattractive. Spend some time tacking them down and ideally hiding them – or reorganize the position of your equipment.

BEDROOMS

- Go through your wardrobe and give to charity anything that you have not worn for a couple of years, get rid of anything that does not fit and mend any clothes that need it.
- Organize your clothes by colour. You will discover several new outfits in this way.
- Praise be to whoever invented duvets. They are so easy to shake out and make a bed in seconds, or at least to turn down and air the bed.

- Invest in several large brightly-coloured stacking boxes for the kids' bedrooms and at the very least get them to throw in their toys at the end of the day. If you are feeling energetic you could segregate the types of toys into different boxes (dolls, train sets, building bricks, etc). This can encourage them to play with toys more effectively as they can find all the 'bits' for each game.
- Bedrooms are places to wind down and induce sleepiness, so make sure that the lighting can be dimmed when needed.

BATHROOMS

- Clear out your bathroom cabinet of all the tubes with dregs of dried up potions in them and put them in the bin.
- Invest in three or four inexpensive small wicker baskets and divide between them your collected grooming items – one for nail varnishes, one for make up, one for moisturizers.
- Keep your vitamins by your toothbrush so you can remember to take them at the same time.
- Stack towels up neatly on open shelves so that they enhance the room rather than detract from it.
- Put a rack of hooks up high at the side of the bath for scrubbing brushes on ropes and bath hats. More hooks arranged along an opposite wall are good for the family's bathrobes and towels and avoids the hook on the back of the door being piled up too high.

GARDEN

- If you just don't have the time to do any gardening, it might make sense to replace a part of a lawn with decking, gravel or flag stones.
- Spend just one day putting up loads of hooks and shelves around your garden shed to clear all the small clutter off the floor. This will leave room for big items such as deckchairs – and allow you to get to them quickly and really enjoy your garden when the weather is fine.
- Get broken lawn mowers, strimmers, etc fixed or throw out what is beyond repair.

PLANNING AND PRIORITIZING

If you aren't a good planner, look on the bright side and think of all the other things you manage to do because you are not always obsessively making lists of things to do! Creative people in particular seem to thrive in a degree of disorganization. However, most people will find their stress levels are brought down to reasonable levels if they can actually find that important phone number or file.

Actually, many of us have split personalities when it comes to being organized. We might be fiercely efficient when at work while our private lives flounder in a mound of clutter and lack of time. In part, this might be a self-defence mechanism. Who wants to be a totally efficient automaton 24 hours a day, 7 days a week? But it can go too far and home disorganization, which contrasts so much with our professional lives, can end up impacting on professional capabilities and encourage feelings of being out of control.

Prioritizing is another vital skill you should learn. It's astounding how, when there is an important job to do, it suddenly seems so important to make the coffee, call your mother or walk the dog. If you habitually procrastinate, make a point of making a daily plan.

Top Tips

- Being organized or disorganized is as much a matter of habit as anything else. If you get into the habit of always checking your diary daily – then you won't miss your dentist appointment for the third time in a row. If you spend just a few minutes sorting out your priorities for the day, first thing, then, for the most part, you can rule your day instead of it ruling you.

- Time spent planning is never wasted, and is actually a major time saver. Planning takes only five to ten minutes daily. When you plan your day, make a point of also prioritizing. Use a star system or use a number from 1 to 5 to indicate how vital it is to complete that day. So if, during the course of your day, you don't even have time to go to the loo – it's time for some planning.

- Initially, you may spend some of the planning time clearing a bit of backlog but if you keep it up, before long you are focusing on moving forwards.

- When you have a list of ten things to do, realistically you won't be able to do more than one 'big thing' in a day, choose that big thing carefully. The other nine items will all need to be small ones.

- If you have a large task ahead of you, plan it out into smaller manageable chunks and prioritize which are the most important. Usually working on a framework is the first item. Break the job down into manageable chunks. Use subheadings to categorize the jobs, and put them into a date sequence — some things may need to run in tandem. For instance, if you need to do some research before writing to someone, list the research areas to check out. If you need to delegate some of the tasks, write a list of who does what and what the completion times need to be. Diarize the jobs. Set regular review times to check you are on course. This way you can focus only on what needs doing at that time, safe in the knowledge that the task won't run out of control. (It will also stop midnight-worrying about the enormity of the job, if you are prone to this.)

- A huge backlog of paperwork is death to any desire to get organized and prioritize as it can engender feelings of hopelessness and lack of direction. If you have a few impossible looking stacks before you, you can either decide to set aside a full day to get through them and then vow they will not build up again, or you can deal with them in half an hour or so as follows (and this is probably more realistic for most people): place a wastepaper basket by your side, and arm yourself with some see-through plastic folders. Go through every item in the stacks of paper and throw out unnecessary items. As you work through the stack make separate piles of: bills to pay, filing, stuff to read, letters needing replies. Put aside any bigger jobs that emerge in separate plastic folders, and put dates in your diary when you will tackle them individually. Then pay the bills (because you know you are going to have to anyway!). Now you must vow to yourself (prioritize) that you will just deal with three or four items each day (reply to a letter, file a couple of items, read something through) until, before long, you will have actually got through the whole lot – probably faster than you think. Finally resolve to not add further to the piles by tackling your morning post systematically when it comes in each day. This method can also be used when you return from a holiday to find a huge stack of post and mail to deal with.

■ There can be differences between your priorities and those of the people you live with. If you can't resolve these differences, learning to respect the differences may be the most peaceful way forward.

More Hints

■ It is easier to concentrate on the 'big thing' if you either: 1) get it out of the way first before distractions set in, or 2) clear the little things out of the way first to free up your mental clutter and allow you to concentrate. If you don't know which method suits you best, experiment with both. I use both systems depending on the task and the day, although there is always a danger with the latter system that it will lead to procrastination. If this is the case, stick to the first system.

■ Bring deadlines forward by a couple of days. This is a bit like always keeping your watch five minutes fast to make sure you get to appointments on time. This way, if there are any unexpected obstacles, you can still meet your deadlines.

■ Keep your promises. If you say you will do something by a given time, do so. On the other hand, think carefully before agreeing to do something if you might regret it later.

DELEGATING

Delegating is an essential planning skill, especially when you have a lot of responsibilities. Some people are terrific at delegating while others will take everything on and end up feeling stressed that they have to do it all – drop the kids at school, finish a report and cook the evening meal. Letting others take some of the burden is not a cop-out, it is a fact of life. Just make sure that both the task and the person are appropriate.

Top Tips

■ If you are constantly 'dumping' on a few selected people remember that you might be pushing your luck – better to spread the load when you can.

■ Make people feel good about accepting jobs or responsibilities. Avoid being confrontational: 'It's your job to take the rubbish out'. Instead, ask in a thoughtful manner: 'I would really appreciate it if you could help me by taking the rubbish out'.

- Remember to say, 'please' and 'thank you'. (Really basic advice but it is amazing how often we take other people for granted, especially those nearest to us.) If people feel appreciated they will always be glad to help. Trade small favours, write thank you notes and give small gifts where appropriate.

- Ask appropriately. There is no point asking the wrong person to do the wrong job – it will only lead to disappointment.

- Remember that nobody is indispensable. If you believe that you and only you can do the job properly then you are setting a trap for yourself.

- Clearly and successfully communicating the standards to which a job needs to be completed is the first step in making sure it reaches your ideal. It could be that your ideal is too stringent, so ask yourself, 'Does it really need to be so perfect?'

- Learn to say 'no'. This is a great skill and will help you to avoid taking even more stuff on. It is possible to say no without giving offence. If you want to play for time, get in the habit of saying 'I'll check my diary' or 'I'll check with my partner' and get back to them efficiently. Be honest but kind, 'I'd love to help out, but I am already over-committed'.

More Hints

- If you want to delegate household jobs this is perfectly reasonable. However, if one person goes out to work all day, while the other stays at home, pick the jobs carefully so that neither person feels overwhelmed.

- Children certainly need to learn from an early age to be responsible for their part of the home. Get them into the habit of laying the table, picking up their toys and putting their dirty clothes in the basket – it won't kill them, and if you are firm and respectful it won't be the struggle you might assume it to be.

- This is a bit of a cheeky tip and smacks of 'helpless female syndrome', but it works for me. I am lousy at DIY (and usually make a mess of it). If I nag my husband to do something the chances are it won't get done – he often has a different set of priorities. I have learned that starting to do the job myself, imperfectly, usually means that he will step in and complete it, with aplomb (this works both ways and he might start half-heartedly doing something and I'll step in).

- Alternatively, save all the jobs up (keep a running list of these) and get an odd-job person along once every six months to spend a couple of hours fixing things and putting things up. It costs a bit of money but saves a lot of tension.

Holistic Help

- If you do agree to do something for someone else, do it wholeheartedly and without moaning. Don't expect anything in return – a trade for a trade. You will be surprised how good deeds have unexpected and wonderful pay-backs.

- Mind map. Because mind-mapping helps you to tap into your subconscious and creative mind by using a pictographic instead of a linear approach to list making, it is a great way of sorting out your thoughts and your priorities – ten minutes spent doing this and they will become self-evident. (See Mind Mapping page 226).

■ When you wake up in the morning spend five minutes stretching out in bed as if you are a cat. Stretch each limb, your back, waist and neck. While you are doing this and starting to wake up, think about what your priorities are for the day. By doing this you programme yourself to get on with whatever it is you have put at the top of your agenda instead of waiting until later in the day to get your mind focused.

ROUTINE

Routine was, in our grandparents' day, something that was taken for granted. Sunday was a day of rest with the treat of a roast after church (or a Friday or Saturday for Moslems or Jews), Monday was washday, and so on until pay-day on Friday meant bills could be paid and food could be bought, and Saturday could mean a family outing. Our domestic lives are a lot less structured now which allows for more flexibility, but also more chaos. Sometimes, just having a routine can free a person up from making decisions all the time about the next thing to do. If you think your life could benefit from a daily or weekly routine to reduce minor stresses, now is the time to apply yourself to it.

Top Tips

■ Set your priorities. Some are so obvious that you do them automatically – such as brushing your teeth, showering and dressing before you leave home. These, and similar, are priorities which we establish without thought. The trick is to identify areas of your life that you need to improve, to reduce stress, and work them higher up the priority list from 'ought to do' to 'must do'. You can then introduce them into your daily or weekly routine. For instance 'I must buy fresh fruit and vegetables twice a week', 'I must plan time out', 'I must keep up with old friends'.

■ Make a 'must do' list. Typically you will need to allow, daily, half an hour first thing for your post, e-mails and minor errands, such as dropping off dry cleaning or buying stamps, half an hour for cooking and preparing healthy meals and half an hour for yourself, so you can exercise, relax in a bath or just cut your toe-nails if you need to! Any less than this and you will be short changing yourself and your pile of mail, unhealthy eating and drooping hemlines will take their toll on how you feel about yourself.

■ Avoid cramming too many things into your daily routine by adding them to your 'must do' list. Keep your list simple and it will be more effective.

■ Allow enough time to complete your list.

■ Don't have too many rules, and ensure that those you do have are well-chosen and vital.

More Hints

- Keep to a routine of eating meals as a family, or with selected friends. If meal times are normally stressful, make them times for exploration and enquiry – discuss non-inflammatory subjects or play word games. Your family will benefit from more meal-time togetherness and eat more healthily at a sit-down meal rather than eating on the run.

- By all means make a plan and form a routine, but if your routine is occasionally thrown out don't let it distress you. Just restructure your routine.

Holistic Help

- Within your newly organized routine, remember to plan for a day of rest. Regeneration is vital.

- Precious weekends are often wasted because of lack of planning. Keep a list of people you want to catch up with, a folder with film, theatre or art gallery reviews which catch your eye, a list of places you would like visit when you get the time. This way you will always be inspired and be able to have weekend mini-holidays when you need to.

SANCTUARY

Everyone needs their own space – a sanctuary to retreat to. A place where worries about work or home can be left behind. Achieving this can eliminate a lot of life's petty stresses.

Top Tips

- Not only do you need your space, but so do others in your household, including children. Respect other people's space and they are more likely to respect yours.

- If you want 'time out' let people know. If not, you will end up feeling resentful that your time is being called upon when you are not really willing to give it.

- If it is difficult to create your own sanctuary at home because of the daily hubbub of life or there's not enough space, find space elsewhere. Take regular trips to the library to read, sit in a hotel lobby and watch the world go by, take a stroll in a park, have your regular table in a café to scan the daily papers.

More Hints

- An ideal place to create your own sanctuary is the bathroom. You can probably lock the door and wallow in the bath for quite a long time before anyone has the nerve to disturb you.

- One friend of mine had a 'red cap' system at work – if anyone is feeling over-pressurized by too many interruptions they can create a mini-sanctuary by donning a red peaked cap for anything up to 20 minutes. During this time no calls are put through, nobody speaks to that person (even to offer a coffee) and they have total peace to do what they wish.

■ Make your sanctuary a pleasing place (see Nest Building page 28).

Holistic Help

■ If you can afford it, check into a health spa for a couple of days from time to time. Go on your own (many people do) and enjoy the anonymity and lack of pressure.

■ Losing yourself in an activity is another way of creating a mental sanctuary – anything that requires concentration will do – crossword puzzles, jig-saw puzzles, embroidery or model-making.

■ Art classes are an ideal sanctuary because you can leave the left side of your brain (the more analytical, judgmental half) outside, and take the right side of your brain (the more creative side) in with you. It doesn't matter if you think you are artistic or not, just give it a go – you might be surprised.

TRANSPORT PROBLEMS

One day we might be able to dematerialize Trekkie fashion and rematerialize at our destination. However, until then, commuting and the stresses of travel form part of most people's lives. We live at increasingly close quarters these days and this is probably a major factor behind the phenomenon of 'road rage'. But you don't even have to go crazy in this way to suffer. Forty-five per cent of people find the rush hour very stressful – yet commuters find themselves embroiled in it five times a week, 48 weeks a year. Allowing for two journeys a day, that is nearly 500 times a year that they are subjected to a serious stressor – it has got to be worth sorting out!

Top Tips

■ So much depends on your attitude to the whole process of travelling. Stay relaxed and view the inevitability of a certain number of cancelled trains or road works as irritations rather than major catastrophes. Changing your perception of the problem is a good first step on the road to a calm travel experience.

■ Minimize your anxiety about being late by letting the people at your destination know what's happening. It may make you feel better if you get out of the traffic jam or off the bus/tube/train to make a call.

■ If you experience constant delays that always make you late and stressed, then there is really no other solution than to get into the habit of allowing more time for your journey. If necessary set your watch forwards several minutes.

■ Remember it is better to arrive at your destination safely than not at all. Rushing raises levels of stress hormones, which can be dangerous.

■ Talk to your boss about flexi-time or staggered working hours. Rethink your daily schedule. You may be able to share school runs for example. Perhaps home-working a couple of days each week is an option, it is worth a little forethought, planning and negotiation.

More Hints

■ Can you do without a car? If you live in a big city with a good transport system, this might be an option. It could even work financially. If you work out how much you spend on repairs, insurance, car tax, petrol, parking, etc you might be surprised by how much each trip is costing you in real terms. You might find that public transport, bolstered by the occasional taxi ride and car rentals for intermittent weekends away can work out a lot cheaper and is less stressful. If you have no car it means you will never be stopped for being over the limit or end up being a taxi driver for other people.

■ Shopping by car can seem convenient but again if you add up the cost of time spent and petrol there are many occasions when well-placed catalogue ordering makes sense – this is particularly the case if you live out of town.

■ For longer trips, consider making travel a part of the experience instead of a means in itself. In earlier days, travel was more leisurely with whole continents traversed by train, and motoring a pleasurable pursuit. If you drive across Europe, don't dash but stop off after three or four hours driving each day and sample the local delights. If you have the option to go by train instead of plane, do so and take a really good book with you. I relish train journeys into the city as I can get so much work done without interruptions, or even better treat myself to a good book. It is astounding how much less stressful leisurely travel is.

Holistic Help

■ Make your journey more pleasant and useful by listening to talking books. You could even learn a language by listening to tapes.

■ It doesn't all have to be mind-expanding learning – music is soothing and can help to switch your mood.

■ Go green, and get fit – cycle instead of driving or taking the bus. But wear a helmet.

WINDING DOWN: 5-MINUTE TIPS

If your home is truly your nest, and you have tamed the chaos you live with – terrific. But if you are wound up you will not be able to enjoy all this. Here are some five-minute tips to use at home to allow you to wind down, relax and de-stress.

■ Change your clothes when you come home to switch mood and get comfortable. It works.

■ A five-minute stretching routine can make you feel energized and calm. Do the following for 45 seconds each with 15 seconds in between to change position.

– Standing up, stretch your arms over your head one after the other feeling the stretch up the side of your ribs.

– Still standing, roll your head slowly around to create a full circle and stretch your neck muscles, two or three times in each direction.

– Holding on to the back of a chair with one hand, with the other hand catch the foot on the same side as your free hand and slowly pull up behind you, feeling the stretch in the front of your thighs. Switch to the other leg.

– On all fours, stretch your back like a cat then cave in the other way.

– Lying down on your back, with your arms in a T-shape, pull your knees up to your waist and lower to the floor on one side, then slowly switch to the other side.

■ Music and lighting changes, the mood immediately. Depending on the atmosphere you are aiming for, put on something upbeat, mellow or calming and adjust your lighting (fix dimmer switches if you need to). Within moments of arriving home you can switch your mood in this way.

■ Candle light is an even more calming and mood altering light, and it is flattering as well!

■ A five-minute shower to freshen up always helps to reset mood.

■ Throw open a window and take five deep oxygen filled breaths to re-energize yourself.

■ The herb *Eyebright* is soothing for tired eyes. Mix one teaspoon with one cup of boiling water. Let it steep and cool, strain and dip cotton pads into the solution and place over your eyes. While relaxing in a chair for five minute with the eyepads on, soak your feet in a tub of hot water mixed with one cup of *Epsom salts*.

■ Colour yourself blue. While you are relaxing with your eyepads and footbath, visualize yourself bathed in light from the relaxing blue, mauve or green spectrums or healing white.

■ Have a gin-and-tonic, glass of wine or a beer. You may be surprised to see this in a health orientated book, but one is never going to hurt. If you go on to have several however, it defeats the object.

CHAPTER 2

WORK AND MONEY

Do you work to live, or live to work? Either way you might find a better way forward. If you work to live, what pleasure do you get out of your work? If you live to work, do you get enough balance in your life and appreciate other aspects of your life? Both scenarios have their inherent stresses if you are not totally happy with them. And then there is money – the source of more stress in relationships than sex or in-laws. Many of us, at best, only get by financially by the seat of our pants, even when earning reasonable salaries.

Since work and money take up so much of our time and mental focus, it is worth most people spending some time working out how they can get these factors to work for them instead of against them.

AMBITION

The words 'ambition' and 'ambitious' have mixed connotations. Ambition is sometimes frowned upon as being something that only highly driven people have, while for some to be ambitious is viewed in a more positive light as being go-ahead and focused.

Having ambitions just means having dreams. And life would be pretty dull without a few dreams to pep it up. However, not realizing your ambitions might be a significant source of stress in your life. Seeing your ambitions through wise eyes allows them to be of more use to you and reduce their potential as sources of stress.

Top Tips

■ A good reason for fulfilling your ambitions is that you don't want to be looking back over your life from your rocking chair in your dotage saying to yourself 'If only I had . . .'

■ Ambition is what drives many people to great heights – don't be afraid to use yours positively.

■ If your ambition means that you are permanently discontented with your current situation, this can be very stressful for all concerned. View the present positively as a springboard for your future.

- If your personal ambitions involve other people, for example when you want a promotion, ask intelligently and in a non-threatening way. If you go in all guns blazing demanding a promotion because, say, you have been at the company longer than others, you will create a situation where you are probably setting yourself up for rejection. If, on the other hand, you set out clearly your value to the company and the talents you can offer to the new position, then you will have a greater chance of success. In other words build bridges and avoid closing doors.

- If your ambitions scare even you, you can still attain them. We all operate within certain comfort zones. If your ambition seems hopelessly out of reach, resolve to make tiny almost imperceptible increments in your comfort zone until you feel able to go full-steam ahead with realizing your dream. If your ambition is to write a novel (apparently we all have one in us) but get dizzy at the idea of actually taking that leap and starting to write it, make small moves in that direction. Start by writing letters, essays and short stories. Join a writing group or a class. Go for a weekend writing retreat. Put together an outline of your book. Start to describe yourself to people you meet as a part-time writer. If publishing seems a huge hurdle, put some stories on a website. Invite editors to look at them. Start writing to agents and publishers with a synopsis. You wouldn't do this last step without having thought of what to write and having samples of your writing, but by taking these small steps to increase your comfort zone you eventually get there. Taking a series of small steps is a strategy that applies to most big ambitions.

More Tips

- Encourage yourself towards your goals by remembering that you don't want to be looking back over your life from your rocking chair in your dotage saying to yourself 'If only ...'

- One way to help yourself achieve your ambitions is to study what successful people do. This approach is obvious, for example, with a budding tennis or chess player who will endlessly study the techniques of the great players. But this strategy can be applied to any area of life. Watch what successful people do, use videos and biographies, see if you can interview them or even to apprentice yourself to them if you are able. Analyse their behaviour and, putting your personal spin on it, emulate what they do to achieve similar results.

- Your ambitions are important – they allow you to fly. However, put crudely, we are often promoted to the level of our incompetence. What this means is that we might be ambitious for a position that we are not really able to fulfil. Put into those situations, we struggle and our bosses are unhappy, and this can lead to a lot of stress for all concerned. Without resorting to being pessimistic, take a long look at offered opportunities and evaluate if you are really right for the job and if the job is right for you.

- If one day you feel absolutely certain about your ambitions, and yet the next feel uncertain, do not allow yourself to be put off your dreams. It is part of the human condition to be troubled by frailties and uncertainties from time to time, but this does not devalue what we wish to aim for. Instead, take note of your uncertainties in a positive light and work out how you can appease them.

- Be careful of your ambitions for your children as you may encourage the opposite. If the temptation is to 'hot house' them in a particular direction they may end up just rebelling, even at quite a young age. The stresses imposed on them may be more than they can deal with. Instead, give your children as many opportunities as you are able and they will reach a level of achievement that they are comfortable with.
- The difference between winners and 'all the rest' is that winners make things happen instead of letting things happen.

Holistic Help

- Consider other people in the rush to fulfil your ambitions. Take your partner or family into consideration and don't fulfil your ambitions by using your colleagues as stepping stones. (There is a saying that the people you meet on the way up, you also meet on the way down – keep them as potential allies.)
- If your partner or child has ambitions, help them to realize them by offering help and support and talking through the challenges with them.
- Dare to dream.

EXAMS AND JOB INTERVIEWS

Some people are particularly wracked with nerves by the whole process of doing exams, or going for job interviews which can seem like another form of exam. The following tips offer a set of techniques for calming anxieties, allowing you to focus on a set of practical tasks that can improve your performance. Keeping your wits about you and shining through for that short but important time is easier if you trust in yourself and think ahead a little bit.

Top Tips

- Believe in yourself. The very fact that you have been selected for interview or have got onto a particular course means that others have confidence in you. Don't let a little voice in your head sabotage you by telling you that you are not up to it – you are.
- If there is something you do not understand, say so. If you don't understand some of your course work, or some of the criteria for an interview, take steps to find out more.
- For job interviews, do a little research on the company you are seeing in advance of the interview – this will make you more confident. Some companies and organizations have very good websites you can use, or you can often speak to your prospective interviewer by telephone before you meet. Such proactive approaches are generally interpreted as a good sign: showing initiative, intelligence and even an ability to do the job. A little work ahead of time will enable you to participate in the interview, instead of making you feel that the spotlight is just on you. Make sure you formulate a small number of questions in advance

to ask the interviewer. Remember this isn't simply a chance to ask about the pay and conditions package, but to also show an interest in the business and operations of the company.

■ On the other hand, it does help if you have an idea of a salary before any interview. It shows that you have an idea of your self-worth. Even if you find the idea of negotiating for your salary awkward, having a ball-park figure in mind will help you make sensible decisions.

■ The first step towards calming exam nerves is to develop a revision timetable. A clearly worked out schedule enables you to see that there is plenty of time to get through every thing you need to know. If you are facing a big exam, say degree finals, a plan will break down what might seem an overwhelming amount of work into daily achievable chunks. Remember to review your progress and schedule weekly – you will find it enormously satisfying crossing off each subject as you finish revising it.

■ People can generally be divided into those who respond best to auditory, visual, kinetic (touch) or analytical information, or a combination of a couple of these (for more information on this, see Neuro Linguistic Programming or NLP, page 228). Experiment with different revision methods to find those that suit you. Take advantage of tapes, videos and the Internet. Taking a tape recorder to lectures, especially those that sum up a whole area of study, can provide you with a useful revision tool. Read around the subject, in journals and magazines, to find helpful short versions of the latest thinking in your area.

■ Some people find it helpful to read through their notes and to make further, condensed notes on file cards. Reduce the note as far as you can so that a single word or phrase will trigger the key information you need to remember.

More Hints

■ Keep the situation in perspective. While the exam or interview might seem to be the most important thing at the moment, in the context of your whole life it is just one stepping stone, with many alternative stepping stones available at different times.

■ If you don't get the job, or place on the course, it does not have to be that you failed, just that another person succeeded. Often it is a very tight choice between two people with little to distinguish the two. Don't think that you have to be perfect. While it is great to be the best you can be, if you are too much of a perfectionist you can set yourself unreasonable hurdles.

■ Being well-prepared will help to boost your confidence, so leave plenty of time for exam revision or interview preparation.

■ Avoid last minute cramming and if possible get a night of really good sleep before the exam (or interview).

■ If you are feeling stressed about an exam or interview, don't bottle it up, find someone understanding to talk to.

■ If you mind goes blank during the exam or interview, don't panic. Move to the next question, or if in an interview be honest and say you are a bit nervous and would like to return to this later. Returning to the question later, you will probably find that you know more than you thought you did.

■ In an exam, keep a scrap of note paper handy to jot down thoughts that flash into your mind before you lose them and you can return to them later.

■ Read the questions properly. Read them through three times each and ask yourself each time — what is the essence of the question that is being asked? Exams are often failed simply because the questions are misunderstood.

■ Keep your eye on the clock so that you can pace yourself during an exam – it is usually better to partially answer the minimum number of questions than to leave some blank.

■ After the exam or interview don't waste energy on reviewing what went wrong or criticizing yourself. Feel good about the things that went well, congratulate yourself on those, and determine to learn from those things that were less than ideal. Then move on.

■ If you are the parent of children who are doing exams, realize that some children bottle up the pressures to an unbearable degree and you may not even be aware of it. To them the exams may be the most important thing in the world and can contribute to depression, eating disorders, addiction, or worse. Avoid adding to the pressure with unrealistic expectations, and let them know you are there for them (see also Concentration and Memory page 85).

Holistic Help

■ Avoid too much caffeine in the form of coffee, tea, colas, energy drinks or caffeine tablets. They will only serve to hype you up and jangle your nerves. Better to go into the exam or interview calm and collected.

■ Eat regular meals, remembering to make healthy choices (see Healthy Eating page 98) to feed your brain with important nutrients.

■ Exercising regularly, but moderately, will boost energy levels, clear stress hormones, and improve clarity of thought. Alternatively, work with some of the more relaxing disciplines such as t'ai chi or yoga. These can improve concentration and sleeping patterns.

■ Just before the exam or interview spend two or three minutes with your eyes closed, as relaxed as possible, taking several slow, deep breaths.

■ Use the **Australian Bush Flower Remedy**, *Confid*, to help boost your confidence (see Useful Resources page 234).

FIVE-MINUTE DE-STRESSING TIPS FOR THE OFFICE

As the pressure mounts in the office, disassociating yourself from it for even a short while helps to preserve your sanity and keep you focused and energetic. People are not automatons and if you don't 'take five' from time-to-time you run the risk of depleting your spirits and your health. Take time out every hour or so to run through a five-minute de-stress routine and make yourself feel better. You probably do this to a degree anyway – many people hang around the water fountain or coffee-machine, or take a trip to the loo, for just this reason. But your de-stressing can be more creative and productive for you.

Top Tips

- Staring at a VDU (computer screen) encourages eye strain and may trigger tiredness and headaches in susceptible people. Take regular breaks by adjusting your eyes and looking into the distance. Use soothing eye drops.

- You can buy amazingly effective gel-filled eye masks which feel cool against the skin and are very good at making you feel alert and refreshed after five minutes use. You can get these from the **Body Shop** and other outlets.

- Sorting out your desk drawer may not be your idea of fun but a fairly mindless task such as this helps to de-stress while also clearing clutter.

- Do a five-minute stretch routine somewhere quiet (the staff room or the stock room). For a short routine see page 42 and choose which exercises are practical for the space. If there is no room to lie down, for instance, you may be able to adapt the exercises.

- Have a look at www.e-stretch.net for ideas of short and easy mini-exercises you can do at your desk.

More Hints

- Change the task you are working on for a short while. A change is as good as a rest.

- Instead of wasting valuable time when you are busy, open e-mails that you know are jokes only when you decide to have your five-minute wind down – a good laugh is always de-stressing.

- If someone is getting your blood pressure up, you can easily transform your stress response instantly. Imagine that person doing something, or looking, silly, say wearing a clown's nose and hat or speaking as if they had taken a breath of helium (all high and squeaky). Such amusing images will instantly cool you down. You can even use this technique to calm you down ahead of time, if for instance you know you have to call a client who you dread speaking to.

- Talk to your bosses about introducing a red cap system (see page 40).

Holistic Help

- Visualize letting go of your stressful thoughts as 'dumping the junk'. Think of yourself standing on a cliff in a warm breeze and the gusts are blowing away all the unwanted thoughts that are cluttering up your brain. (See Creative Visualization page 222.)
- Take a brisk walk around the block.
- Take five to ten deep breaths every hour. It is invigorating, calming and reduces lethargy.

HEALTHY OFFICE

We spend a third of our day in the office, yet often give little thought to how our environment affects our health and stress levels. Follow these ideas to make your office a healthier environment.

- If you are sitting at a desk all day, you may be storing up postural problems. Back and neck ache, repetitive strain injury (RSI) and tension headaches can all result. Check out the following.

  Your chair should give good back support and allow you to sit comfortably with the computer screen just below your eyes and tilted back at 15 degrees.

  Sit with your hips and back at right angles to the chair, with both feet resting on the floor or on a foot rest.

  Avoid cradling your phone under your chin or against your shoulder.

  Change positions and get up and move around frequently.

- Many items of office equipment give off ozone, a hazardous gas which can worsen asthma and allergic attacks for many people. Even non-allergic people might be adversely affected by ozone emissions and experience headaches, tiredness and itchy eyes. Photocopiers, printers, fax machines and computers are all to blame. Keeping green plants nearby can help to mop up some of these gases – ferns and spider plants are particularly good at this. If your exposure is high, and you experience adverse symptoms you might consider *Nozone* which is a relatively inexpensive desk-top vaporizer which reduces ozone levels and is available from larger **Boots** and other chemists. Look up www.atmospherics.co.uk

- Keep a 1.5 litre bottle of water on your desk and keep topping up your drinking glass until you get through the bottle each day. Staying hydrated will help to keep dry skin, dry eyes, headaches and muscle aches at bay.

- Keep a bowl of fruit on your desk and nibble your way through this when you feel peckish for a snack. Fruit are also watery and will keep you hydrated while also providing power packed nutrients.

- If your office does not yet have a no-smoking policy, lobby your managers to implement one. Most large offices have a no-smoking policy, but you may work in a small office with a chain-smoking colleague.

- In an ideal world, companies would always provide facilities to allow employees to unwind when necessary. A staff room which can be used for eating meals and taking rest periods away from your desk, a water fountain and herbal teas to be offered alongside the usual tea and coffee can all make your work life more pleasant. If you feel you lack such facilities, get together with colleagues to lobby for them. Alternatively, make your own work station as pleasant as possible with plants, photographs and other pictures.

- Office striplighting does not provide full spectrum light needed for optimal functioning. The people who are most likely to suffer as a result of this are those who are prone to Seasonal Affective Disorder or SAD (see page122). However, everyone can benefit from a half-hour stroll outside in full light even in winter.

- See Five-Minute De-stressing Tips for the Office (page 48).

LET'S DO LUNCH

Eating healthily at work can sometimes be a rare achievement. Business lunch menus are tempting. Sandwiches are guzzled hurriedly at desks, afternoon sugar-boosts are craved, and meals are often skipped when under pressure. Forty per cent of calories are consumed out of the home these days, and the meals we eat at work form a large part of these. Because take-away foods tend to be higher in fat and calories than the foods we eat at home, this means it is a great idea to brush up on the skill of making healthy fast food choices. For more ideas on how to choose healthy take-away options see Disordered Eating (page 88).

With a little forethought and planning, healthy eating at the office can be quite easy. As a result, you will improve your energy levels and ability to concentrate and feed your body the nutrients it needs to deal with work-day stresses.

Top Tips

- It all starts with breakfast and if you are always running to get to the office on time, you might well be tempted to skip this vital meal. If you habitually grab a coffee and Danish pastry on the way in, you are just giving yourself an adrenaline hit (which perpetuates stress) and a meal of empty calories. Ideally allow an extra 15 minutes each morning to eat a bowl of muesli cereal and a piece of fruit or a couple of slices of wholegrain toast and a glass of juice. If you are convinced that breakfast is not your thing, you could be wrong. It is a classic sign of blood sugar imbalance that the person does not feel hungry until mid-morning — and of course this perpetuates the disordered blood sugar cycle. Quite often, hunger signals will be suppressed by several cups of coffee. You really need to make yourself eat something (see tip above) and keep it up for about four weeks, to retrain yourself, and you will then see how you feel better for it, and feel worse if you skip breakfast after that.

■ If you can't break the habit of eating on the run, grab some of the following as healthy options: a banana or other piece of fruit, a bio-yoghurt, a few oatcakes, some rye crackers spread with nut butter or a toasted bagel with cheese and a cup of tea from a sandwich shop. Any of these will sustain you for longer and be gentler on your body than the caffeine- and sugar-laden coffee and Danish.

■ Snacking helps to keep energy levels up and to keep you alert. But a sugar-laden chocolate bar will just perpetuate your stress levels and lead to energy dips later by perpetuating the blood sugar imbalance cycle. A couple of cubes of chocolate or one biscuit is really not the point, it is when you are inexplicably drawn to eating the whole pack and feeling exhausted soon after that you know it is draining you. In your desk drawer keep some muesli bars (you can find healthy choices amongst all the sugar-laden ones), packets of mini rice cakes or oatcakes and nuts and raisins. You can keep an attractive fruit bowl on your desk to munch from. If you snack healthily there is a greater chance that you will avoid the post-lunch 2–4pm energy slump that so many people suffer from.

■ If you haven't made your own lunch then seek out the healthy take-away lunch options. Enjoy a baked potato stuffed with baked beans or tuna, sushi boxes, sandwiches made with wholemeal bread, salad boxes (avoid those drowned in mayonnaise), and tortilla wraps with healthy ingredients.

■ There is a wide range of healthy home-packed lunches that are simple and quick to make. Sandwiches made with wholemeal or pumpernickel bread with tomato salsa, hummus or Branston pickle used to moisten the sandwiches instead of butter or mayonnaise. Vegetable soup or left-over casseroles can be taken in a flask. Make your own salad box adding in, for example, chick peas, sunflower seeds, strips of lean meat, grilled peppers, sun-dried tomatoes – a trawl through the left overs in your fridge will often dictate which extra ingredients you can add to the basic salad. Keep a packet of rye crackers at the office then eat them with whatever is easy to hand as you rush out the door: a can of sardines and a couple of tomatoes, a boiled egg, tinned tuna, hummus. Pitta bread and crudités (chopped fresh vegetables) are easy and are also good with hummus, tzetsiki and guacamole.

■ Choose the healthier options in restaurants at lunchtime. Order a salad with the dressing on the side (so you can control how much goes on) or a vegetable soup. Healthy meals include: baked fish or chicken with a selection of vegetables or a side salad, pasta with a low-fat sauce such as tomato, tandoori chicken or chick pea curry with plain rice. Favour fresh fruit salad with a little ice cream for dessert.

■ If you have a works canteen and are unhappy with the choice, get together with a few like-minded colleagues to press for change and give them ideas of what they could offer.

MONEY MANAGEMENT

Money makes the world go round, whether we like it or not. Yet it is the source of misery for many people, often because they don't think they have enough of it, and just as often because they are simply disorganized about managing their money. Added to this, we live in a society of buy-now-pay-later and this, for some people, has caused their debts to spiral out of control. We also live in a time when property prices have risen to a level that makes it hard to 'get on the ladder' and when jobs-for-life are no longer a reality. If any of this affects you, and you are stressed by the situation, some of the pointers in this section will help.

Top Tips

- Understand what your financial priorities are. Do you tend to live for today – where you are happy to spend what you earn and save little for the future – or do you mostly live for tomorrow as a conscientious saver and investor, foregoing costly fun and frolics now? For many of us these issues are age related – we are the former in our younger years and the latter as we age. One way of reducing the stresses this might create is to realize what your habits are. There is no point in doing one and regretting the other. By deciding which you are and embracing it you are likely to be happier with your lot. On the other hand, you could work towards a middle ground between these extremes!

- Don't confuse need with want. The more we have the more we often think we need – a new sofa to go with the new curtains. Yet if you take time to question your 'need' you may find that it's really a 'want'. Monitoring your material desires will save you money and avoid feelings of frustration.

- Increasing use of freelance workers has created a more insecure labour market. But looked at in a more positive light, this work-fluidity also creates new opportunities for those who want them.

More Hints

- Advertising. Don't fall for it. As you know, whole industries exist to part you from your money. And it is not they who tremble when you open the bill, it is you. Rather than follow trends, create your own style and supersede fashion in favour of lasting style and chic classics. Instil the same discipline in your children to avoid buying the latest, and most expensive, trainers three times a year. Give them the confidence in their own taste and approach instead of needing to follow the herd. (I realize this may sound simpler than it is to really achieve, but if they understand what branding and advertising is all about, and how it is more cool to have a unique style, they just might go for it!)

- We are lucky enough to live in a time where we have excellent design and production methods. This means that we can afford to take some time to research products we wish to buy rather that buying impulsively. Large white goods (hoovers, washing machines etc) are often to be found more cheaply if you use consumer magazines or subscribe to the

Which? website (www.which.net) for information on the best and cheapest items. Fashion and decorating magazines are great for ideas, inspiring you to be creative and get the 'look' for a lot less than your more hasty friends might pay.

- Make regular forays to browse for things you need in rural or out-of-the-way antique shops, auction houses and markets, including car boot sales. It takes time but can be fun. In my local 'retro' shop, the people have an unerring eye for good household stuff, but dealers from London regularly come and buy from them at their shop prices and then triple or quadruple the price when they sell it on. By turning the whole exercise into a hobby you turn it into a much lower stress activity than cruising the high streets and paying through the nose.

Holistic Help

- Focus on some truths when you meditate: 'I am impoverished when I yearn for more, not when I have little'. 'Without the concept of thrift no amount of money is ever enough'. 'On a global scale, we are the lucky ones'.

BUDGETING AND BILL PAYING

- If you have never worked out a budget, now is the time to do so. Working from your cheque stubs, bank statements and credit card bills, write down what you spend on all the basics of life: rent/mortgage, utilities, insurance, travel, food, etc. Also work out what you spend, on average, on large but occasional expenditures such as holidays and furnishings. Then spend two weeks meticulously keeping a note of every penny you spend – every round of drinks you buy, every newspaper and magazine you purchase, presents for other people, treats for yourself, meals out, clothes. At the end of these two exercises, you will have a good picture of your spending patterns. Working out your income will probably be a little simpler especially if you have a single employer. Now there is nothing else to do but marry the two up and find out why you are fortunate enough to be able to save, or why you are always in debt.

- Credit cards may be your flexible friends but if you lack self-control they are also a cause of many sleepless nights. These days we average, per credit card owner, debts of £5000 spread over store cards, credit cards and personal bank loans. If you are not able to control your spending on them or, more importantly pay them all off each month, then cut them up. Store cards have notoriously high interest charges if you do not pay the bill off on time. One credit card, carefully used, only when you really need it, such as going abroad and booking tickets, is enough for anybody.

- If you have a large credit card debt, possibly spread over a range of cards, you need to find out about transferring all the debts to one source. You will find that refinancing your debt at a lower rate of interest through a bank, or other loan, will work out cheaper than leaving interest charges to mount up on your cards. Make sure you work out realistically how much you can afford to pay back and over what time.

- In the old days, people would keep envelopes or jars in which they put money to save up to pay utility bills or for big expenditures like holidays or furniture. There is something in this. While envelopes might be a little low-tech these days, at least work out how much you need to put aside, each month, into a savings account for regular expenditures.

- Check your bank statements regularly. If they sit unopened because you fear what is inside, it really is not going to change the situation for the better. Ask for your bank statements to be sent to you two weekly instead of monthly so you don't get too far out of control. Or check your bank balances weekly by going on-line.

- It might be an old-fashioned idea, but there is something in the saying 'never a lender nor a borrower be'. This was obviously the forerunner of modern stress-management!

EARNING POWER

- Value yourself and others will value you. Those who consistently do well are those who are not afraid to ask for top prices and who give a good service (you can't have one without the other for very long). There is always a market for high quality goods and services. This is even true in an economic downturn when people still want quality and it is the lower-quality things and services they dispense with. If you dare to charge more than others for your service several things are likely to happen. Firstly, you will automatically be perceived to be better than the others. Secondly, people will be serious in their dealings with you. Thirdly, you will probably attract even more business.

- All this presupposes that you are professional and provide a good service – and if this is the case you need never have a conscience, as some do, that they are 'ripping people off' – if the customer is not satisfied they simply won't come back. (Incidentally I have put this principle to the test on several occasions and it has never let me down). Never feel bad, guilty or unworthy of your full earning potential. If you have more, you are then in the position of helping others – in your family or to help charities.

- If you are looking for a raise remember to ask intelligently (see Ambition page 43). Also avoid disempowering terms when you think about getting a raise. Avoid saying 'I hope I will get a raise', and say 'I know I will get a raise'. And if you don't? Avoid thinking 'What will I do now?' And say to yourself 'I'll handle it'.

- You can always move jobs to improve your income. But remember that salary is not the only thing your working life is about. You also need to evaluate how you feel about the location, your colleagues, your job satisfaction. Sometimes there is a hidden price to a job move and you have to ferret out what this might be in advance and then decide if you can accept it?

- Creative Visualization (see page 222) can be used for the following affirmations (and remember to always express the affirmations in the present tense even if you have not yet got what you are hoping for financially). 'I am enjoying great financial prosperity now'. 'The more I prosper, the more I am able to share with others'. 'My life is filled with abundance'. 'Financial success is coming to me effortlessly'. 'I value myself, I value those around me, and I am valued by others'.

INVESTING AND SAVING

- It is important to realize that investing is not the same as saving. If you invest in, say stocks and shares, or in a company start up scheme, you risk losing that money. If you put money into a savings account you do not risk losing that money (except in very rare circumstances where banks have folded and not been backed up by governments). Invest or save your money according to your needs and according to how much you could afford to lose if the worst came to the worst.

- However, remember that if you invest £500 in a stock which then rises to £5000, but you leave it there and it eventually crashes to £250 – you have lost £250 and not £4,750. If you never cashed it in, you never had it and it was just paper. This might help you to be more philosophical if you are ever in this situation.

- Work out where you want to be, financially, five, ten, twenty years from now. Do you need to get through higher education? Do you want to buy a flat or house? Do you want to plan for your children's future? Do you want to ensure a secure retirement? By working out what your needs are, you can decide how to achieve these with saving and investing.

- As a general rule, it is a good plan to save at least ten per cent of your net income for future needs and contingencies. Planning for life's unexpected events is wise because nobody knows what the future holds. Ill health, the roof caving in, unexpected additions to the family, being responsible for an ageing parent and other events can all stretch finances to the limit.

- Don't be frightened of the whole question of managing money in the belief that you don't have a mind for it as, with very little perseverance, you can change this around. Most of the newspapers, particularly the weekend editions, have excellent money sections that simplify the whole issue of money, saving and investment. At budget times, tax year ends and when new financial products become available they explain it all in simple terms. They also regularly feature different types of bank accounts, different spending profiles and investment plans. They may also have informative questions and answers pages. Six months spent reading the money sections of a selected paper can make a huge difference to your confidence and your understanding. You might also want to tune into the Moneybox programme on BBC Radio 4.

- Get professional advice, but always be aware that financial advisers are usually paid commission (though they are controlled by regulations). Truly independent advice is available only from advisers who are paid a fee. The more you know, the more you will be able to use your educated judgement.

SPEND, SPEND, SPEND

- Learn to walk away from potential purchases. Take a day to decide if you really want or need the item. Your desire will often wane, but sometimes will be enhanced and this will provide the answer about whether to buy it or not. On the other hand, if it has been sold when you get there learn to be fatalistic about it. It wasn't meant to be. And in truth when you look back ten years from now the chances are that you won't even remember it.

■ Our desire to buy something is usually in direct proportion to its availability. All sales people know this which is why you will be pressed with 'this is the last one in the shop' and similar lines. Resist this and examine your feelings around loss and deprivation. In reality it is rarely the case that you will experience serious loss or deprivation if you do not get this item.

■ Overspending is all about instant gratification in exactly the same way that eating a cream cake is. You want it, and you want it now. You are putting off the pain of worrying about the credit card bill, in favour of avoiding the pain of not getting what you want this instant. It is only when the pain of the bills landing on the doormat gets too great, that it affects the consciousness of the overspender at the cash till. Understanding this pain/gratification pattern can help to break the habit.

■ It used to be that debts would arise because people got into difficulty over unexpected events such as illness or major property repairs. However, these days it is more likely that the cause is borrowing too much money. If you get into financial difficulty, the Citizen's Advice Bureau can often help with free advice to help you get on top of your finances.

■ The following are tips for getting out of debt. Don't take on further debt (especially to make payments on your existing debts). Make a list of all your debts. Which are most pressing? These are the ones where there are sanctions such as repossession of a property or cutting off services, or legal penalties such as council tax or child support. Negotiate repayments on your most important debts. You can refinance your non-urgent debts such as credit cards to spread out payments and rationalize the interest you are paying, but do not be tempted to increase your debt load.

TAXES

It's corny but it's true – the only certainties in life are death and taxes. Despite the fact that we always know that tax-form-filling time and settling-up time will come around 'as sure as eggs is eggs', many still manage to be caught out by this inevitability. So, given that there is no getting away from it, these steps will help you deal with the inevitability of tax returns.

■ If your tax is deducted at source by your employer that is one stress you do not have to deal with. However, if you are self-employed, immediately set up a separate bank account, if you have not already done so, and decide how much money you need to put in on a monthly basis to meet your tax commitment at the end of the year. Each year re-evaluate whether you are putting in sufficient funds.

■ Keeping accounts is easy if you stick to a few simple rules. Always keep a record of your income in the form of invoices. Keep all the receipts that show expenditure which can be partially or wholly claimed against tax, such as capital investment in equipment like computers, copiers etc. Either write everything down in a book or computer spreadsheet on a weekly or monthly basis, or file your bills and receipts in a 12-pocket concertina file, working out the costs regularly. Set aside sufficient time – some people find themselves spending at least a day doing their accounts once a year!

■ For most people filling in their tax form is about as appealing as having teeth extracted without an anaesthetic. But this does not make it any less of a fact. The first step in doing what you know you have to do is simple – open the envelope. This may sound obvious but many people will leave it wallowing at the bottom of a pile of papers until the deadline looms or even, when it passes. The procrastination of filling in tax forms simply puts off the pain of getting on with the job, but come the day when you have to get the form in suddenly the pain of not filling it in becomes greater – so you get on with it. You can use this information in future by saying to yourself, at the point where you are tempted to procrastinate, 'If I don't get on with it now, what will the ultimate cost be to me (in money, sleepless nights, anxiety, etc)'.

■ Once you have opened the envelope, check immediately that you have the right forms. Not having what you need is a non-existent excuse as far as the Inland Revenue are concerned. If you have not received a form at all, and think you should have one, call the tax office with your tax reference number and national insurance number.

■ Now get your diary out and set aside a half-day or, worst case, a day when you will definitely sit down to do your tax return. Make sure this date is well within the time limits so if anything goes wrong or you need more information you have time to sort these out.

■ Each year make sure you keep a copy of your return. This will facilitate future returns as you will probably have income from much the same sources – your work, bank or building society accounts, and investments.

■ If there are any new sources of income or if you have switched accounts, make a note of these.

■ Ask your employer for any forms you need to complete your returns.

■ Getting the information together is probably much worse than completing the form. Keep a file for this and keep it up-to-date. If you have not done this up until now, you can start immediately. Into this you can pop all mid-year and end-of-year statements you receive.

■ Now you just need to get on with it!

OFFICE POLITICS

Wherever you get two or more people who work together you have the potential for office politics. Research shows that one of the major causes of stress is unhappiness at work, and this is often the result of office politics. Objectively, office politics are completely unnecessary, but they are frequently an integral feature of working life involving gossip, petty resentments, favouritism and anxiety about promotions. The following advice will help you to avoid a lot of time wasting and worry.

Top Tips

■ Don't gossip – ever. If you don't get drawn into chatting about other people then you can't also get drawn into the office politics game. While exchanging information on work-related matters might be valid, gossip often involves individuals and is often damaging to that person.

- Don't moan to colleagues. If you have a complaint, deal with it in a professional way and take it to whoever will realistically be able to deal with it. Taking positive action is likely to be most rewarding either in real terms or in the sense that you have done something positive about your situation.

- If colleagues who have less self-control get irritated by your lack of involvement in the office politics game don't give them the opportunity to believe that you are aloof. Stay friendly, open and honest, but still don't gossip.

- Notice what influence your behaviour has on your colleagues and environment. Learn to be confident in your requirements. This is usually called assertiveness, and while this is correct, I hesitate to use the word directly because of the negative connotations this often has for people.

- Being confident in your requirements is particularly important if you are up against 'glass ceilings', 'jobs for the boys', 'closed shops' or various forms of protectionism.

More Hints

- If your boss is claiming success based on your work this could be a major source of work-based stress. To a degree your boss has the right to do this because you are a part of his or her team, but if credit is never being given where it is due, you need to do something about this or suffer the consequences in your self-esteem. Work out what your choices and options are and then make an action plan. If your boss is a bully this might mean planning to leave.

- Take responsibility for all your actions, that way when you refuse to take responsibility for the failings of others they can't be irritated. If there is collective responsibility for team activities however, you have to take your part of the blame.

- Discrimination of any sort is never acceptable. Deal with it, but retain a sense of humour and fair play or else you lose out as well.

- Remain true to yourself. If you are honest, focused and kind to other people, you can set an example and lead from a position of strength without getting dragged down into the petty details of others' concerns.

Holistic Help

- Nurture a more communal, caring environment in your office by focusing on constructive activities, such as supporting a charity as a group or setting up a book club. Communal activities can prevent the seeds of discontent – office politics of course – taking root.

PROBLEM SOLVING AND DECISION MAKING

Problem solving and decision making are inescapable facts of life. We are faced with choices on a daily basis, and thank goodness we are. Those who do not have choices, or who feel they do not, are most prone to the effects of stress. You need to hone your decision-making skills if you react to challenges with anxiety and usually struggle to come up with the best course of action to take. There are easy ways to speed up and ease the process which, if applied consistently, can lighten the load.

Top Tips

- Those who agonize most are those who see problems in every answer. Instead focus on being someone who sees answers in every problem.

- Change the use of the word 'problem' to 'challenge' and the phrase 'problem solving' to 'decision making'.

- Arm yourself with the information you need. If you don't have this information, find it. If you don't know where to find it, do some research.

- Spend no more than 10–20 per cent of your time on examining the problem, or challenge, and 80–90 per cent of your time on coming up with solutions.

- Life is full of 'ifs', 'ands' and 'buts' which complicate making decisions. The most difficult part is often the actual process of arriving at a decision. Once you have arrived at that point it will usually seem quite easy. Once you have made that decision, don't spend energy on worrying about what would have happened if you had taken another course of action.

- Remain flexible and if one avenue of exploration ends up being a dead end, or not appropriate for other reasons, don't waste time on worrying about this, but just get on with the next approach (see Mindset/Flexibility page 159).

- Get into the habit of changing your limiting thoughts. Thoughts such as 'I am not good at this', 'I don't understand this', or 'I don't want this' are more crippling than you probably realize. They limit your potential and your enjoyment. As a specific exercise, spend the next week checking yourself whenever you are tempted to have a limiting thought. Have only empowering thoughts such as 'I can do this', 'I am able to find out the information needed' and 'I know what I want'. If a week seems too much, start with one day. And then do it for another day and so on.

- One of the main reasons why decisions might be hard to reach is because of the chatterbox in your head saying 'What if it goes wrong?' or 'What if I make a bad choice?' If you keep repeating these disempowering thoughts, ask yourself another question immediately: 'What is the worst thing that can happen if it goes wrong' – 99 per cent of the time you will realize that nothing too bad will happen. This can help to get the challenge into perspective.

- Remain true to your convictions. Whether you are taking big or little decisions stay true to yourself.

- Time spent worrying about things is time wasted. Time spent planning solutions is time well spent.

- Problems (challenges) don't resolve themselves by thinking about them. You have to take action.

- Don't be afraid to ask for help (see Delegating page 36).

More Hints

- There are four main types of response when people are faced with a challenge. Understanding which category yours fall into can improve your response.

  - Fight response (external): you meet challenges head-on in a positive manner and often deal with problems before they arise. You are assertive and positive in your approach. Often this person is a high achiever but may find it hard to relax.

  - Fight response (internal): you appear calm and in control. You might have a fixed method of how to do things and do not welcome change as it undermines your idea of how everything should be ordered. This lack of flexibility can be stressful.

  - Flight response: you pretend the problem doesn't exist, find it easy to give up and are happiest letting someone else handle it. This can lead to feelings of lack of self-determination (see page 61).

  - Flow response: you accept problems without either fighting them or running away from them. However, you often find it difficult to make decisions which can be stressful.

- If you decide that a change needs to happen, it will be a temporary one unless you make yourself totally responsible for the change (this does not mean that you can't bring in other people as resources, but that you recognize the buck stops with you). For lasting results, you must make the following decisions: a) It must change b) I must change it c) I can change it.

- Get into the habit of always writing down the pros and cons of a situation. If you keep these in your head they tend to swirl around in an unfocused way, but if you commit them to paper, a clear solution will often emerge. Quite often one of the lists (of either cons or pros) will be longer than the other and automatically provide the answer. Mind Mapping (page 226) is an ideal technique for this. (See also Cognitive Thinking page 219.)

- If your decision proves to be less than perfect, do not get frustrated but learn from the experience.

- Often the best decision making happens after team work, or at least asking others for input. Use the wealth of experience and information around you. However, for some people this will serve to sway them in several different directions, depending on who they are talking to at the time, so stay centred and pull in all the information to come to a decision. If necessary use the pro and con list (mentioned above) once you have talked to people.

- When talking to people, ask relevant questions. Be clear about what you are seeking and spend some time jotting down notes before you survey them. Throughout your conversations with others remain curious about how they picture the challenge and adopt the elements you find useful.

- If your decision making is clouded by emotional issues see the relevant section in Chapter 4, Emotions.

Holistic Help

- Stay centred and calm throughout the process. Getting flustered or being anxious will not help to resolve the debate but will just serve to exact a toll on you as your stress levels rise. If you feel overwhelmed, take time to do deep breathing exercises and refocus your mind on looking for solutions.

- Work on the positive affirmations 'I am a resourceful person' and 'I have an innate creativity which helps me to find answers'.

- Tap your instinctive creativity by closing your eyes and visualizing yourself standing in a circular forest glade, in lovely weather, from which radiates a number of paths. Hanging from trees at the entrance to the paths are notices with one solution on each. Walk along each of the paths in turn and see where they take you. In your visualization you always remain safe and can return to the glade. (See Creative Visualization page 222.)

- Use the homeopathic **Australian Bush Remedy**, *Cognis Essence* (see Useful Resources page 234).

SELF-DETERMINATION

It is an absolute fact that the people who feel most stressed are those who feel they have no control over a situation. For instance, you might think that a high powered executive with a busy lifestyle would be most likely to feel stressed if the company is in trouble because the need for trouble-shooting falls to her or him. But, as it happens it is often the blue-collar workers who are the ones that feel the stress – they feel they have little or no influence about which way the company goes, and therefore over their job security. The most innovative companies recognize this and encourage forums for 'the workers' to participate in the direction of the company.

Of equal importance to having actual control or influence over a situation, is the 'feeling' of control. One of the important things to restore in people who are depressed is their feeling of control over their lives – their feeling of self-determination. They may actually have a reasonable degree of control, but because they do not feel they have choices and are unconfident about their decision-making abilities, they feel out of control and this can fuel depression and anxiety (this sequence of events is referred to as learned helplessness).

While this section deals with self-determination in the work place, you can of course apply these principles to any area of your life.

Top Tips

■ Establishing the belief system that we all have choices and can determine our future is the best way to achieve self-determination. These words will sound hollow to the person who is in the throes of a difficult situation but for the most part we really do have the ability to determine our fate. For instance, if you are about to be fired you have the choice about whether to feel defeated about this or determined to use it as an opportunity to take a new direction in life. If you have an overbearing partner who is occasionally violent, you have a choice about whether to stay or not. If your teenage child has addiction problems, you have a choice about whether to find out about help organizations and to find out about how family and friends might be inadvertently facilitating this. Nobody said these choices are easy, and they are indeed often complicated. There are nearly always many facets to the decision-making process and you may need to explore them, but you do have choices in most things. (See Cognitive Thinking page 219.)

■ Make a list of your personal strengths – work on the list over a few days if necessary and as you have fresh thoughts add them to the list (see Mind Mapping page 226). This exercise will help you focus on your abilities and see yourself in a positive light. Your strengths could be anything at all: 'I am highly organized', 'I have a good relationship with my colleagues/family', 'I enjoy new challenges', 'I am outgoing and friendly', 'I am a good person'.

■ Keep a diary of problems which tend to recur in your life. This gives you the ability to root out the causes and to be very realistic about how to resolve them. It stops you being an ostrich! If you are always late for work figure out what your morning patterns are and what needs to change. If you are always overdrawn keep a diary of spending and analyze your spending patterns. If you regularly fall out with your kids, work through your typical conversations and see where they tend to break down. By going through these exercises, you regain control over the various threads of your life.

■ It is usually the case that attempts to change have only a temporary effect as a result of failing to find an alternative way of behaviour. It is essential to replace old patterns with new ones and not just to eliminate them.

■ If you are in a job that you find unrewarding — you do not like your colleagues, the job is not satisfying, you are not appreciated and the money just is not worth it — you need to do something about it to put yourself back in control of the situation. Sit down now and plan your future by reading the section on Goal Setting (page 16).

■ Confronting a bullying boss is never easy, and takes guts, but in the long run may be necessary to retain self-esteem. If your boss is the type who talks down to you in public, who consistently expects you to sacrifice your personal life for your work life, or who undermines your work at every opportunity, you need to start taking notes about the instances where you have found the behaviour unacceptable. Once you have some notes, you can think about the issues in a constructive way. Be clear that you are not going to put up with being treated in this way and that if you are to be criticized it needs to be in private and it needs to be done in a constructive manner. You may, of course, find that this backfires on you and you need to plan for this eventuality. However, putting up with bad behaviour because of your fears (typically of losing your job) will, in the long run, exhaust you and cripple your self-esteem. You may need to look for another job.

More Hints

■ Some people have a misguided way of finding self-determination within the work environment. They themselves have limited scope for manoeuvrability, and so they inflict the same on their subordinates, or on customers. They are the 'jobs-worths' – the ones who suck air through their teeth and claim 'it's more than my job is worth'. They become, in effect, mini-dictators presiding over their domain with all the ferocity they can muster. If you work for someone like this, it will be a debilitating situation and you will quickly lose all sense of self-determination if you allow it. (For more on this see Office Politics page 57).

■ Assertiveness can be perfectly healthy and can be thought of as a middle ground between being unhealthily passive and unhealthily aggressive.

■ The same as the above is true in some domestic situations. (For more guidance see Self-Esteem, page 169).

■ If you find it initially difficult to take control of the major areas of your work, or personal life, start small. By working on small things and succeeding at making improvements, you can do wonders for your self-esteem and create the belief system that you are indeed able to make changes and positively influence your future.

Holistic Help

■ Create a positive visualization that helps you to 'bounce' bad events off you. (See page 222 for details of how to work at visualization.) See yourself as surrounded by a shimmering white light hovering just outside your body, from top to toe. This light does two things, one of which is to fill you with warmth and energy, giving you the strength to deal with whatever comes your way. It also creates a protective shield around you, off which bad events, bad feelings and unpleasant comments just bounce back out into space. They can't touch you.

SUCCESS BRINGS NEW CHALLENGES

We may dream of success, in whatever is our chosen sphere, but when that success comes – what then? Success can be every bit as difficult to deal with as failure, but knowing about the possible challenges can help you to avoid these stresses.

Top Tips

■ Working your way up the company ladder can include unexpected hurdles. You may find you are responsible for others, it might be perceived that you can take an even greater workload than you were prepared for, or a job that you went into because you enjoy being 'hands on' has turned into a management job. Once you've got to where you wanted to be, you may find that it is not all you dreamed it would be. Find out beforehand what is involved in a promotion and work out if you are happy with the terms.

■ If you are self-employed, you are not necessarily immune to similar events. You might find that you have more demand than you can keep up with and are forced to decide if you need to employ an assistant (with all the differences in working methods that this requires). You might find that demands are made on your time which are not actually cost-effective – being asked to give talks or to do some fund raising are typical examples. It is surprising how these can build up and require a lot of preparation. You may get something out of these activities, such as networking or feeling good about helping others, but if they are an unacceptable drain on your resources you need to learn to say no in a kind way.

■ When you've planned and worked hard to achieve your dreams, it can be a cruel blow to find that far from just being able to relax and ride the tide of success that you have to work just as hard. For instance, success may bring all sorts of practical problems for the owner of a growing business, such as staffing levels, having to juggle stocking levels (with large amounts of money tied up with stock), problems with multiple premises, and distancing from the end-customer. Often all the ideals that you started out with, such as giving a good service or a good product at a good price, can fly out of the window when the company gets to an unwieldy size. Anticipating such problems in a reworked business plan is essential.

More Hints

■ You would also be wise to talk to your bank or financiers about contingency plans if you find that success brings a greater short-term financial drain. Avoid mortgaging your house against any financial drains that crop up with your business activities – even if you seem to be riding high at the moment. Sometimes people do this and win through but many lose out. If you are seeking finance for a strong enough reason usually the banks will be interested – if they are not then they consider it too great a risk. Are you prepared to risk you home if this is their view?

■ By keeping other aspects of your life in focus, such as family, friends, leisure activities and interests, and not sacrificing them to the god of success, you can maintain balance in your life and avoid feelings of disenchantment. (See Work/Home balance page 72.)

■ The culture in which we live suddenly throws some people into the limelight. As a result, we have a chance to see some challenges of success in graphic detail. Film, rock and media stars gain overwhelming success, and then have to cope with the consequences of this. Often the way to deal with it is to use a large chunk of their new-found wealth to prop themselves up and not infrequently we hear tales of descent into alcoholism or drug addiction. You have to be a very strong person with a very level head to deal with this sort of fame, and many are simply not mature enough for this. If perchance, you have even a small percentage of this thrust upon you, take a deep breath and keep your wits about you. Take financial advice, understand that a rich alcoholic is just as miserable as a poor alcoholic and decide early on in the game if this is really what you want, or what you think you want.

■ Some people and businesses are successful even during economic downturns. Smaller companies often do better, if managed properly, than larger, more unwieldy ones. They have a flexible approach and see it as an opportunity to excel over their competition, to expand and to acquire premises and expertise at lower prices. Recessions are opportunities to lighten up operating structure and negotiate harder. Keeping tight credit control at these times is vital.

Holistic Help

■ No matter how successful you become, remember those you love and people who helped you along the way. We are all a sum of the experiences and people we meet during our life.

■ If you have succeeded, you can be an inspiration to others. Take time to give back to the system by giving talks at a local school or helping out youngsters.

■ If you are a high earner, you can support those who are less fortunate and who are unable to look after their own interests.

■ If you have succeeded once, you know you can do it again when you need to. Use this as an affirmation when you need to (see Creative Visualization page 222).

TIME MANAGEMENT

Do you find that you struggle to juggle your time? You might feel that there never seem to be enough hours in the day – or are there? Sometimes it is easy to be busy being busy. Rationalizing what you do could free up a lot of spare time – to enjoy yourself.

Top Tips

■ Remember to be selective. We have many labour-saving devices but are busier than ever. Where once an executive would have had a secretary, now that person has a laptop and e-mail and does all their own correspondence. Because of the ease of photocopying and sending electronic info, we are bombarded with more and more copies, memos and circulars – and then we have to read and file most of these! This means that we need to be more and more selective about how we spend our time and what we keep and what we chuck out. Otherwise we run the risk of drowning in paper and stuff to do.

■ Make a point of taking five minutes at the start of each day to plan your day, and also glance at how it impacts on the rest of the week.

■ If you are over-stretched, take a long hard look at your daily schedule and decide if you are expecting too much of yourself. Make cuts if you need to.

■ Do a time audit. Keep a diary for three or four days and meticulously write down how you spend your time. You may find that you spend more time than you think on irrelevant tasks, such as filling in questionnaires in magazines that are hanging around the office, spending 20 minutes reading all the joke e-mails you have received or phoning to check the cinema listings at five different cinemas, with the result that you are creating undue pressure on yourself to complete more important tasks in less time. Or you may find that you are underestimating the time taken to complete the necessaries of life, and so feel pressurized. A time diary will help you see where your time is going and help you to prioritize tasks and allocate time sensibly.

■ We are subject to different biorhythms (energy cycles when we are more, or less, productive) and you may be aware of these. In most people, brain power peaks before mid-day, so handle difficult jobs between 8am and 12pm. Avoid difficult jobs in the evening. The exception to this seems to be with some creative people who like to use the quiet night-time hours as thinking time. If you do work later on in the day, avoid alcohol which will deaden your ability to focus.

■ Delegate where appropriate. If you tend to do everything yourself investigate why. Use the techniques described in Cognitive Thinking (page 219) to uncover more reasonable alternatives to statements such as 'I can't trust anyone else to do the job properly' or 'I don't like to be a burden'.

More Hints

■ If you find that you are repeatedly logging-on to check your e-mails the chances are that this is distracting you from other activities. Make a point of only checking your e-mails a maximum of three times a day at pre-set times (morning, after lunch and clocking off time). Avoid opening jokes and other distracting e-mails until you are ready – set aside time to unwind and then you can really enjoy them.

■ Keep your paperwork in order and files up to date. A small amount of time spent on getting organized will save huge amounts of time later on when trying to find things you need in a hurry.

■ Write contact details down on the inside of each folder you create, right at the beginning, to save you flicking through reams of paper to find names and numbers.

■ Regularly sweep through your computer files and delete or store on disc any you don't need. This will make it easier to access those files you really need.

■ If you have a large project to tackle, break it down into smaller chunks and put the resulting plan into your diary.

■ If you allocate time to a task and can't afford for it to put your day out, stick to this time allotment and don't be tempted to work late and eat into your down-time. If you overrun you will need, of course, to reorganize priorities for the next day or the rest of the week, but at least you will be rested from a good night's sleep and will have topped up your energy levels, before you tackle it again.

■ If you can't change it, don't sweat it. Once you have completed a task, you might reflect on it and want to make a change, and that is fine. But if, for whatever reason, you can't change it, don't waste valuable time and energy worrying about it. Always remember to ask yourself the question 'What is the worst that can happen if it is not perfect' and the majority of times the answer is – it won't be a big deal.

- Don't waste valuable time thinking up excuses for why you haven't finished something. Come clean and get on with the task, but hiding behind excuses never works in the long term. It just creates stress for you, uncertainty for the person on the receiving end, and uses up valuable energy.

Holistic Help

- 'Mindfulness', where you really concentrate on a single activity, fully interacting with it and appreciating the essence of it, is a useful thing to bring into our lives even if we do not practice it as a set exercise (see Meditation page 224). You have heard of Parkinson's law that work expands to fill the time allotted to the task. Yet many of us feel we do not have enough time for anything. It can seem as if the past was a time when we were able to engage in a host of restful and enriching activities, such as letter writing or playing music. Despite our labour-saving tools we have less and less time on our hands. Being 'mindful' helps us to recapture some of this time.

- Keeping in touch with friends is vital for a rounded and happy life. However, avoid chatting in the middle of your work day as this will inevitably throw your day out. But do set aside time to chat to people at a time when you can relax and really focus on the conversation.

TRAVELLING FREQUENTLY

Some jobs require a significant amount of travel. Whether this is disproportionate or not in the context of your life depends on your circumstances. All sorts of people spend a lot of time travelling: business executives, salespeople, lorry drivers, health professionals who are on call, and others. If you do travel frequently it is worth thinking about how to reduce the impact of this stress on your life.

Top Tips

- Things that go wrong when you travel frequently create huge stresses and can send blood pressure soaring. Think ahead about what can go wrong and have action plans ready.
  - Have a good book available to deal with flight delays.
  - Keep copies of your medical insurance with you.
  - If there are baggage restrictions find out about them in advance.
  - Check out the arrangements for taxis at your destination.
  - Ensure your checked-in luggage has your name and address in it.
  - Make sure you have roadside insurance in case your vehicle breaks down.

■ Think about the people you have left behind. Invariably they will be making changes to their routine to accommodate your travel. Be thoughtful. Always call from your destination if you are able. Drop a card in the post to say 'I'm thinking of you'. Find out if there are aspects of your travelling lifestyle that they find difficult and discuss these with them.

More Hints

■ Always have your bag packed the night before, when money, passport, tickets, credit cards, keys and any vital paperwork can all be assembled calmly, and the next day will not be as rushed.

■ If your travel involves time-changes and jet-lag, see page 105.

■ If your travel involves long journeys in the car, make sure you stop frequently for breaks – this could be a life-saver. Invest in a back rest to help reduce the potential of back strain.

■ Do you travel more than you need to? You might investigate the merits of conference calling and discuss them with your boss.

Holistic Help

■ Transform your hotel room with a little bit of home, for no matter how short a time. Take photos of your family, a favourite pillow case or your favourite tea.

■ Pack an emergency health kit which includes tea tree oil and grapefruit seed extract – two of the best natural anti-bacterials.

■ Carry an eye mask with you if you are to stay in a hotel room to stop any light interrupting your sleep.

■ On long-haul flights, take a bottle of water with you (the flight attendants are never around when you want them and give tiny glasses anyway), go easy on the alcohol, do stretching exercises (you'll need to go to the loo with all that water anyway) and do deep breathing exercises periodically). For more tips on how to avoid jet-lag and ease travel symptoms see Jet Lag page 105).

UNEMPLOYMENT

Our reaction to unemployment has everything to do with how involved we were in the process of losing a job. If unemployment is a result of taking voluntary redundancy or 'constructive dismissal', retirement or a deliberate decision to take a sort of sabbatical, then the effect is not likely to be so intense. However, if unemployment comes out of the blue, as a result of illness, or from not getting a job in the first place when leaving education, then it can have quite an impact.

The main problems of unemployment are usually threefold: the financial impact; a knock for self-esteem; and lack of time-filling skills to benefit from the newly available stretches of time. One, or any combination of these, can be enough to bring on depression or other stress-related problems such as acute lethargy.

Many people are used to measuring their self-worth in terms of their productivity or ability to meet sales targets or close deals. Transferring this need for productivity to other areas of life is the obvious way forward. But if you are knocked back because you can't even get a job interview then being productive with your time can be a bit more difficult. Interestingly, many people get through recessions, which are times of highest unemployment, emotionally and financially intact even though they have been subjected to the same events and pressures as everyone else.

Top Tips

- Aim to turn around your perception of unemployment. Instead of viewing it as the end of a road (which it isn't) or as a major step back (which it might be), view it differently. Take the view that it is the beginning of another road, an opportunity to change direction and that life is now full of exciting possibilities (even if you don't feel particularly excited at the moment, you can become so).

- Take time out to make a daily and weekly plan. Structure your day and avoid floating aimlessly from activity to activity. Spend structured time researching options, networking and planning. However, do not be dismayed when things don't go according to plan – remain flexible in your approach (see Flexibility page 159).

- When thinking about new options and opportunities think laterally. List all your skills that are transferable – any expertise that you can transfer to new challenges in the job market. Could you become a consultant (see Working From Home page 74)? Could you become a specialist in one area of your previous job (such as training people to do what you did previously)? Could you design websites linked to your speciality? Many people are even re-employed by their old companies on a freelance basis – it may be worth approaching them. Become a master (or mistress) of reinvention!

- Put a CV together as soon as possible, or if you are selling your services design a marketing brochure.

- As soon as you are able, sit down and draw up an emergency financial strategy (do not wait until you have worked through your notice period). Find out about available benefits and grants.

More Hints

- Banish the word redundancy from your vocabulary. You are NOT a redundant person. There is a reason that actors use the word 'resting' when they are temporarily out of work (they may be working as waiters and not see an acting job from one end of the year to the next, but they know they must stay positive). Acknowledge the power of language and describe yourself more positively such as 'I'm looking for opportunities' not 'I'm out of work'.

- Speak positively about your activities to other people. Avoid complaining about being out of a job, instead talk about opportunities and look for ideas of new avenues to follow. People respond to positive people. I found myself describing myself as a writer, when I was thinking about moving in that direction – it wasn't a lie, it was just projecting myself into that role. Before I knew it, people were offering me work!

■ Focus your mind on the good things that are apparent in your life such as social support and love from your family. Enjoy the time you can devote to enhancing these important aspects of your life, such as spending more time with your kids or nephews and nieces, nurturing your relationships with parents or siblings or developing new friendships.

■ Take the opportunity to retrain if you would like to do so. Now may be the time to learn a new skill. Do you need computing skills, training skills, report-writing skills? Future employers will be impressed with your determination, and learning can reinvigorate you and trigger new ideas. Find out about courses run by the unemployment services or the local authorities – many practical schemes are available such as learning to do your own accounting, how to draw up a business plan and how to market yourself.

■ How you view 'loss' is important. Immigrants to other countries will often leave behind everything – jobs, financial security, culture and even, sometimes, family. Yet some of our most successful people have been immigrants. If you have lost your job it is, of course, serious but you CAN use it as the opportunity to make a new life.

Holistic Help

■ Remember to allow some time in your day to have some fun – join an art/crafts class, indulge in an afternoon matinée, make time to read those novels you've never had time for. You need all the mood boosters you can at the moment.

■ Make time daily for exercise and healthy eating to nourish your body and brain. Exercise can lift your spirits and food can have a direct impact on how you feel – both positively and negatively. Don't 'feed' depression (see Healthy Eating page 98).

VOCATION

One of the stresses that can drag you downwards faster than anything is if you dislike or just tolerate your job. It might be that your job is a means to an end – earning enough money to live – but if you are unhappy in your work, both your work and your spirit suffer. However, if you can follow a vocation – a passion, a calling, an occupation you really love – many common work-related problems cease to exist – feeling put-upon, not wanting to give that extra 10 per cent, and so on. If you get out of bed on Monday and think 'only five more days until the weekend' you could probably do with finding your vocation. Not everyone has a vocation and this section is not necessary for everyone to have a satisfying work life. But if you do have one and it is not realized, you may find yourself getting frustrated in your work life. Some people just know from the beginning they want to be nurses, surgeons, circus performers, artists or to work with children. Even if you do have a vocation there is a time in life to work on the treadmill (perhaps to earn a good salary) and a time to pursue your vocation (where you may be doing it for the love of it).

Top Tips

■ We can't always do exactly as we want. Nevertheless, if your work can be as close to your ambitions as possible, you are more likely to be inspired by what you do. You might want to be a footballer but have two left feet. Maybe you could find job satisfaction by working at a sports equipment company.

■ Not everyone is lucky enough to have a burning ambition which leads to a real vocation in life, however don't assume that because you don't have one now, that you will never have one. One day you might be inspired to change the course of your life, and it is never too late to retrain. We are living longer, more active lives than previously, and instead of thinking of retirement you may well find a calling that takes you into a second career.

More Hints

■ It is not ideal to be too analytical about a vocation, it tends to be more of an inspiration. However, if you are more analytical by nature you may find it helpful to mind map (see p226) your likes and dislikes, talents and skills, fantasies and limitations, to seek out what your vocation might be. To realize what your vocation might be, you might find it useful to consult a career counsellor.

■ If you are fascinated by the theatre, perhaps you could train for set-design or costume making. If you are a train enthusiast, perhaps you could work in the railway system. If you enjoy talking to people, perhaps you could retrain as a counsellor.

■ Following your vocation might mean taking risks or a drop in income – are you ready for this? Following a vocation often means a drop in income, and often involves retaining. In order to pursue this, you may have to plan quite a while ahead and restructure your life in the meantime. This may seem daunting at first and is long term but if you have chosen well the dream of doing something that inspires you can keep you motivated. (Incidentally, I know this is possible because I did exactly this myself — it took me 3 to 4 years but in the end I am much happier).

Holistic Help

■ Even if you are in a job you don't absolutely love at the moment, find other things to enjoy about your job and concentrate on those. Do you particularly get on with a few colleagues? Do you like the area your workplace is in and want to explore what it offers more thoroughly? Can you get your company and colleagues interested in other activities that inspire you such as starting an amateur dramatics club, a regular football game or supporting a particular charity?

WORK/HOME BALANCE

A great myth of our time is 'You Can Do It All'. We work hard, we play hard, we give 'quality time' to our children. But if you find that you are becoming exhausted by attempting to keep all these balls in the air, it is probably time to make some choices.

Failing to find an acceptable balance between work and home life is one of the most common causes of stress. We work long hours at the office, weekends can vanish in a mass of tasks, and taking time off when the kids are unwell becomes a major time-negotiation nightmare. Not surprisingly this can lead to many stress-related health problems including depression, anxiety and physical strains. The Japanese even have a word, KAROSHI, which means 'death by overwork'. Karoshi is listed on 10,000 death certificates each year in Japan! (It is most often heart failure or suicide). These individuals clearly have not got the balance right between their work and home life.

Top Tips

■ If your vocation is your vacation (see Vocation page 70) then you have got the best of all worlds because you really enjoy what you do. But even if this is the case it is easy for work to creep over into other areas of your life and create an imbalance leaving you feeling drained. It also does not take into account the needs of your partner and family who might hope to spend more time with you. If you are married to your job, you probably need to discuss with your family how they feel about it.

■ Sometimes it is easier to value successes at work rather than at home. This is, in part, because it is how we earn our living and also because there are recognized reward schemes (such as salary increase, promotion and customer/boss satisfaction). Valuing your successes at home, as well as at the office, is an excellent step towards recreating some balance. Successes might be a loving relationship, enjoying your children, a vibrant home atmosphere or a few really good friends to count on – think of those successes that are relevant to you.

■ If you find that you are always bringing work home see Time Management (page 65). You may need to develop the ability to compartmentalize your various activities and get into the habit of creating cut off times.

■ Set yourself a fixed time beyond which you do not stay at work. And stick to it.

■ Of course this can all work the other way round. If your home and family or social life are most important to you, you might be not giving your best to your work life. You might be in temporary employment, drifting from job to job or just getting by in what you feel is an uninspiring job. This is just as imbalanced, and perhaps you might benefit from getting more excited about your job, no matter how short term and giving it all you've got while you are there. You will reap the reward in a more fulfilling experience.

■ In the same way that you go off to an office or work place to concentrate on your job, make specific commitments to concentrate on your partner, family or friends. Time spent with family and friends is important for stress reduction.

■ All working parents have to ask themselves one important question at some point or other. Will my job or my children come first most of the time? The answer to this question helps to determine how you structure your life because it is really not possible to do it all. You have to ask yourself what you really want, and what is really achievable.

■ It can be particularly difficult to juggle parental responsibilities with work life. Rather than wait for a crisis to happen (illness, feelings of guilt, tiredness, needing to attend sports days/school plays), evaluate what you need to do for your children and negotiate in advance with your employers about how you are going to handle this. A site to help parents deal with the conflict between childrearing and work is www.parentsatwork.org.uk

■ No one ever went to their grave saying 'I wish I had worked harder'. It is more likely to be 'I wish I spent more time with my loved ones or doing things I enjoy'.

More Hints

■ If work worries are keeping you awake at night, you definitely need to improve your compartmentalization skills and the best way is to use the techniques covered under Cognitive Thinking (page 219). For example, if you are worrying about getting a project in on time, 'I've got to get that report in on time or else it'll be a complete screw-up and everyone will be mad at me.' 'Why do I always let it get so late with everything? 'I'm just running out of time.' 'Help!'. Write down the thoughts and then work out the 'antidotes' to each one.

– It'll be a complete screw up — an overgeneralization and it is unlikely to be a complete screw-up, just a partial screw-up!

– Everyone will be mad at me — they probably value the work you've done and have been in similar situations themselves. If you forewarn them that it may be a little late, they can reorganize their timing accordingly.

– You probably don't always get late with everything, and you probably do plenty of other things on time — another overgeneralization. Seen in a positive light you know you can work specifically on your time management (see page 65).

– Help! — unnecessary panic is not constructive. Who are you asking to help you? Is this a suggestion you could take up and can you draft in someone to take some of the load?

– If you are running out of time, you have two choices — you can do some extra work on a one-off basis to catch up — or you can delay the deadline and talking to people might make it more workable than it seems at 1am.

– If you have written all these things down you may now have a plan instead of an unstructured worry.

– You can now compartmentalize the worry and get on with your home life and your night's sleep.

- Don't volunteer if you don't have to when you are over-stretched with other stuff to do. Some people are always the first to put their hand up and give of their time, but, while this can be commendable, it is often at the expense of their home life. If you want to volunteer, don't do it impulsively but after taking time to consider all of the issues, and do it on your own terms.

- If you are using the workplace to escape from problems at home then this needs to be addressed. For example, if you argue a lot at home, or you find that you can't get any down-time because you are always having to do stuff for others at home, these are specific problems that need addressing. If you just spend time at the office, you don't solve the problem and by ignoring it you may tip it into a crisis. Look through chapter 1, Home and chapter 5, Relationships.

- Realistically there is a limit to how much you can burn the candle at both ends (even if you think you are handling it well it usually catches up with most people). Keep your fun and frolics to evenings when you don't have to be at work the following day – you'll enjoy your nights out even more!

- Aim to not feel guilty about how you achieve balance between work and home. While you are bringing a better balance to your life, silence the little chatterbox in your head that makes you feel inadequate about what you are not doing. Focus on what you are doing and feel good about it. Work on positive affirmations (see Creative Visualization page 222) such as 'I am a rounded individual with many interests in life' or 'I enjoy my home life and also make a valuable contribution at work'

Holistic Help

- Take the time to smell the roses – whether at work or at home.

- Do something positive to unwind and, if you are able, get away. Changing the scenery is one of the best ways to alter your behaviour patterns, which is why holidays are so valuable. If you can't get away, switch to an activity which has positive associations for you such as walking in a calming place or playing a football game. And if you still can't do this, at the very least spend some time relaxing and visualizing a calming place.

WORKING FROM HOME

The last twenty years have seen more and more of us working from home. The age in which we live demands flexibility and cost effectiveness, and provides us with communication capabilities to capitalize on this new approach. And it does not look as if this is likely to change in the near future. This means that willingly or unwillingly many of us are having to learn new strategies for home working.

Working from home can have advantages. It cuts the need for expensive and time consuming travel and, in theory, lends us these hours for increased productivity. It can allow us to combine child rearing and a productive work life. You are your own boss and can prioritize your workday in any way you wish – time to be creative, time to get organized, time to meet deadlines. It also has some potential disadvantages including being distracted by domestic events and losing the camaraderie of workmates. Working from home suits some and not others. Many people embrace this discipline enthusiastically and yet months later return to the traditional workplace, desperate for office routine.

Whether you are working at home voluntarily or because it has been thrust upon you, there is a range of particular stresses engendered by this, which can be minimized or eliminated. The following tips will enable you to handle any strains more calmly, leaving you free to focus on the life-enhancing benefits of your situation.

Top Tips

■ Don't jumble up your work with your domestic clutter and create a separate work space. Ideally set aside a room to work in, but if this is not possible ensure that you at least have a desk with sufficient bookshelves and a filing cabinet which is dedicated to your work needs and you can literally or metaphorically shut the door on your work when you need to.(Order Out Of Chaos page 29 for more tips.)

■ Avoid sharing your computer with others in the household if you can. In this way you can access what you need when you need it.

■ If you can afford it, have a separate telephone line for work with an answering machine that clearly delineates when you are available for office calls. It is more professional and also stops work intruding on your personal life.

■ Decide that your time 'in the office' is sacrosanct time.

■ The greatest burden of working from home is that you may find you don't know when to stop. It can be too tempting to catch up by working late at night or sitting at your desk in your pyjamas at 6am. This is fine if you really enjoy what you do (see Vocation page 70) or to meet the occasional deadline, but for most people this then becomes a vicious spiral of increased work, less productivity and more stress. Decide what your working hours are and stick to them. This is the first step towards making a healthy division between work and home time.

More Hints

■ The temptation to fiddle around with home life when working can seem overwhelming. But if you have decided that you need to be at work by 9am – stick to it. Do whatever domestic chores you can before you sit at your desk and then forget about them. Structured interruptions, on the other hand, can work for you (see following hint).

■ Structured interruptions can break the day when you have no work colleagues to chat with around the water fountain. Take regular breaks – mid-morning, lunchtime and mid-afternoon. Decide what you are going to do with them. A short walk can provide an invigorating change of scenery. Use breaks constructively to make a couple of personal calls or take something out of the freezer and chop some vegetables for the evening meal.

■ If you are able to do so, answer calls when they come in – it often takes twice as long, and costs more in phone bills, if you always have to reply to a long list of messages. Use e-mail whenever possible.

■ Use an answering machine to screen calls when you have a piece of work that requires absolute concentration. You then have the advantage of being able to finish that report without dealing with phone calls.

■ In the traditional office the chances are that you would attend regular meetings of one sort or another. While businesses often err by having more meetings than they need, it is important to take stock from time to time and a lesson can be learned by the home worker. Put in your diary regular planning sessions and stick to them. This will enhance your confidence in your own efficiency by preventing you just responding to incoming events, and feeling 'not in control'.

■ Schedule your work-load realistically. The common cry of the self-employed is that they are terrified of saying no to a project because they don't know where the next offer will come from. Get this into perspective and recognize that you can only do so much.

■ We all need human contact in our working life. Make a point of joining an association linked to your work in some way and attend events. Keep up with old colleagues in your line of business.

Holistic Help

■ Make your home/work environment a pleasing one. Take some time to organize the space around your desk or work area. Put up a picture you like, pin some humour on your noticeboard, make a point of having a vase of scented flowers or a plant on your desk along with a photo of a happy moment in your life.

■ Ensure your desk height, computer angle and chair are comfortable.

■ Remind yourself regularly of the advantages of home working, such as being free from people wandering by your desk for a chat at inappropriate times.

■ Take regular time out from work – do take your weekends and put holidays into your diary well in advance. That way you can plan around them (see Holidays page 189).

CHAPTER 3

HEALTH

Your physical health is one of the first things to suffer when you are feeling stressed. Tense muscles, disturbed digestion, sleepless nights, headaches and susceptibility to frequent colds and 'flu can all conspire to drag you down. Stress also places a heavy demand on your nutritional resources. The basic stress reaction is a physical one, and the long-term effects shut down efficient digestion, wear out body tissues and imbalance brain chemicals.

Investing in your health is a most profound way of ensuring you have the necessary reserves when you find yourself in stressful situations. A holistic, balanced approach using nutrition, fitness, relaxation and, where necessary, supplements and herbs pays the best long-term dividends.

Changing habits while currently in a stressed frame of mind may seem difficult and even seem to be an added burden and stress. But as rewards can often be felt fairly quickly, you might find that dealing with physical symptoms lightens the burden and inspires and motivates you to tackle other areas of your life.

ADDICTIONS

Addictions are a chicken-and-egg situation as far as stress is concerned. Chemical dependency – whether it be to drugs, nicotine, alcohol or food – is vastly exacerbated by stress, and additionally the addiction itself is a serious source of stress, both mental and physical.

All addictions share a common feature with a 'high' being harder and harder to achieve, requiring more and more 'hits' and leading further and further into addictive behaviour patterns. Much time is spent thinking about how to get the next 'fix' and it will often involve subterfuge. The pointers in this section are designed to be of use for those who find that they have the mild to moderate forms of addiction which are sufficient to impact on daily life and be a source of anxiety.

The information can also be used in conjunction with other therapies for more serious addictions, but should never be used as an alternative to professional and medical advice. I would urge anyone who has a serious addiction to seek the advice of their doctor and the relevant support organizations. To be addicted to any substance is to be in a lonely situation and it is vital to realize that you need all the help you can get. There are plenty of people out there who can help you through the experience and who understand the problems, you just need to seek them out. At the end of this section is a list of such organizations.

Top Tips

■ The first step in dealing with any addictive habit is to recognize it exists. The second step is to have a genuine desire to overcome it.

■ There is a biochemical aspect to all addictions. Even a thrill from something that does not have an obvious chemical aspect to it, such as gambling or shopping, results in a type of electro-chemical activity in the brain which is typical of addiction. What this means is that all types of addictions have both a behavioural and chemical effect, and that both have to be addressed in order to beat the habit. Diet can often help with the biochemical aspects (see below) and relief from the behavioural effects can be gained by working on some of the tips in this section and also, possibly, seeking out one of the listening therapies such as counselling.

■ Some people are able to make that quantum leap from a person who has a habit, to someone who doesn't. The process by which they arrive at that point is one of self-discovery and understanding the problem, even though the actual moment of making that irrevocable decision appears to happens in an instant. You can accelerate this process just by knowing this and actively looking for the one motivating factor that might make the difference to you personally.

■ Be kind to yourself and congratulate yourself on every small achievement. You can support yourself through the journey you are on and feel a lot better about the process if you are not always being self-critical.

More Hints

■ If at first you don't succeed, don't let it put you off. You are not a failure, you just need to do it again until you achieve the results you want. If you do not get the result you want, treat it as a learning experience to apply the next time around.

■ Make a plan by using the techniques covered in Goal Setting (page 16). Describe in detail what your goal is, how you are going to get there, what will help you and what might hinder you.

■ You may find it helpful to make a 'contract' with a friend who is in the same boat as you with an addictive problem. Meet regularly, once or twice a week, and agree between you on the measures you are going to take this time around. Discuss any successes or failures since your last meeting. Discuss what worked and what went wrong. Sharing the experience makes you realize that you are not alone.

■ Keep a private journal in which you can write down your wins, what has helped and what has not. Be honest with yourself, but also remember to keep your sense of humour. Put in an entry every day, even if it is just one word!

- Some people need to hit rock bottom with their addiction before they can move towards recovery. They need to see themselves as others see them – as they are caught up in self-deception. Such clarity of vision usually eludes those who can't kick a habit. Awareness can help an addict turn towards recovery, before it is forced upon them by circumstances.

- Addiction is a form of compulsive behaviour. In this case you might be able to substitute another non-damaging intense activity for the damaging compulsion. You might take a serious interest in a particular hobby or sport, which will distract you from your compulsion. Staying active really does help to deflect your focus from seeking out another 'hit'.

- Nurture yourself through the process of getting off your addiction by applying the principles of mindfulness discussed in Meditation (page 224). Concentrate on nurturing activities. For instance, make delicious fresh juices to drink and really enjoy the process of making juices, as well as the final juice to drink, and feel great about treating yourself well. The same goes for writing a letter to a friend, taking a relaxing bath, enjoying a meal or a walk. You can change your mental emphasis from self-abuse to self-nurturing.

Holistic Help – Diet

- Dietary adaptations are not just for those with dietary addictions. By dealing with diet you can influence the balance of brain chemicals which govern addictive tendencies. This section is for everyone who has a habit they want to give up.

- Having some protein with each meal and snack can reduce the impact that carbohydrates have on feeding brain chemical imbalances. Protein sources are eggs, lean meats, fish, lentils, beans and other pulses, soya, yoghurt, cottage cheese, other cheeses, nuts and seeds.

- Blood sugar imbalance is one of the main dietary contributors to addictions. You may not be aware of this tendency but it could be appropriate if you exist on coffee, strong teas, colas, sugary snacks, cigarettes, and even foods you might consider healthy but which have a dramatic effect on blood sugar. For instance, lots of dried fruit, large glasses of orange juice, large bowls of pasta or rice. You will probably suffer from accompanying drowsiness which makes you feel like you need an energy boost, which you resolve with yet another coffee, or chocolate. Make sure that all the carbohydrates you eat are complex such as wholemeal bread, wholegrain brown rice, porridge oats and quinoa. Stimulants such as coffee and sugar are just as bad.

- Alcohol lowers resolve to avoid whatever it is you are addicted to. It might be best, while you are on the journey to kick your habit that you also avoid alcohol.

- The brain needs very specific fats for optimal functioning. It is particularly important to consume the healthy omega 3 and 6 essential fatty acids (EFAS) found in oily fish, soya, walnuts, linseeds and pumpkin seeds, which help to normalize the functioning of the brain chemical serotonin (see page 80).

- Antioxidants in the diet are vital to help your liver through the process of detoxifying any substances to which you have been addicted. Eat plenty of fruits and vegetables, at least five portions daily and ideally more.

■ If you are a chocoholic but are worried about 'death by chocolate', take heart as it is not all bad. The unhealthy stuff is the typical chocolate that is sold at most confectionery counters. Instead find good quality 60–70 per cent cocoa mass dark chocolate and enjoy this in moderation. Cocoa in chocolate is actually a perfectly good food and is very rich in antioxidants, but it is the high sugar levels that are the real problem. However, remember that chocolate with a high cocoa solid content is also relatively high in caffeine compounds. The best chocolate and drinking chocolate, in my opinion, is **Green & Black's** which is now widely available. (It is also free of the high amount of pesticides found in most chocolates, as well as being part of the Fair Trade organization which ensures that Third World farmers get paid a decent price for their products.)

■ If you are attracted to colas, energy drinks or the herb guarana, these are really just caffeine and/or sugar in another form. Caffeine is the most widely consumed drug and in high amounts, or if the person is sensitive, perpetuates other addictions. Substitute non-caffeine drinks such as dandelion coffee, fruit or herbal teas or fruit juices diluted with sparkling water.

■ Read *Natural Highs* by Patrick Holford and Dr Hyla Cass (Piatkus).

Holistic Help – Supplements

■ All addictive substances, including alcohol, nicotine, sugars, over-the-counter and illicit drugs, deplete certain important nutrients. The most vulnerable are B-vitamins, vitamin C, magnesium and chromium. If you have not yet kicked your particular habit, it is certainly a good idea to take a good quality, daily multi-vitamin and multi-mineral.

■ *B-vitamins* are vital for all aspects of mental health and are most often depleted when someone has been taking any addictive substance for a while. Take a 100mg supplement daily (do not worry about your urine turning bright yellow, this is just the B2 part of the supplement).

■ *L-glutamine* is helpful to reduce cravings. Take 3–5g twice a day. It is easiest and cheapest to take in powdered form, mixed into water or juice. (**Higher Nature** supply it in powdered form, www.highernature.co.uk) Avoid it if you have liver or kidney damage.

■ *5-HTP* is very helpful for reducing cravings, as it helps to balance serotonin levels in the brain. Take 100 –200mg daily (but do not take it too late at night, as it might interfere with sleep).

■ If you don't like to eat fish (see dietary advice page 79) I would urge you to take 1–2g of *fish oil* supplements daily.

■ *Kava kava* is called natural valium (see warning on page 234). If you need a relaxant to help you through your journey, it is best to turn to kava instead of benzodiazepines (anti-anxiety medication) or sleeping aides as these are highly addictive. Do not take kava kava with other drugs or alcohol and only take it for a month at a time. However, if you are already dealing with an addiction to these you need to come off them with medical supervision.

HELPFUL ORGANIZATIONS
- Alcoholics Anonymous 01904 644 026 www.alcoholics-anonymous.org.uk
- Alcohol Concern 020 7928 7377 www.alcoholconcern.org.uk
- Alcohol Recovery Project 020 7403 3369 www.arp-uk.org
- Narcotics Anonymous 020 7251 4007 www.ukna.org
- Addiction Today 020 7233 5333 www.addictiontoday.co.uk
- Debtors Anonymous 020 7644 5070
- Gambler's Anonymous www.gamblersanonymous.co.uk
- National Drugs Helpline 0800 776600 www.ndh.org.uk
- See Giving Up Smoking (page 94) for relevant organizations.
- See Disordered Eating (page 88) for relevant organizations.
- See also the various counselling organizations listed under Useful Resources (page 234).

ALLERGIES AND STRESS

Most allergies, such as asthma, eczema, allergic colitis and others, are made worse by stressful events. Allergies occur when a reaction, to a particular substance, group of substances or food, triggers an allergic immune response. This immune response leads to inflammation of whichever tissue is affected by the allergy such as the nasal passages, lung bronchioles, skin or colon. The inflammation leads to reddening, weeping, mucus production and broken skin. The body's natural way of dealing with this is to counter it with steroid hormones produced by the adrenal glands to reduce the inflammation. This becomes clear when you realize that many of the anti-allergy medicines, prescribed by doctors, are types of steroid. However, steroids cannot usually be used long term as they have serious side effects. Encouraging healthy adrenal gland function is a way forward. However, if the person is stressed, it is these very glands which are overtaxed and so are unable to respond adequately.

There are many natural means by which you can improve the prognosis for allergic reactions, reduce the negative effects of stress and bring down inflammation. If you have serious allergies you must not discontinue or lower the dose of medication prescribed by your doctor without first consulting them.

Top Tips
- Managing your reaction to stress is obviously important. You will know this if your allergy worsens when you are feeling anxious or when you lose your temper. Learning to pace yourself and relax is important. See the relevant sections in Chapter 4, Emotions.
- For some allergies it is very important to reduce the stress of pollution in the home. Most asthmatics know that house dust mites create problems, but those with hay fever and

eczema also frequently react. Contact The Healthy House 01453 752 216 www.healthy-house.co.uk for ideas on how to get your environment dust-mite free.

■ Avoid chemicals in the house (see Housework page 20) but also avoid dry-cleaning fluids, paint solvents and garden chemicals. Also avoid smoky atmospheres.

■ Check your house for areas of mould growth. Damp areas such as basements, bathrooms and kitchens are the worst culprits. Mould spores can exacerbate allergies. Dealing with the damp at source is essential and leaking gutters or rising damp need to be addressed. In the meantime, there is nothing for it but to get out the rubber gloves, a strong scrubbing brush and a bleach or borax solution and get scrubbing.

■ Office equipment such as photocopiers and computers can aggravate allergies such as asthma in some people. See Environmental Stress (page 91) and Healthy Office (page 49). Avoid sitting right next to a photocopier all the time, and switch off your computer when it is not in use.

■ Meditation can be a potent way to reduce allergic reactions (see page 224). For instance, if you have a respiratory allergy, use visualization or meditation to focus on easy breathing and on drawing air into your lungs through an invisible filter that cleans the air of allergens. Imagine your lungs working efficiently and the billions of tiny protrusions lining your airways efficiently trapping and cleansing the air your draw into your lungs. Feel the air being warmed so that cold air does not put your lungs into spasm.

More Hints

■ Often the stress that worsens a predisposition to allergy may not be apparent. For instance, it could be a physical stress such as intense exercise. Some people with asthma are aware that they can eat a food, say egg, and be fine, but if they exercise shortly afterwards it will lead to an attack. Take 1–3 g of *vitamin C* before exercising and this may help by stopping the allergic reaction.

■ I have seen many children dragged from therapist to therapist in a quest to find out what is causing their allergy when it is reasonably apparent the parents are communicating, inadvertently, all kinds of anxieties to the child. It is common for a child to have, say, an asthma attack when there is discord in the home. Be aware that your behaviour and attitudes may influence your child's allergy.

■ Avoid fan heaters, convection heaters and open bar heaters as these just recirculate dust in the home.

■ Avoid open fires and bonfires which can have a negative effect by irritating lungs and nasal passages.

■ If you have asthma, hay fever or rhinitis (consult an aromatherapist before using aromatherapy oils).

Holistic Help – Diet

■ Nearly all allergies respond to highish levels of fish oils in the diet. This is because they are rich in EPA and DHA which turn readily into anti-inflammatory substances. Eat oily fish, such as mackerel, sardines, tuna and salmon, and shellfish, three times a week (or even more). You need to keep this up for at least eight weeks before expecting to notice a difference.

■ Often a sensitivity to wheat or dairy products can exacerbate many allergies. Experiment with giving these up for at least two weeks and then carefully reintroducing them one at a time to see if it affects how your allergy responds. (The only people who should do this in a controlled hospital setting are those with brittle asthma.) Other common food sensitivities are to soya, citrus fruit, eggs and yeast.

■ Alcohol and caffeine will usually make allergies worse. They are responsible for depleting nutrient levels and interfering with the manufacture of anti-inflammatory substances called prostaglandins in the body. The exception to this is the effect that caffeine has on asthma. It can reduce symptoms which means that if you give up caffeine, your asthma could get worse in the short term. Nevertheless, while it may be fine to have one or two cups of coffee daily, having more than this could adversely affect general health.

■ Histamine-rich foods can worsen allergies for some people. These are red wine, champagne, other wines, some beers including non-alcoholic ones, very ripe cheeses such as Emmenthal and Gouda, continental sausages, fish such as tuna or mackerel and pickled foods such as sauerkraut and chutneys.

Holistic Help – Supplements

■ Antioxidants are important for mopping up free-radical activity generated by inflammation and help to keep skin and mucus membranes intact and help them to heal. Take a daily supplement containing *vitamins A, C and E* and the minerals *zinc and selenium*.

■ If you are not eating fish, take 2g of *fish oil* capsules daily.

■ *Quercitin* is a bioflavonoid which helps to support adrenal function and is a potent supporter of lung health. Quercitin and vitamin C also have an anti-histamine action. Other good general anti-allergy supplements are the herbs *echinacea* and *devil's claw*.

■ *Liquorice* acts to boost adrenal function and has a mild steroidal effect which reduces allergic reactions but does not adversely affect adrenal health. Avoid liquorice if you have high blood pressure.

■ *Nettle tea*, in the form of both tinctures and supplements, is very useful for hay fever. *Eyebright* can also reduce itchy eyes. *Luffa (sponge cucumber)* helps to alleviate hay fever and allergic rhinitis. On the other hand, *camomile* is a relative of ragweed and may set some people off.

■ An Ayurvedic (Indian) herb *Coleus forskohlii* works to relieve psoriasis and asthma.

CARING FOR OTHERS

Caring for family members or close friends who are unwell, disabled or elderly and frail can be stressful. Part of the stress often comes from feeling guilty about wanting time off from the sick room, especially when you are the only carer. Here are some pointers to remember.

Top Tips

■ If you are in a caring role, remember that you cannot care for someone else if you are also unwell. Take care of your own health and do not exhaust yourself.

■ Constant proximity can sometimes make it difficult to empathize with the unwell person, especially if you they are being a demanding patient. Do not be too hard on yourself about this – it is a human reaction and may be a sign that you need a break.

■ I recall when, for the first and only time ever (so far!), I put my back out for a week, I finally realized what my sister had being going through for the previous couple of years. Empathy with another's pain can be hard – it is difficult to really understand someone else's pain, but remembering your own illnesses will help you to help them.

■ It is often the case that someone who is seriously unwell will not want to make demands on the other person, or to worry them unduly, which rather forces the carer to be a bit of a mind reader. Ideally it is best to gently discuss these issues periodically – it could well be a great relief for all concerned.

■ Avoid trying to compensate by doing too much – this can often be exhausting to the unwell person on the receiving end. Again good communication will help to get the balance right.

■ Some people do, it has to be said, hang on to their illness. By being ill they become the centre of attention. This may seem a cruel thing to say, but it is true in some instances. In these cases, they need to be given some of their self-confidence back so they can go back out into the world.

■ If someone is unwell or disabled long-term, or even in the short term, do find out about community services and carers' facilities and allowances. They can make a real difference and, for instance, allow for special fittings in the home, intermittent nursing care or for the carer to go on holiday.

■ Take a look at the dietary advice above, which can be relevant in many cases, to see if this will help the person you are caring for.

■ On the other hand do not force nutritional advice on those who patently do not want it. They may be a lot happier eating cream cakes and chocolates and have no interest in how foods might help to heal them. However, if you can persuade them to do just two things, get them to drink water regularly and take a multi-vitamin and multi-mineral supplement to give them a nutrient boost.

■ One word I avoid whenever possible is 'patient'. It seems to pigeon-hole people into the situation where they are victims, where they are 'done to' by other people and ignore the fact that they are people.

■ There are different views about whether to tell terminally ill people of their true condition. By and large nowadays, it is generally the case that people are told. It may be more appropriate for the family to tell the person, or for the medical staff to do so. In cases where mental capability has diminished to the point where they do not understand, they are not told. How the information is imparted is important, but it usually gives the person the ability to come to terms with their situation and say what they need to their friends and relatives. It also allows them to get their affairs in order if they wish to.

CONCENTRATION AND MEMORY

The stress of having too many things to do really plays havoc with your ability to focus. Stress has a lot to do with reduced concentration. Often, lack of concentration is attributed to laziness in children, or put down to reduced mental capability in older adults, when stress may be the actual reason. And sometimes lack of concentration is quite simply a bad habit which can be worked on. It can be dispiriting to forget things, at times embarrassing, and can also affect self-esteem.

Top Tips

■ If you need to concentrate, say to finish some revision or similar, you will find it hard to concentrate if surrounded by hustle and bustle – find a quiet place where you can hide away for as long as you need to.

■ For many people, their ability to concentrate is seriously impaired by blood sugar swings as their brain simply does not have the fuel to keep focused. This is particularly the case if you are subject to mid-afternoon energy slumps. See diet tips page 87.

■ If you are not really interested in what you are doing, concentration will not come easily. This may be a hint that you need to change your study course, job or activity.

■ Stay interested in life. Those with the sharpest mental acuity in retirement years are people who never give up learning.

■ Alternatively, fall back on your inner resources and find something about the 'dull' activity that you find interesting. It may be that you respond better to a different medium. For instance some people are better at listening to tapes, while others prefer to read books, or watch a video, and others will be better off copying down text or browsing the Internet. And many people improve their powers of concentration by mixing some of these media.

More Hints

■ If you know that you generally find it easier to concentrate, say in the morning, then plan your day accordingly. Try to undertake the more demanding tasks at the best time of day for you.

- Get a good night's sleep if you know you need to concentrate the next day.

- If you always have trouble remembering the names of people to whom you have been introduced, this is likely to be related to lack of concentration rather than to failing memory. Get into the habit of really paying attention, and not worrying about other things, such as what they think of you or what you are going to say to them. Make a memory link – such as imagining Mary with a lamb under her arm (Mary had a little lamb) – or repeating their name a couple of times when you speak to people.

- The same goes for misplaced items. If you are not consciously aware when you put your keys down or put your wallet in a drawer you could spend many fruitless hours looking for them. Aim to get into the habit of noting where you put things down. Or have a place where you always put things, such as a hook for keys in the hall.

- Give your brain a work out with mental gymnastics. By breaking normal thinking and concentration patterns, which exercise your brain, you can cause positive changes in brain functioning. You can challenge your normal patterns by, for instance eating breakfast with chopsticks, brushing your teeth using the wrong hand or reading a book upside down. This may sound crazy but it can help! Other mental exercise can be done by doing crossword puzzles and jigsaw puzzles. Good sources of ideas can be gained from Brain Gym, www.braingym.org; or practitioners of Edu-K (Educational Kinesiology), Kay McCarrol 020 8202 9747 or David Hubbard 01453 759 444.

- If you are doing research for a project beware of being sidetracked. It is all too easy to go off at tangents when sitting in the library, browsing the Internet or interviewing people. To a degree this will keep you interested and might lead to other interesting avenues. However, if it gets out of hand, you need to pull yourself back and decide to concentrate on the job in hand. Keep a piece of paper next to you and note down any extraneous thoughts.

- Transfer lists to paper rather than keep them in your mind. A cluttered brain can slow you down as much as a cluttered desk can.

- An active life is the best way to preserve brain health for the future. People of retirement age who have interests, hobbies and are physically active not only live longer but also hang on to their mental faculties for longer.

- If you need to remember anything, break it down into memorable 'chunks'. If you are memorizing a shopping list of ten random items, it is more difficult than if you remember a few items from each shop — so three items from the baker, two from the butcher and five from the grocer. A series of numbers, such as 392503557, might be difficult to remember, but 392-503-557 is much easier.

- Use it or lose it. If you want to remember something, practice, practice, practice.

- Read *The Sharper Mind* by Fred B. Chernow (Souvenir Press).

- If you are worried about your power of memory contact **Neurologica** on 0870 066 0286 or www.neurologica.co.uk who offer a simple set of memory tests. These can set your mind at rest, or if necessary, they will refer you for specialist advice.

- Pregnancy can certainly make you more fuzzy brained than normal – it isn't just a myth. First of all you may be doing more than usual, sleeping patterns may change and the effects of the pregnancy hormone progesterone is a relaxing one. But also brain size shrinks slightly and then recovers about six months after the birth. No one is absolutely sure why this is but it is believed that the developing baby is literally taking the fats that make up the brain for its own development. It could help to eat lots of oily fish, eat fresh nuts and seeds, and take a *GLA* and *EPA fatty acid* supplement.
- Cannabis and other recreational drugs definitely impair concentration and memory if used regularly.

Holistic Help – Diet

- If you know you need to concentrate at a particular time of the day or evening, make sure you avoid alcohol which will play havoc with your resolve.
- Blood sugar swings lead to drowsiness, often just when you need to concentrate and particularly mid-afternoon. If this is the case, make sure you eat whole foods and whole grains and avoid sugary snacks. Snack instead on fruit or vegetable sticks with a little yoghurt or cottage cheese for protein, or a small handful of nuts or seeds.
- While coffee may keep you alert in the short term, if you regularly drink too much of it (more than two cups a day) you are likely to find that it has the opposite effect by playing havoc with your brain functioning. Substitute alternative coffees such as dandelion, chicory, barley or acorn coffee – there are many different types available at health food shops.
- Antioxidants are vital for brain health and might slow down degeneration of brain tissues. Eating a diet rich in fruits and vegetables is the way to achieve this, and an antioxidant supplement might be a good insurance.

Holistic Help – Supplements

- *Ginkgo biloba* can be useful when you need to make sure your concentration is at a peak, say for an exam, interview, presentation or difficult meeting. Take between 60–300mg 2 hours beforehand.
- As ever, *B-vitamins* are vital for brain health and concentration. Take 100mg daily (do not worry about your urine turning bright yellow which results from high doses of B2).
- *Phosphatidyl serine* is used as a building material for brain tissue. Take 100–300mg daily. **Higher Nature** make this product.
- *Lecithin* contains a high amount of *choline* which is used to make an important neurotransmitter. Take 1 tablespoon daily (in yoghurt or straight off the spoon), or a *choline* supplement of 300–600mg daily.
- *Vinca minor* is a herb which increases the tone of blood vessels and improves circulation in the brain.

DISORDERED EATING

Disordered eating covers a range of factors that are familiar to those with eating disorders including bingeing and stress eating, but could also be as simple as just not being organized or knowledgeable enough about food. Disordered eating is often a result of busy lives where take-away food is eaten on the run (see Let's Do Lunch page 50). Extreme faddiness about food and a lack of attention paid to eating in a balanced way – for whatever reason, all come under the heading of Disordered Eating. If your eating habits are disordered here are some tips to help you.

Top Tips

■ The following will help bring order back to your eating habits.

– Eat with family or friends.

– Make the table (or just your own plate) inviting, attractive and friendly.

– Make your food attractive even if you are at work.

– Take time to really savour the food.

– Never eat on the run or fridge-graze. Sit down and make eating an event.

■ Stress plays a big part in disordered eating. Some people just forget to eat when they are under duress, sometimes for days at a time. If this is you, make a point of observing eating times (breakfast, lunch and dinner) quite deliberately even if you don't actually eat very much. Take time out to use the experience to nurture yourself quite consciously by eating healthily.

■ Stress also causes some people to hoover up anything they can lay their hands on when feeling the pressure. This is invariably (and I use this definitive term quite deliberately) about anaesthetizing pain. The foods we crave, particularly carbohydrate and sugary foods trigger endorphins and serotonin which make us feel better in the short term. Just knowing this can make you more aware of the process, helping you to resist that afternoon chocolate bar. Nurture yourself consciously by choosing healthily options such as nuts and seeds, vegetable sticks or fruit as a snack.

■ In Italy, a movement was started called 'Slow Food', where people were encourage to choose a proper, preferably home-cooked meal instead of a burger. Initially this was a slightly tongue-in-cheek offensive against 'Fast Food', but it grew to have significant impact. We can all learn from this.

■ You might eat reasonably healthily at home, but find that when it comes to take-aways you are a junk-food addict. Take-aways tend to be higher in fat and calories than home prepared food, so concentrate on making healthier choices at every opportunity. Some of these might be the following.

– Choose grilled or steamed over deep fried.

– Choose tomato and herb-based sauces over cream-based sauces.

– Choose lemon, balsamic or mustard over mayonnaise.

– Choose leaner add-ons such as seafood and tomato on pizzas instead of double cheese and salami.

– Ask for salad dressings on the side and measure out the minimum amount you need to flavour the dish.

– Choose tandoori and plain rice over masala and pilau.

– Choose stir-fried vegetables and seafood with plain rice over spring rolls, fried prawn balls and fried rice.

■ Bingeing usually involves switching off the conscious brain until after the binge has taken place. A sort of numbness takes over as you go to the shop and consume what you buy soon after, cook a meal sufficient for two or three people to eat on your own at a sitting, or raid the freezer and tuck in. Become aware of this and at least observe the process. This is the first step to doing something about it.

■ The newly coined term, 'orthorexia', has been used to describe people who are over-fanatical about eating health foods. If you feel that you are on the slippery slope of cutting out too many foods from your diet and can't even eat out for fear that foods might have chemicals in them or be processed in a way that you don't know about, then this could be you. It might even be a first step to anorexia. Those who are overly worried about healthy eating usually end up not actually enjoying food – if you are eating egg-white omelettes over sprouted seeds as one woman of my acquaintance was, this is not enjoying food. It is important to seek some sort of balance.

■ So much about food and eating is tied up with self-esteem (see page 169). You also can look at Healthy Eating (page 98), Nutrition (page 230) and Order Out Of Chaos, Kitchen (page 29).

■ Thinking about being unattractive, overweight or uninteresting is a great way to send yourself straight to the biscuit jar. Replace such thoughts with something positive such as 'my hair is looking terrific today' or 'I have a lovely smile' (people remember a stunning smile more easily than a flat tummy).

■ If you are permanently dieting, this is likely to be another source of stress. If dieting is a source of worry, then it is likely to rebound and not be successful in the long term. Concentrate on healthy eating (see page 98) and making more fundamental changes in eating habits for a long-term result.

More Hints

■ Feeling deprived is really not the point about changing eating habits. Instead of giving yourself a long list of foods you 'ought not' to be eating, concentrate on foods you can eat and which you enjoy.

■ If you overeat habitually, observe how much food other people eat (those who do not overeat) when you are out or at friends' houses, or when you have visitors, and emulate them.

- If you overeat only when you are on your own, make a conscious decision to eat as if others were with you.

- Bingeing often takes place in the car. There are not many places where you can eat and not be seen and the car fits the bill for 69 per cent of those with eating disorders (against 20 per cent of those without eating disorders). Make a rule of no food in the car.

- If you find it difficult to give up whatever it is that you are hoping to avoid – say a family-sized bar of chocolate each afternoon, make a deal with yourself that you will at least eat a piece of fruit first and then see if you still want it.

- If you tend to overeat, clean your teeth or chew gum to change the taste in your mouth at the critical moment when you want to add second helpings to your meal. Some people find pausing before diving in for second helpings can diminish the desire for more food.

- Treat yourself to non-food rewards. You could treat yourself to a glossy magazine, a video rental, a new accessory, a book or a theatre ticket.

- For inspiration and advice look at www.comfortqueen.com

- If you feel you have a real eating disorder then you need to contact the National Centre for Eating Disorders 01372 469493 (www.eating-disorders.org.uk). Other useful organizations include, Overeaters Anonymous 01426 984 674 or Anorexia and Bulimia Nervosa Association 0811 808 6555.

Holistic Help – Diet

- Make a point of eating three meals a day. Not one meal a day. And not six meals a day.

- Include fresh fruit and vegetables whenever you can. When you look at your plate it is ideal if it consists of one-third protein (fish, eggs, meat, pulses, etc), one-third complex carbohydrates (bread, pasta, potatoes) and one-third vegetables.

- Carbohydrates have the worst reputation for perpetuating the bingeing cycle (Have you noticed that STRESSED is DESSERTS spelled backwards? Hmmm…) If you head for starches and sugars all the time, greatly moderate your intake of bread, rice, pasta, biscuits, sugar and other carbohydrate sources and concentrate on eating lots of fresh vegetables, fruit and protein and see if this makes a difference.

- Don't cut out fats from your diet, you need them for brain function and hormones. Low levels contribute to depression and eating disorders. See Healthy Eating (page 98) for more information.

- It is thought that one reason we crave fats is that we are deficient in essential fatty acids. Making sure you get enough in your diet – the best source for this is flax oil, 1tbsp daily – might help to reduce fat cravings.

- Take a healthy eating cookery course to really begin to appreciate and develop your understanding about how to prepare delicious and healthy food.

- Get more involved in other areas of food health such as how it is grown and distributed. You can visit your local farmers' markets and talk to the traders about how their food is produced, you could grow vegetables in your garden or if you have only a windowsill, some herbs, lettuces and radishes, or go hunting for edible mushrooms or blackberrying in the countryside in the autumn. You could even gather (unsprayed) nettles in town for nettle soup!

Holistic Help – Supplements

■ The mineral *chromium* helps to balance blood sugar balance. Take 200–500mcg daily. It works best if you take a *B-complex* alongside it.

■ *Zinc* has a good track record with helping people with eating disorders, especially severe undereaters. Zinc is needed for brain health and may help to normalize thinking patterns. Take 25mg daily.

■ Other useful supplements are *L-glutamine*, 5g daily and *5-HTP*, 100–200mg daily to improve food cravings (see page 80 for contraindications).

■ *Liquorice root* helps to normalize blood sugar levels (do not take if you have high blood pressure).

■ If you are terrified of calories, in the first instance at least make sure you get sufficient nutrients. Take a *multi-vitamin and multi-mineral* supplement and a *free-form amino acid* mixture (a protein supplement usually sold for athletes). These have no, or very few calories, and can help to normalize brain chemistry which helps if you are engaged in counselling for an eating disorder. I do not want to suggest you can subsist on these – you can't – just that they will help if you are seriously undereating.

ENVIRONMENTAL STRESS

We are used to thinking about stress as related to events in our personal lives or bad reactions to those events. So it can come as a surprise to realize just how negative the impact of our environment can be. Among the worst offenders are noise levels and air pollutants which impact on our mental and physical equilibrium, but EMFs (electromagnetic fields) have also been proven to have an adverse affect on wellbeing. The food we eat, produced with pesticides or heavily processed, is another source of environmental chemicals that increase the stress our bodies have to deal with. While many of these factors may be beyond our control there are ways of countering, and so minimizing, the effects of these environmental stresses.

Top Tips

■ Noise, particularly in inner cities, can be a remorseless source of stress. If you live next to inconsiderate neighbours or directly under a flight path, you may just have to learn to live with it. Letting it get to you is just going to wear you down. You need to alter your reaction to that stress by altering your thought patterns. Now is the time to practice your meditation! Alternatively, invest in a pair of earplugs.

■ You may also have to brush up on your diplomatic skills to talk to the neighbours without starting a row. It may be simply that they are unaware. Offer practical solutions such as moving their TV away from the wall, instead of just criticism which will escalate into a row.

■ Get a noise break as often as you can by getting out of town – this is also a good opportunity to catch up with friends who live further afield.

■ According to research, your home is likely to have up to ten times the amount of chemical pollution than you will encounter out of doors. There are approximately 400 chemicals in the average home creating a cocktail effect which can worsen allergies, tiredness, anxiety and moods. Artificial chemicals are another source of stress on your body.

■ Some ways of reducing pollution in your home include the following.

– Leave your shoes by the front door (neatly of course!). Shoes are the major source of lead pollution build-up in houses as it persists in the soil and pavement dust in cities.

– Ask people to smoke outside.

– Put out a bowl of aromatherapy scented wood chips instead of using air fresheners.

– Stop using aerosol cans. Use spray products that do not use propellants.

– Avoid using domestic pesticides such as wood treatment or chemical head lice products. To avoid head lice, comb through tea tree oil which the lice seem to hate. **Chinese Whispers** Lice X products, available from health food shops or call **Nature's Store**, (01782 794300), work well against head lice. For headlice, use products based on Tea Tree or on Neem. For neem-based products, call 01294 277 344 or www.neemco.co.uk

– When replacing or building cabinets or other furniture avoid using foam, chipboard or MDF as the dust produced when cutting these is toxic as are the toxic chemicals used in the glue which release formaldehyde.

– Use hard flooring such as stone, tile or wood which can be easily wiped down and which do not trap and re-circulate chemicals.

– Use water-based paints.

■ Skin products can be another source of unhelpful chemicals we take into our bodies, particularly those containing SLS (sodium lauryl sulphate). This is a compound used industrially as a de-greaser but which can irritate skin and be absorbed through the skin as a dioxin (a carcinogenic substance). Take these measures.

– Buy skin and hair products that are free of SLS – I buy these from **The Green People** 01444 401 444 (www.thegreenpeople.co.uk) but there are other manufacturers as well. Ask your local health food shops.

– Favour unscented products. You can always mix your own scents using aromatherapy oils in a base using grapeseed oil.

– Use household products which are chemical free (see Housework page 20).

– If you are happy to eat it, you can be happy to put it on your face. Check out **Liz Earl's** range *Naturally Active Skincare* 020 7306 3295 www.lizearl.com

– Use unbleached paper and sanitary products. See **Natural Woman**, 0117 946 6649.

More Hints

■ You might be able to tune out of irritating sounds, such as noisy building work outside your home, by putting on some calming music upon which you can focus. Try listening to the radio with headphones.

■ Sources of EMFs (electromagnetic fields) include all electrical equipment including mobile phones, fridges and computers. Serious concern is being raised about the EMFs from pylons and there seems to be reasonable evidence that some types of cancer are higher in those who live near them. If you feel unrefreshed when you awaken, you need to see if EMFs are contributing and try sleeping without a radio/alarm clock by your ear and an electric blanket for at least a couple of weeks. Even those security devices placed at shop entrances to pick up tags attached to clothes have been shown to induce twice the allowed level of EMFs in small children whose heads are at precisely the level of the devices. Of course the effect will be minimal as the child passes by quite quickly, but it is the accumulation of all the EMFs from such a wide array of equipment that are thought to affect health. If you feel the need to monitor the EMFs near you, you can get electrical field meters from **Healthy House** 01453 752 216 www.healthy-house.co.uk

■ Open up a couple of the windows of your home for at least an hour once a day to create a cross draught. Tightly sealed windows and doors means that chemical levels build up inside the home and cannot escape.

Holistic Help –Diet

■ Some of the ways to reduce pollution that you ingest with food and drink includes the following.

– Buy organic food wherever possible to reduce the number of agricultural chemicals you are exposed to. Some of these foreign chemicals have been termed 'gender benders' as they have hormonal effects on the body which are linked to several cancers including prostate, testicular and breast cancers.

– Avoid using flexible plastic food wrap as this is a source of chemical forms of the hormone oestrogen, which some researchers believe may be a cause of falling sperm counts in men. Other plastics such as those used in food containers also present a problem. Instead, use ceramic or glass containers and use greaseproof paper (if necessary secured with foil or plastic wrap, but an elastic band will usually do just as well) to wrap food.

– Restrict your dependence on canned foods and those in cartons as they are lined with a thin layer of plastic (see above).

– Use stainless steel, ceramic or glass cookware in preference to non-stick pans or aluminium pans.

– Filter or distil the water you drink. Also use this water for cooking and in kettles.

- Pectin, found in apples, pears and bananas, and alginic acid found in seaweeds are powerful detoxifiers. You will also find these compounds in specially formulated supplements aimed at detoxifying.
- Avoid buying produce that has been sitting by the roadside and soaking up all the traffic pollution.

Holistic Help – Supplements
- A good detoxifying supplement will contain the antioxidant nutrients *vitamins A, C and E* and minerals *calcium, magnesium, zinc and selenium*. All of these help to either rid the body of pollutants, or help it to cope with them.
- **Health Plus** do a good detox formula.

GIVING UP SMOKING

Many people smoke to relieve their stress and the idea of giving up smoking, which is one of the most potent addictions we know, can itself be incredibly stressful. But you have decided to quit, so how can you help yourself through the process?

There are around 4000 toxic chemicals in cigarettes and the average smoker gets through 5,500 cigarettes each year. But all the health warnings in the world are not going to make you give up unless you really want to do so. A multi-faceted approach taking behavioural, nutritional and herbal methods into account is probably the most effective way forward.

Top Tips
- Look up the organizations who can help you: www.quit.org.uk or call 0800 002200, and www.ash.org.uk
- Just cutting back will usually just lead to increasing the amount you smoke later on. Better to go cold turkey and give up totally.
- Women in particular link giving up smoking with putting on weight and this can interfere with their resolve. Studies show that those women who had counselling for this fear while giving up smoking not only were significantly more likely to be successful with kicking the habit but they also were less likely to put on weight.
- Avoid situations that trigger the craving for a cigarette – particularly having an alcoholic drink or a coffee. Drink tonic with lime and Angostura bitters, tomato juice or green or herbal teas instead. After meals can also be difficult moments. Having a replacement such as gum ready may help (see below).

More Hints
- You may find that keeping your mouth and hands busy helps. Chew gum (with xylitol in it for healthy teeth) and take up fiddling with a squeezy stress ball or worry beads.

- Imagine what it is like to kiss a dirty ashtray. Really imagine this in full detail – go as far as rubbing your nose in a real dirty ashtray. This sounds disgusting (don't do it in public or everyone will think you have gone crazy) but it is a graphic way of bringing your other senses into the process and helps with sensory memory.

- Some people find that acupuncture or hypnotism are highly effective at reducing cravings for nicotine.

Holistic Help – Diet

- The desire to smoke is usually worsened by poor blood sugar control. Smoking is often just one prop among many – coffee, alcohol, sugar and carbohydrate cravings. The yo-yo assault on blood sugar is one reason why so many ex-smokers exchange one fix, tobacco, for another, such as sweets. By eating a diet based on lean meats, beans, lentils and other pulses such as chick peas, nuts and seeds, wholegrains, vegetables and fruit, blood sugar balance can be improved and the desire to smoke reduced.

- When you give up smoking there is often an outpouring of mucus as your body finally has the chance to throw off years of accumulated toxins. This can be exacerbated by a diet high in milk and cheese, so during this time it may be best to significantly or reduce these.

- A diet rich in antioxidants is vital to counteract the damage that smoking can do. Eat between 7 to 10 portions of fruits and vegetables daily. For instance, you can have one piece of fruit and a glass of fresh juice for breakfast, a couple of tomatoes and a piece of fruit at lunchtime, a bowl of vegetable soup and a portion of broccoli with your evening meal, and a couple of pieces of fruit as snacks mid-morning and mid-afternoon. It isn't too difficult.

Holistic Help – Supplements

- Each cigarette robs the body of about 25mg of vitamin C so a diet rich in this nutrient from fruits and vegetables is vital. Taking at least 500mg daily can help to counteract some of this loss.

- The herb wild oats, *Avena sativa*, has a calming effect on the mind helping to reduce the craving for a cigarette.

- The herb *Acorus calamus* was once used by miners to keep their lungs clear, though this herb should not be used for more than a couple of months. Another herb which should be used only under the supervision of a herbalist is *lobelia* which has a similar chemical structure to nicotine and helps to wean off cigarettes. Contact the National Institute of Medical Herbalists 01392 426 022.

- *St John's wort* helps to ease depression and low moods associated with giving up nicotine. Levels of the brain chemicals serotonin and dopamine fall when giving up cigarettes and this herb helps to counteract this.

- The mineral *chromium*, at 200mcg daily, and the amino acid *L-glutamine* at around 5g daily, can help to reduce cravings by helping to balance blood sugar levels.

HEADACHES AND MIGRAINES

Suffering from headaches or migraines can be a sign of mounting tensions and stresses. The stresses might be emotional, often with a feeling of being out of control, and can also relate to physical and dietary stresses. Migraines are different from headaches in that they are often one sided, and may involve nausea or visual disturbances. There are also different biochemical reactions in the brain that are thought to cause migraines. If you are prone to regular headaches or migraines there is a lot you can do to prevent them interfering with your life.

Top Tips

■ Keep a diary for a couple of months and work out the triggers for your headaches or migraines. Keep a note of major events (looking for stresses that lead to attacks), poor sleeping patterns, bright lights, what you eat, whether you are pre-menstrual (see page 116).

■ Bad posture or spinal misalignment might be a contributing cause. A few appointments with a chiropractor, osteopath or physiotherapist can make a great difference for some people. Other help for muscle tension can be found from massage, shiatsu, acupuncture or cranial-osteopathy. Posture realignment from Pilates or Alexander technique classes might also help.

■ Migraines are very common pre-menstrually (see Pre-menstrual Health page 116) and are also linked to the contraceptive pill and to hormone replacement therapy (HRT). If either hormone preparations do not agree with you, speak to your doctor about an alternative prescription or seek natural methods of contraception or hormone balance (see supplements below).

More Hints

■ Taking pain relief medication may stop an attack from developing, but in one in ten cases the medicine, particularly paracetamol, will worsen the headache, through a rebound effect as it creates more work for the liver to do.

■ The essential oils peppermint, lavender and rosemary can wipe away headaches as they are developing. Put a drop of one or two, one on each temple, before the headache intensifies too much.

■ A word of caution: if you have been headache-free and are suddenly beset by frequent headaches you must see you doctor to rule out more serious causes.

■ Contact the Migraine Action Association 01536 461 333 or www.migraine.org.uk and The City of London Migraine Clinic website at www.colmc.org.uk

Holistic Help – Diet

■ Missed or inappropriate meals are the most likely dietary cause of headaches and migraines. Skipping breakfast or lunch, or eating meals centred on stimulants and sugary foods, such as coffee and a Danish pastry for breakfast, or a cola and chocolate for a snack, are a recipe for suffering.

■ If necessary, eat a small snack just before bedtime to keep your blood sugar even throughout the night and to avoid an attack the next day. A couple of oatcakes, a banana, some yoghurt or a small handful of nuts should be sufficient.

■ A diet which consists of whole grains, beans and lentils, lean meats, and lots of fruits and vegetables can help.

■ Most people who suffer migraines are usually aware of particular foods which are their triggers. The most common are: chocolate (particularly dark), cheese (particularly mature and blue, but not cream or cottage), red and white wine and citrus fruit. Foods rich in amine such as Horlicks, Marmite, liver, sausage, broad beans, pickled herrings and beer are also triggers as are nitrate-rich foods such as salami, bacon and frankfurters. Avoid coffee and other caffeinated drinks and medication containing caffeine such as cold and pain medication. Other elements found to cause migraines are colas (even caffeine-free), MSG (monosodium glutamate, E621) and Aspartame (artificial sweetener). Not all these foods trigger attacks in all migraine sufferers all the time and keeping a diary may pinpoint if any are a problem for you.

■ You may need to wean yourself off caffeine slowly to avoid rebound headaches.

■ Food sensitivities, most commonly to wheat or dairy products, are a frequent cause, especially if the person also suffers from other health issues such as digestive or bloating problems, or unexplained lethargy.

■ Magnesium-rich foods can help. This mineral is found in all green leafy vegetables, wholegrains, brewer's yeast, sunflower and pumpkin seeds, dried fruit and nuts.

■ Oily fish eaten three times a week can bring relief from migraines by reducing blood platelet clumping. Choose from mackerel, sardines, tuna, salmon, shellfish and other oil-rich fish.

■ You may find that you can tolerate spirits in moderation if you have to give up wine. Experiment with vodka or gin mixed with juices such as tomato.

■ Headaches are often linked to bowel problems and if you tend to be constipated and also get headaches it is valuable to resolve the former. The best remedy is usually to make sure fluid (and particularly water) intake is kept up to around the 2 litre level daily, avoiding coffee, taking one to two teaspoons of *psyllium husks* daily as well as an *acidophilus and bifidobacteria* supplement.

■ Keep a jar of crystallized ginger handy and treat yourself to a cube or two if you feel a headache coming on – it really works and tastes delicious – or take a ginger supplement.

Holistic Help – Supplements

■ The most effective anti-migraine herb is *feverfew*. The active compound, parthenolide, has the effect of reducing the platelet clumping that contributes to migraines. You need to take two capsules daily (or take 50 drops of *feverfew tincture* in water) for about 2 months before you are likely to see an effect. If you grow feverfew, make sure it is the right variety *Tanacetum parthenium*. Add one or two leaves daily to salads or sandwiches.

■ Butterbur root, *Petasites hybridus*, is effective where migraines are linked to muscle tensions in the neck and back. Trials show between 60–75 per cent reduction in the incidence of attacks. Take 50mg twice daily, and again you need to take it for two months before you are likely to see an effect.

■ *Magnesium* is often linked to migraines, particularly those triggered pre-menstrually. Take 400mg for two months and then reduce to 250–300mg daily thereafter.

■ Trials have shown that *vitamin B2 (riboflavin)* helped up to 60 per cent of migraine sufferers. A high dose was used, 400mg daily for three months, but this is quite safe. It is best to also take a general *B-vitamin complex* alongside this or some *brewer's yeast*.

■ For pre-menstrual headaches and migraines experiment with the herb chasteberry (*Agnus castus*) which has the effect of balancing female hormones. You need to take it for two to three months before you see an effect.

■ *Camomile tea* drunk four or five times daily can be very soothing and helps to eliminate toxic build up which might contribute to headaches.

HEALTHY EATING: 5 STRESS-FREE STEPS

The food we eat determines our health at the most fundamental level – 'you are what you eat'. The modern diet, filled with processed ready meals and junk food, is a proven factor in the escalating numbers of people affected by illnesses such as tooth decay, diabetes, arthritis, and bowel and heart disease, among others. The terms 'healthy eating' and 'balanced diet' are bandied about, but many are not really sure what these terms mean and how they can achieve these ideals.

It is monumentally off-putting and threatening to be given a long list of what not to do. Being told to give up salt and saturated fats, cut down on the booze and avoid sugar, can seem a daunting list of injunctions because they get to the very core of our dietary addictions and poor eating habits. Changes can be stressful if they lead to feelings of deprivation – a negative approach which does not give people the tools they need to make necessary changes. So here is a different approach. Make sure that you eat positively by consuming more of the foods which your body needs to carry out its normal functions and repair itself, and, of course, protect you from stress. The habits that serve us less well are then automatically crowded out. That cream cake and coffee will not kill you. What will make you feel progressively worse – is if you have them day in, day out. So moderation is important, as is variety, which is an important mainstay of excellent nutrition. If you eat the same foods all the time, you will be getting only the nutrients (vitamins and minerals) that those foods give you. However, if you eat a range of foods you will consume a wider choice of nutrients.

Here are five easy steps:

STEP 1: Eat loads of fruits and vegetables

■ We are advised to eat at least five portions of fruits and vegetables daily. A portion means:

- one apple, banana, orange or pear

- a couple of kiwis, tomatoes or plums

- a large slice of melon or pineapple

- a small bunch of grapes or a handful of berries

- a wineglass of fruit, tomato or other vegetable juice

- a cup of loosely packed chopped vegetables

- a small side salad.

It does not mean potatoes, which are mostly starch.

■ Fruits and vegetables are our principal sources of antioxidants, such as the vitamins A, C and E, which are protective against a variety of degenerative diseases. The role of antioxidants is to neutralize damaging molecules called free-radicals which oxidize our body tissues – in the same way that iron rusts or an apple turns brown when exposed to air. An antioxidant-rich diet can reduce the onslaught of time, protect our body tissues against stress-induced damage, and help keep skin in good condition and to protect against eye damage. Ideally, eat and prepare fresh or frozen fruits and vegetables, and if you occasionally have canned produce make sure that you rinse off salty water and avoid sugars and syrups.

■ To get five portions, eat at least one serving with each meal (for instance chopped fruit on cereal or a glass of juice at breakfast, a side-salad or a couple of tomatoes at lunchtime, a portion of vegetables or pulses in the evening), and snack on fruit, or dried fruit, between meals mid-morning and mid-afternoon. By snacking on health-giving fruits, you will reduce the desire to have biscuits, chocolates or crisps at breaktime.

■ And remember, if five portions of fruit and veg is good, more is even better so don't stop there! Ideally go for 7–10 portions. As a minimum this just means one extra vegetable at lunch and with your evening meal.

■ Finally, fruit is excellent as a sweet-tasting substitute for sugary foods, and a mashed banana on toast or chopped dried apricots in cereal can go a long way to satisfying a sweet tooth and so cutting dependency on sugar. Sugar is a nutritional void with no nutrients to recommend it (and no, you do not need sugar for energy – quite the opposite in fact as, in the long run, excess sugar leads to depleted energy).

STEP 2: Eat foods which are sources of healthy fats

■ Low-fat, no-fat, trans-fats, cholesterol … don't let this confusing array of fats scare you. The first thing is to realize that cutting out all fats is unhealthy. We all need a certain amount of fats, and problems only arise when we eat too much of the wrong sort, such as the saturated fats found in meat and dairy products. Certain fats, such as the omega 3 and 6 EFAs (essential fatty acids), are needed for vital body functions such as building all the cells in our bodies, sex and stress hormone production, brain cells and nerve insulation.

■ An important source of beneficial unsaturated fats are oily fish such as mackerel, sardines, sprats, anchovies, salmon and tuna (not canned tuna). The omega-3 fats found in these are particularly important for brain and eye function, but are also needed for other purposes such as making anti-inflammatory prostaglandins and anti-coagulation substances. This is why fish oils are so useful for helping to treat conditions such as arthritis, eczema and high blood pressure.

■ Other vital fats, the omega-6s and some omega-3s, are found in all fresh nuts and fresh seeds which can be chopped or ground and added to yoghurts, cereals and casseroles, or just eaten as satisfying snacks with some fruit. Seeds which you might like to experiment with include sunflower seeds, pumpkin seeds, linseeds and pine nuts.

■ Other healthy fats can be found in naturally fatty foods such as avocados, olives and coconut. Olive oil is probably the best oil to cook with, particularly if you use extra-virgin oil, because it is more heat stable than other oils and is a good source of antioxidants. This lends itself to all the wonderful Mediterranean dishes that you will want to create as you experiment with eating more vegetables, as mentioned previously, and which have heart-disease- and cancer-protective properties.

■ The two main types of fat to cut back on are excessive saturated fats and hydrogenated fats (commonly found in processed foods, especially margarines and other butter substitutes). If you substitute between three and four meat-based meals with fish and vegetarian dishes (using pulses) each week, you will automatically cut back on your intake of saturated fats. Easy choices would be to order a chick pea curry instead of a lamb curry, to make a lentil patty instead of a beefburger, to stuff a pitta bread with hummus instead of ham, or even just good old baked beans on wholemeal toast. The rest of the time, eat lean cuts of meat such as chicken or turkey breast or game meat such as pheasant.

■ You can reduce your consumption of saturated fats derived from dairy produce with delicious half-fat or low-fat milk and yoghurt or experiment with soya milk and other products. Get into the habit of using plain yoghurt instead of cream on desserts, as well as in salad dressings and to replace cream in cooking.

■ If you have already started following the advice above about snacking on fruits or nuts, or low-fat yoghurts, you will automatically be reducing the main sources of hydrogenated fats which tend to lurk in processed snack foods such as crisps, cakes and biscuits. Some margarines are also sources of hydrogenated fats. Marketed as 'healthy' these alternative spreads have been linked to the rise of some cancers. In fact a little scrape of butter instead or a drizzle of olive oil is a better option.

STEP 3: Eat more fibre-rich foods

- Fibre is the indigestible portion of plant foods which we need to regulate our digestive system. Eating fibre-rich foods encourages the growth of beneficial bacteria in our bowels which keeps digestive disturbances, irritable bowel syndrome and even bowel cancer at bay. Fibre is also needed to slow down the absorption of carbohydrates which are our main source of energy, ensuring more sustained energy levels throughout the day as our blood sugar level is kept in balance. This process is also thought to protect against diabetes, as well as hormonal imbalances which lead to pre-menstrual syndrome/pre-menstrual tension (PMS/PMT) and menopausal problems.

- Some of the most valuable and also versatile fibre-rich foods are pulses, beans and lentils. If you immediately think that they are likely to cause you digestive upset, do not be put off as increasing the fibre content of your diet is the best way to resolve this. You will just need to add them in more slowly. Enjoy all sorts of dishes from familiar baked beans and peas, to lentil soup, Mexican refried beans, black eye beans with rice, flageolet beans (traditional in France) and others. Add them to soups, stews, casseroles and salads. They are really very versatile, low in fat, nutritious, satisfying and delicious.

- The final step is to choose wholemeal versions of grains whenever you can. In the refining process, much of the fibre is removed from bread and rice to make the white varieties. At the same time, they lose many of the vitamins and minerals, and while some are put back into flour (iron, B vitamins and calcium) many are not. The antioxidant vitamin E and minerals such as selenium and chromium are lost when the wheatgerm is removed from flour. Any grain eaten whole is better than its refined relative. This means choosing wholemeal bread over white bread, brown rice over white rice, whole porridge oats over instant oats. Potatoes are a starchy food and jacket potatoes, boiled potatoes or potato wedges with their skins on, are to be preferred over peeled potatoes.

- If you find that adding more fibre into your diet means you suffer more bowel problems, instead of less, you will need to increase your fibre levels more slowly by easing into eating wholegrains over a period of a few weeks. In the short term you may also find that you are reacting badly to more wheat in your diet, in which case concentrate on other grains such as oats, rye, barley, rice, buckwheat, millet and amaranth.

STEP 4: Enjoy drinks which are hydrating

- Our bodies are 70 per cent water and dehydration contributes to a wide variety of problems including overeating, joint pain and headaches. Part of the problem is that instead of drinking hydrating drinks such as water and diluted fresh fruit juices, we drink dehydrating drinks such as coffee, colas, strong tea and alcohol.

- Weak tea is OK, or try *Rooibos* or green tea. Make yourself a large jug of fruit tea, add slices of orange and lemon and sprigs of mint and keep chilled as a refreshing drink, or keep a large (preferably a 1.5–2 litre) bottle of water by your desk and drink it all each day.

- If you want to put the kettle on, have hot water and lemon with a teaspoon of honey.

- All of these will keep you hydrated but remember that, if you find you are thirsty, you have let it go on too long – you are already dehydrated and need to make sure that you get your 1.5–2 litres of water a day (not 1.5–2 litres of coffee!).

STEP 5: Use healthy flavourings

- Herbs are amazingly hardy and grow successfully in pots even if you don't lavish as much love on them as you ought. A few snipped fresh herbs (such as chives, thyme, mint, coriander, basil or tarragon), a sprinkling of dried herbs or spices such as turmeric, chilli or cinnamon, not only make the simplest dishes and salads more delicious, but more importantly help to cut back on salt levels. You can also use a squeeze of lemon or a dash of vinegar or balsamic vinegar. Add garlic to everything you can as it is a delicious flavouring and has many health properties.

- We eat about twice as much salt as we need (a lot of it in the form of bought ready meals and snacks), and by cutting back on processed foods and using more herbs and spices you will be able to cut back your salt intake to a healthy level. Excess salt consumption (an average of 10–12g per person against the recommended 6g daily) is linked to high blood pressure and heart disease as well as water retention.

- Get out of the habit of reaching for the salt cellar when you are cooking but, if this is difficult, use a potassium-based salt such as *Solo*, which is also a source of valuable trace minerals (www.soloseasalt.com).

- Another ideal alternative is to replace the salt in your grinder with seaweed granules (available from health food shops) which have a mildly salty taste, but are also rich in many other minerals such as iodine (www.seagreens.com).

- You will quickly find that a diet such as this, with its fresh varied ingredients and cleaner taste, will lead you to cut back on sugary and processed foods. Over time many convenience foods will taste greasy and unpalatable.

- For more information about healthy eating, as well as using medicinal herbs and supplements see pages 98 and 230.

INFECTIONS/IMMUNE SYSTEM

If you dread the coming of winter because you always seem to catch every bug going, you can prepare a couple of months ahead by tuning up your immune system. The immune system is easily depressed by stress. This is quite apparent when we become ill at just the time when we need all our resources – when moving house triggers the flu, a promotion brings a heavier workload along with chronic fatigue syndrome and students develop glandular fever around exam time (a very common phenomenon). By supporting your immune health you give it the resources it needs to fight off infections.

Top Tips

■ Laughter is one of the best immune stimulants known. Keep your sense of humour.

■ If you feel ill don't fight it, but operate at a level at which you feel comfortable and if necessary take to your bed for complete rest. By ignoring the warning signs and working through it, you do not allow your body to mount the necessary immune response as energy is diverted into other activities. One or two days at home or in bed might be a good trade off against several days of bed-rest when you are finally incapacitated.

■ Smoking is guaranteed to bring immune health to its knees. Give it up (see Giving Up Smoking page 94). If you continue to smoke, then take at least 500mg of *vitamin C* a day to partially compensate and eat loads of antioxidant rich fruits and vegetables.

More Hints

■ Excessive use of antibiotics (more than once or twice a year) ultimately suppresses immune function. Taking *acidophilus and bifidobacteria* (also found in live yoghurt, see below) can help to redress bowel bacterial balance which in turn supports immune health.

■ Keep moving. Moderate exercise improves immune health. It also improves the flow of lymph throughout the body. The lymph system can be thought of as the body's waste disposal system and helps to excrete immune-dampening toxins.

■ A polluted environment can reduce immune health. At work avoid standing or sitting near the photocopier all the time (see Healthy Office page 49), avoid smoky atmospheres and at home cut back on the number of chemicals used around the house (see Housework page 20).

■ If you have had two or more pregnancies close together, your immune health might well be suffering. Follow the dietary advice even more closely and make sure you get at least two full nights of sleep (without crying babies) each week.

Holistic Help – Diet

■ There is no substitute for eating at least five portions of a variety of fruits and vegetables daily. The antioxidants in these will be used to improve immune health. Vitamin C-rich foods, probably the most important, include citrus fruit, blackcurrants, kiwis, dark green leafy vegetables such as cabbage and broccoli, and potatoes and sweet potatoes in their jackets.

■ Aim to include at least one portion of dark berries in your diet daily – autumn and winter options, to help protect against colds and flu, include blackberries, blueberries (frozen or canned are fine), cranberries and elderberries. *Sambucol* is a tonic made from elderberries and a teaspoon once or twice a day is a delicious way to keep infections at bay available from health food stores or call **Nature's Store** 01782 794300. **Biona** make a cranberry juice sweetened with apple juice instead of sugar.

■ If you are low in zinc not only are you more likely to get an infection, but it is likely to last longer. Zinc-rich foods include lean red meat, shellfish, wholegrains, seeds and nuts.

- A clove of garlic a day, added to food, is a painless way to improve immune health. It is antiviral, antibacterial and antiparasitic. Garlic has even been shown to prevent the growth of antibiotic resistant MRSA (*Streptococcus aureus*) which kills many hospital patients. The allicin it contains has been well studied as an immune enhancer. If you find it easier you could take garlic supplements, but I find the herb itself so delicious that I prefer the food.

- Fresh ginger root is known to enhance immunity. Together with garlic, ginger is an essential ingredient for Chinese style chicken broths or healthy vegetable stir-fries. Grated with lemon and honey, ginger makes a comforting drink, useful for promoting sweating and lowering body temperature when you have the flu.

- Making fruit and vegetable juices is a delicious way to support immune health and get a boost of antioxidants. Aim to make three or four fresh juices each week. The quercitin in apple is particularly useful for lung health, and the beta-carotene in carrots keeps mucus membranes functioning well. A healthy gut also promotes overall immune health and eating pineapple and papaya helps to maintain the health of the digestive tract.

- Eat one live yoghurt each day. The beneficial bacteria will help to keep your bowel health optimal, which in turn boosts immunity. Alternatively, take a beneficial bowel bacteria supplement daily.

- Oriental mushrooms such as maitake, shitake and reishi contain powerful immune stimulating polysaccharides. You can buy them dried and add a couple a day to soups and stews or make an immune supporting, delicious and very warming broth with them by adding to some miso boiled up with chopped onion and garlic. The **East West Herb Shop** sells mushroom-based supplements (020 7379 1312).

- Seaweeds are rich sources of minerals and the alginic acid they contain helps to clear out toxins. Fill a pepper grinder with seaweed granules (available from health food shops) and add to savoury dishes for a mildly salty taste (www.seagreens.com)

- If you tend towards a lot of mucus with colds in the winter, avoid dairy products. Soya foods can also create mucus build-up in some sensitive people.

Holistic Help – Supplements

- Balance your immune system by taking plant sterols and sterolins (found naturally in plant matter), such as **Nature's Store's** *Moducare* (01782 794 300). Taking Moducare is a safe, natural means of supporting the body's immune system.

- A good quality antioxidant supplement once a day during autumn and winter is a good investment. I like **Solgar's** *Antioxidant Nutrients*, though there are many good brands.

- *Echinacea* and *astragalus* are potent immune boosting herbs. Use tinctures, about 30–50 drops of each in water, or take a capsule of 1 of each once a day. One excellent formulation for winter ills combines echinacea with eucalyptus (an antiseptic to clear sinuses), liquorice root and aniseed (expectorants), peppermint and cloves (to soothe ticklish throats) and fennel (a natural stimulant). You can find this in *Revitonil* from **Lichtwer** (01803 528 668, www.lichtwer.co.uk).

- *Cat's claw*, a Peruvian herb, is drunk as a tea and provides strong antioxidant protection for boosting immunity.
- Tickles in the throat respond to *zinc* and *echinacea* from **Bioforce** (see page 232) and *Propolis lozenges* (for **Propolis** products see www.comvita.com).

JET LAG

If you travel across time zones, you are likely to be affected by jet lag as your body struggles to adapt to the day/night cycle in your new location. Even experienced air crew suffer from jet lag. Jet lag seems to be worse flying west to east around the globe, rather than the other way round. The following tips will help to reduce the effects of jet lag.

- As soon as you are able on the flight, adjust your watch to the time at your destination.
- If your stay is a short one, say two or three days, keep to your home time schedule and make appointments and go to sleep accordingly.
- Keep hydrated on the flight by drinking lots of water and avoid alcohol. This will make you less likely to suffer from jet lag.
- Avoid caffeine which often increases jet lag.
- Take an eye mask with you to help you sleep when it is light.
- Taking 0.3mg of *melatonin* for two to four nights half an hour before you want to sleep until your sleeping patterns right themselves.
- You may find that a pillow slip fitted with integral magnets helps to reduce jet lag. These are available from www.homediscs.uk.com
- At your destination, walk around out of doors in daylight for a while each day, and particularly on the first day, to reset your body clock.
- Homeopathic *arnica* has jet lag reducing qualities that may help you.
- On arrival, have either a soothing or a stimulating aromatherapy bath as required. Restful essential oils include rose, neroli, camomile or lavender while more enlivening ones are pine, grapefruit, lemon, eucalyptus, rosemary, lemon and bergamot.

LOW ENERGY (TIRED ALL THE TIME)

Many people actually believe it is normal to feel washed out most of the time. They rationalize that with their frenetic pace of life that burnout is inevitable and that exhaustion is just something they have to put up with. But it is not normal to feel this way and there is a lot that can be done about it. Of course it helps to not burn all your candles at all their ends all the time, but you can also shore up your body's reserves to help you to cope with a busy life. If you are feeling exhausted take this as a wake up call to look after your health. (It might be a good idea to ask your doctor for a blood test to rule out such physiological conditions as an underactive thyroid.) Don't ignore extreme tiredness – or you may find that you tip over into serious depression or chronic fatigue with only a little push from a stressful event such as moving house or changing jobs.

Top Tips

■ Eat three meals a day and make sure you are making healthy choices (see page 98). You would not expect your car to perform without the right fuel, so do not expect this of your body.

■ It is best to take a multi-disciplinary approach when dealing with exhaustion. The best results are achieved by using a combination of diet, nutritional supplements, stress management or counselling, physiotherapy, massage or gentle exercise and perhaps another discipline such as homeopathy or acupuncture.

■ If you are feeling chronically burned out over a period of time it is important to rule out possible causes such as anaemia, glandular fever, thyroid problems or diabetes with your doctor. More and more doctors are becoming aware of the diagnosis of chronic fatigue (also variously called ME, post-viral fatigue and adrenal syndrome depending on the symptoms). Chronic fatigue involves a diagnosis of at least six months of symptoms, summarized on a check list, which includes excessive fatigue, which is worsened by physical or mental exertion, possibly with muscle weakness, painful lymph nodes, depression, sleep disturbance, memory and concentration problems or digestive problems.

■ The greatest mistake that many people make when they are on the road to recovery and begin to feel better is to do too much, too soon. If you have been exhausted or ill for a while, it takes time to build up your reserves again, so take it slowly to avoid another setback.

■ If you are staying up late to catch up on domestic or work-related jobs, or are out clubbing into the early hours, and getting up early to go to the office or to deal with family needs, and pushing yourself between times, and are feeling tired, you really need to take a long hard look at your lifestyle.

■ If you are not inspired by what you are doing, and find your life a bit of a drudge, that can be as tiring as having too much to do. Use mind mapping techniques (page 226) to find out what it is you really want to be doing with your time. People who enjoy what they do are less likely to feel tired.

More Hints

■ Exercise can seem impossible if you are exhausted. Nevertheless it is important for wellness to keep moving, no matter how gently. Find a programme that works for you. Slow walking, yoga, gentle swimming and gentle stretches are all ways to slowly get yourself moving again.

- Having eliminated various possible complications with your GP, if you consult a nutritionist they can look for various 'loads' which are placed upon the immune system – for instance pollution, toxins, candida, allergies, food intolerances and others can have an effect, and they can advise on measures to take to reduce these.

- If you think you might be affected by chronic fatigue or ME you are not alone and you can find support by contacting the support organizations: ME Association 01375 642 466 www.meassociation.org.uk or Association of Youth with ME 01908 373 300 www.ayme org. uk

Holistic Help – Diet

- A healthy diet is essential to improve energy levels and promote recovery. Eat plenty of high energy foods such as fruits, vegetables, lentils, pulses, brown rice, oats, barley and fresh fish.

- Favour oils which provide you with healthy EFAs (essential fatty acids), such as cold-pressed, linseed and walnut oils. Totally avoid hydrogenated fats which are found in margarines and in packaged foods such as crisps, biscuits and pies (vegetarian packaged foods are also often sources of hydrogenated fats).

- Eat to balance blood sugar levels and make sure you eat five small meals and snacks daily. In this way you will reduce the energy taken to digest large meals.

- I strongly recommend that you avoid all sources of caffeine and alcohol to replete your energy levels. You may want to reduce coffee gradually over a couple of weeks to avoid a rebound reaction and headaches.

- Drink 1.5–2 litres of water daily for hydration and cleansing of your body tissues and organs.

- Keep sources of sweetness to fruits, a little honey, a little *fructose* or *FOS*, a sweet-tasting fibre available from **Biocare**, **Higher Nature** and others in powder form to use as a sugar substitute (it is actually a fibre which helps bowel health).

- Sprinkle cracked linseeds or psyllium husks on your cereals or in drinks daily to improve digestive function and to help the elimination of toxins from the body.

- Food sensitivities can be a particular problem for people who seem to be perpetually exhausted especially if there does not seem to be any other obvious cause of their fatigue. It often pays dividends to follow a wheat-free diet for a few weeks, and possibly also to investigate other sensitivities, such as dairy products.

- A typical Western diet means we generally eat twice as much salt as we need, with all the linked problems of high blood pressure and water retention. However, if you have been on a salt-restricted diet for a long time and have very low blood pressure, which can lead to exhaustion, you may actually need to increase the salt in your diet. Do not do this if you have been on a 'normal' diet.

■ Another possible cause of tiredness is an overgrowth of an opportunistic yeast organism called *Candida albicans* which is normally resident in the bowels. But if the immune system of the person is weakened there is a greater chance of candida spreading. Most commonly this manifests itself as thrush which leads to a white discharge and itchiness in the vagina or anal area. Thrush of the mouth, eyes, under the nails or other areas is also quite common. Occasionally, however, the candida manages to invade higher up the digestive tract, in the small intestines and to invade other body tissues. In these cases, the person can feel quite debilitated, with energy problems being one of the most severe effects. There are often a host of other related problems such as food allergies, sensitivities to moulds and damp environments, and headaches and migraines.

■ The main dietary advice for getting rid of candida is to avoid all sources of sugar rigorously because the yeast feeds on sugar. In addition to cutting out sugar, fast-releasing carbohydrates (which turn into sugar quickly) and alcohol, it may also mean cutting back on over-ripe fruit and sticking to fruit such as green apples and pears.

■ The other main dietary treatment to deal with candida is to avoid all yeasts. These include bread (apart from breads and crackers which do not use yeast, such as soda bread and oatcakes), alcohol (again), most cheeses (cottage cheese is OK) and in extreme cases mushrooms, *Quorn* and vinegars. It is also necessary to avoid stimulants and any foods to which you may be sensitive or allergic.

Holistic Help – Supplements

■ The most important nutrients to combat energy depletion are the B-group of vitamins which are involved in all aspects of energy production in the cells. Either take a 50mg *B-complex* or some *brewer's yeast* daily (although not if your problem is candida, see above).

■ Other important energy production nutrients are *magnesium*, *vitamin C* and *iodine*, which helps to produce the thyroid hormone which regulates metabolism and so is important for energy. Maintain healthy Iodine levels by taking 150mcg of *kelp* daily.

■ If you have been chronically tired for a while you might want to see if the supplement *NADH* works for you. NADH (nicotinamide adenine dinucleotide) is the co-enzyme of vitamin B3 and has proven ability to replenish depleted cellular stores of ATP (which is the name we give to cellular energy) and in this way can improve fatigue and boost mental function. The brand name *Enada* (NADH) is available from the **NutriCentre**, 020 7436 0422, or try their website (www.nutricentre.com). The amounts recommended for use as supplements vary between 1 and 5 mg. If you suffer from stress-induced palpitations don't take this supplement.

■ *Liquorice root* can help to stabilize blood sugar and also help to improve low blood pressure (which can be linked to tiredness). In order to elevate your blood pressure you need to use liquorice which contains glycyrrhizin rather than the DGL (deglycyrrhized) version. You can also find compounds which combine liquorice and Siberian ginseng (see below). Do not take liquorice root if you have high blood pressure.

- Herbal adaptogens are used to help the body adapt to stress and have even been used on space programmes to help cosmonauts adapt to the stress of being in space. The ginsengs (*Siberian*, *Korean* and *American*) are the best known adaptogens to improve energy and reduce the harmful effects of stress. Ginseng should not be overused as it can lead to over-stimulation and insomnia, and this is particularly a risk if it is taken with sources of caffeine. It should also not be used by those with high blood pressure.

- Another useful adaptogen is *Rhodiola* (available from **Solgar**, see Supplements page 233).

- Taking a 'probiotic' supplement which includes *lactobacillus acidophilus and bifidobacteria* is helpful if you are dealing with candida.

MUSCLE TENSION

Frequently, we hold tensions in our body as an alternative to voicing our stresses. We may also find ourselves sitting at desks and hunched over computers for hours at a time causing tight neck and shoulder muscles. Working on muscle tensions, whether short or long term, can have profound effects on relieving stress and improving overall health.

Top Tips
- There is nothing quite like massage to relieve muscle tension. It is even more effective if you have a massage after a heat treatment such as a sauna. For very bad muscle tension make sure you go to a properly trained remedial massage therapist.

- To see if posture may be at the root of your tension problems, strip to your underwear and stand in front of a full-length mirror with legs together and your hands hanging loosely by your side. Look carefully to see if one shoulder is higher than the other and if your hip alignment is out. If so (and it is in so many people) you will probably benefit from a discipline such as Alexander technique, yoga or Pilates (see Useful Resources page 235).

- If you are worried and are holding tension in your neck and back as a result, work on the source of your concerns (see Anxiety page 135 and Problem Solving page 59).

- Posture is a very good indicator of our internal emotional state. If we are depressed, we round our shoulders and if we are anxious, we tense our shoulders, yet if we are happy, we tend to throw back our shoulders and look the world in the eye. Try this experiment: throw back your shoulders, walk briskly and look ahead while you are smiling. It is actually quite difficult to feel low and depressed when you adopt this posture. Now you know what to do when you are feeling fed-up.

More Hints
- Heat treatments can relax muscles and relieve pain. These simple treatments can be done at home. A warm shower followed by a cream containing essential oils of lavender and rosemary rubbed into the affected area is warming and relaxing. A hot-water bottle wrapped in a fluffy towel may also bring relief.

- A well-trained kinesiology practitioner can pinpoint the reason for muscle tensions and use a form of acupressure to rebalance the tautness of muscles so that they work in better balance.

- Holding tension in the jaw is common, as is teeth grinding at night. Your dentist may be able to give you advice about this, or a kinesiologist (see above) who is familiar with temporomandibular joint (TMJ) work can help to sort it out.

Holistic Help – Diet

- Dehydration is a common reason for muscle tension. Low back pain is often particularly related to dehydration which affects the strength of the muscles. Drinking 1.5–2 litres of water daily, while cutting back on dehydrating caffeine and alcohol, can make all the difference.

- Magnesium is vital to help muscles to relax. Food sources include green leafy vegetables,

Holistic Help – Supplements

- The minerals magnesium and calcium help to relax muscles, which can be involved in back spasm and other muscle tensions. While both minerals are important, the bias is often towards needing *magnesium* at around 400mg daily to relax muscle tension. It has a marked effect on cramped leg muscles, can be effective at treating back pain, and is very useful for migraines.

- Another useful anti-spasmodic and muscle relaxant is the herb *cramp bark* which can be taken as a tea or in capsule form.

- *Devil's claw*, a South West African herb, can provide fairly fast-acting relief for muscle tension due to its muscle relaxant action.

- The herb *butterbur* (*Petasites*) is a useful anti-spasmodic supplement for muscle tension. It can relieve tension-related migraine, menstrual cramps and muscle spasms. In about half to two-thirds of people it is fairly fast acting (within half-an-hour). Take 50mg twice daily for chronic muscle tension. *Petaforce* is the name of **Bioforce's** butterbur.

NERVOUS TUMMY

Nervous tummy, butterflies in the stomach, collywobbles – we all know that stress affects digestion faster than anything else. Stress is linked to heartburn, indigestion, bloating, stomach ulcers, irritable bowel syndrome (IBS) and wind among other digestive tract problems.

When we experience stress one of the first symptoms is a tight, fluttering feeling in our stomachs. This happens because the blood supply is shunted away from the digestive tract towards the skeletal frame, a response that evolved to help humans to escape from danger in prehistoric times. But in this day and age, stress is more likely to be triggered by a late train or a row with the kids. Stress also has the effect of encouraging the breakdown of the tissues lining the digestive tract. This reduces absorption of nutrients from food and creates a vicious circle where we don't have an adequate supply of the nutrients needed to combat the effects of stress on the body. Additionally, acute stress can encourage painful spasms of the gut wall which are one of the effects of irritable bowel syndrome. Stress also lowers immunity and stomach acidity which allows the bacteria *Helicobacter pylori* to get a foot-hold which encourages ulcers.

Obviously the best way to reduce the impact that stress has on digestion is to reduce your stress load. However, much can also be done to use diet to compensate for the worst effects of stress on the digestive tract.

Top Tips

■ Make a point of eating in a relaxed, non-stressful environment. Eat slowly, chewing food properly and concentrate on enjoying your meal. Do this even if you are just having a snack, and especially if you are eating at work.

■ If you are prone to not eating when nervous make sure that you at least have a small, healthy snack, such as a banana, to keep you going. Your digestive tract mostly feeds directly from the contents of the tract, rather from its blood supply, and needs to be kept nourished to function well. Eating a series of small healthy snacks throughout the day helps to alleviate nervousness.

■ Relaxation or yoga classes can improve digestion if you apply yourself over time.

More Hints

■ Use visualization techniques (see page 222) during quiet moments to imagine your digestive tract functioning normally. Imagine the food going through, being broken down thoroughly, and the nutrients being absorbed across the healthy mucus membranes lining your tract. Now visualize a stressful situation and see what effect it has on your digestion in your mind's eye. Work out a visual way in which the stress 'bounces' off your digestive tract and does not interfere. Imagine a healing light coursing through your digestive tract and restoring normal function.

■ Autogenic training, which is a form of intense relaxation (see page 140), focuses on different parts of the body and can help to calm stressed digestion.

Top Tips

■ Wheat is the food which most commonly stresses the digestive tract, which may find it hard to break down a protein called gluten contained in wheat among other cereals. In Western diets, wheat is commonly eaten several times a day and can lead to bloating, stomach cramps and IBS. Alternatives include rye, oats, barley, rice, buckwheat, corn and quinoa. Good health food shops, and increasingly supermarkets, stock many standard foods, such as bread and pasta, made from these grains. Try the website www.allergyfreedirect.co.uk for many wheat-free products available by mail order.

■ Food combining has been found to help many people to normalize nervous digestion. This involves eating proteins OR carbohydrates with vegetables or salad at a meal and eating fruit separately from meals. This is said to work with the efficient process of digestion rather than against it. So a meal might consist of either meat/cheese and salad and vegetables OR pasta/bread and salad and vegetables, but not the meat/cheese and pasta/bread together. Fruit such as melon is eaten either as a first course and 20 to 30 minutes allowed to pass before eating the main meal, or as snacks between meals.

■ If you have irritable bowel syndrome, make sure you keep your water intake up by drinking 2 litres daily. It will help to reduce constipation and will replace liquids lost with loose bowel movements.

■ Peppermint tea drunk after meals – four to five times a day is ideal – is a great normalizer of digestive function and reduces gassy bloating.

■ Essential fats are needed to repair the digestive tract and good concentrated sources are nuts, seeds and oily fish.

■ Coffee, tea and alcohol interfere with the absorption of nutrients particularly minerals and B-vitamins. Coffee also raises stress hormone levels making digestive problems worse.

■ For more advice on digestive problems, read my book *Banish Bloating* (Simon & Schuster Pocket Books).

Holistic Help – Supplements

■ All bowel problems will benefit from taking 1–2 teaspoons daily of *psyllium husks*, available from good health food shops, to normalize bowel movements. This gentle fibre provides a great 'work-out' for the muscles of the digestive tract. Mix it with water, pinch your nose and swallow it down – it tastes like sawdust. However, if you mix it with apple juice and let it swell up for five minutes, it takes on the consistency of apple sauce and is quite pleasant. Follow with another glass of water.

■ Take a good quality antioxidant supplement containing *vitamins A and C* and the mineral *zinc* to encourage healing of the digestive tract.

■ *Digestive enzymes* taken with each meal can ensure that you actually absorb nutrients from your meal if your digestion is disturbed. Take between one and four capsules with each meal depending on the size of the meal. To test if the supplement you are taking is working properly put one in half a cup of warm porridge and it should turn it to liquid in 15 minutes or so. Digestive enzymes will not reduce your digestive capability but will allow you to absorb nutrients to improve your own digestive enzyme output.

■ An excessive growth of *Candida albicans*, a yeast that occurs naturally in the gut and other areas of the body, can also cause bloating and constipation. Taking *acidophilus and bifidobacteria* supplements can normalize the bacterial balance in the bowels, replacing the healthy, yeast eating bacteria which are depleted by stress.

- *Aloe vera* is a potent healer of the digestive tract. Buy a good quality brand and take 20ml before meals.

- *Slippery elm* is also a proven digestive tract healer and protects against ulcers and is a soothing drink for after meals.

- The amino acid *L-glutamine* is used by the digestive tract directly as fuel and helps to heal stomach ulcers. Take 5–10g daily. As this is a large amount it is easiest to take as a powder mixed in water in two doses, 5g in the morning and 5g in the afternoon (not too late or it might interfere with sleep).

PAIN

Even though many people will simply try to suppress pain by taking analgesics, most will recognize that you can think of pain as a messenger. The pain from a sprained ankle tells you not to put weight on that foot. Your toothache is a warning that a visit to the dentist cannot be delayed. That arthritic twinge is telling you to find out what might be causing the inflammation. But what many people do not realize is that stress can certainly worsen pain. And of course pain is in itself a major anxiety in people's lives which is sometimes, in the case of injury or arthritis, a very long-term stress.

We spend more than £270 million on painkillers each year. But not everyone can take over-the-counter (OTC) pain killers – aspirin can cause gastritis or ulcers. If you are asthmatic, aspirin can trigger an attack, and a recent study concluded that those who take paracetamol once a week increase their risk of developing asthma by 80 per cent. Painkillers have also been found to induce 'rebound' headaches when more than 12 doses are taken weekly. Prescription steroids which suppress inflammation can have far reaching consequences from long-term use, including osteoporosis. It is far better to treat the source of the pain if at all possible and to use side-effect-free painkillers whenever possible (do not stop prescribed medication without first consulting your doctor).

Top Tips

- Pain should never be ignored as a sign of stress. It is often the case that, subconsciously, people will feel it is OK to admit to physical pain, but will not find it easy to admit that they feel frightened, anxious or depressed. The psychological pain they are feeling may well be manifesting as physical pain.

- Acupuncture is proven method of pain relief in the short term. It is also a treatment that can eventually restore harmony and balance to your whole system, eliminating or vastly reducing pain.

- Consider osteopathy or chiropractic help to resolve back pain.

- So much pain and discomfort, particularly that of the joints and back, is related to poor posture and inappropriate footwear. As a first step, get yourself checked out by a qualified podiatrist for foot alignment and to find out if you have fallen arches. **Dr Scholls** is the most well known company (www.drscholls.com). Then find out about **Alexander Technique** classes for posture.

■ Check your bed and mattress to make sure they are not contributing to the problem.

■ A transcutaneous electrical nerve stimulation (TENS) machine is another way to help to block pain in a drug-free way and available from large pharmacies, or you can rent one. They are best known for use during childbirth but are used for all sorts of pain management.

More Hints

■ Many people find that copper bracelets offer relief from arthritic pain.

■ Magnets placed on the affected joint have been found to relieve pain. Magnetism is thought to increase the blood flow, thereby increasing oxygen and relief from pain. You can buy mattresses and pillows containing magnets or more economically buy plasters and straps designed for specific parts of the body (such as the elbow or knee). For information on magnets to help combat pain look up www.homediscsuk.com

■ Patients with chronic pain can be referred by their doctor to the Walton Centre for Pain Relief, NHS Trust (www.wcnn.co.uk).

■ The British Chiropractic Association 0118 950 5950 or www.chiropractic-uk.co.uk; the McTimoney Chiropractic Association 01865 880 974 or www.mctimoney-chiropractic.org; The General Council and Register of Osteopaths 020 7357 6655 www.osteopathy.org.uk; The National Back Pain Association 020 8977 5754 http:/homepages.nildram.co.uk/~backtalk are all organizations concerned with pain relief.

Holistic Help – Diet

■ Hormone-like chemicals produced in the body called leukotrienes and prostaglandins regulate inflammation. Changing the type of fats that a person eats is usually the first step in a nutritional programme. Saturated fats, found in meat, butter, eggs, cheese and full- and half-fat milk, are rich in a substance called arachadonic acid which produces leukotrienes, and these promote inflammation. Conversely, unsaturated fats found in oily fish, fresh nuts and seeds – for example walnuts, almonds, pecans, pumpkin seeds, sunflower seeds and evening primrose oil – are rich in omega-3 and omega-6 fats which promote anti-inflammatory prostaglandins. Fish oil switches off the COX-2 enzyme which kills joint pain. Aspirin also does this but with the unwelcome effect of also inhibiting COX-1 which also triggers gastrointestinal upset.

■ Some people find that inflammation is worsened by certain foods to which they are sensitive, such as wheat, dairy products, citrus fruit, coffee, sugar and alcohol. Food sensitivities have been associated with arthritic pain in a significant number of cases.

■ Histamine is the chemical involved in inflammation and allergies. The ever-popular vitamin C has a mild histamine-reducing effect and also appears to help stabilize the structure of cartilage. Another antioxidant substance, quercitin, found in apples and onions and also available in capsule form, blocks histamine release as well as stopping the release of leukotrienes, and is often used alongside vitamin C for pain relief. Ginger has a long history as an anti-inflammatory compound (do not use if you have stomach or duodenal ulcers) and also acts as an antihistamine.

■ Substance P is a neurotransmitter responsible for the pain message. Elements that can block that message include curcumin – the active agent in turmeric – a potent antioxidant which gives the spice its dark yellow colour and is said to work as well as the steroid cortisone in relieving acute inflammation. Chillies are another powerful blocker of substance P, but if you can't take the heat there are capsicum supplements available.

■ Some specific foods might be helpful. One study found that 20 cherries contained between 12–25mg of anthocyanins, which has more potent pain killing capability than an aspirin tablet, and this has to be one of the more pleasant pain relief options.

■ For a couple of books that are helpful, check out *Foods That Fight Pain* by Neal Barnard, (Bantam Books) and *The Back Pain Bible* by Anthony J. Cichoke, (Keats), (a US book available on www.amazon.co.uk).

Holistic Help – Supplements

■ The enzymes *bromelain*, found in pineapple, and *papain*, from papayas, are known to break up a substance called fibrin that collects in areas of inflammation and is one cause of painful swelling. Available in capsule form, these substances are proteolytic enzymes (which digest proteins), high doses of which have been used successfully to treat back problems and acute strains. Capsules are normally taken with meals to aid digestion but, when taken between meals, it is believed that they remove waste products and fibrin in the area of the injury, helping speed up the healing process. Bromelain also seems to block the formation of inflammatory prostaglandins. Do not take enzymes if you have ulcers or gastritis. *Curcumin* and *ginger* also promote the breakdown of fibrin and as well as adding them liberally to your diet you can take supplements (avoid ginger if you have stomach or duodenal ulcers).

■ 600mg of *Boswellic acid (Indian frankincense)* can help with arthritis pain. You can also get it in a cream for localized inflammation, strains and back pain.

■ *Borage oil* is a more potent source of GLA than *evening primrose oil* and is a potent anti-inflammatory agent. Take 300mg of GLA daily.

■ *White willow* is really herbal aspirin, but as it contains the full spectrum of complementary (synergistic) compounds it is less likely to cause gastro-intestinal upset.

■ *Nettle tea* is particularly helpful for rheumatic pain. Drink three cups daily or take a supplement.

■ *Devil's claw* is a powerful anti-inflammatory for pain relief and is suitable for long-term use.

■ *Knotgrass* breaks down painful deposits in joints. It needs to be taken for at least four months to gain benefit.

PRE-MENSTRUAL HEALTH

The defining characteristic of pre-menstrual problems is that they occur days, and possibly up to two weeks, prior to a period. The symptoms then resolve themselves shortly after the onset of a period. If your symptoms happen at other times of the month then it is not pre-menstrual tension (PMT).

There is a wide variety of symptoms associated with PMT ranging from bloating and breast tenderness to headaches, depression, and even cold symptoms and nausea. No wonder many women feel that they can't cope at this time of the month. Such feelings only promote stress which is a major player in worsening pre-menstrual problems, because it serves to further unbalance hormone and blood sugar levels. But pre-menstrual problems are nowhere near as bad in many parts of the world where they have a different diet to us, particularly in Asia, the Middle East and parts of the Mediterranean where little or no dairy and wheat products are eaten and the emphasis is on fish, pulses, vegetables and fruit. Dietary and lifestyle changes can make a profound difference to the degree of PMT you suffer from, but realistically you usually have to persevere for at least two and possibly three cycles to achieve full benefit.

Top Tips

■ If you think that stress may play a big part in your pre-menstrual problems, either as a cause or an effect, take steps to address the stress in your life (read the relevant chapters of this book!) and learn to pace yourself. At the very least, plan to do more of what you enjoy in the week before your period. It isn't always easy to rearrange your schedule with work and kids to think about, but factoring in some restful times for you to unwind and work on your stress levels can be very important until the effects of changing diet and taking supplements kick in.

■ Sign up for some relaxation therapy classes such as yoga or t'ai chi, some stress management classes such as autogenic training (see page 140), or indulge in some massages.

■ Some women find that using magnets placed near their womb just before and during their period can help with cramps. Contact **Ladycare** 08000 838 645 or www.magnopulse.com

More Hints

■ The contraceptive pill can adversely affect period problems if your brand contains too high a dose of oestrogen. Speak to your doctor if you suspect this, or investigate non-hormonal contraception such as barrier methods and ovulation awareness.

■ Periods that feature cramps and heavy blood flow may be a sign of endometriosis or fibroids, both conditions of which are on the increase. Endometriosis is when womb tissue attaches to organs outside in the organ cavity, and fibroids are benign (non-cancerous)

growths in the womb. This is a notoriously difficult problem to diagnose and many doctors simply don't recognize it as a serious condition. However, your GP should always be your first port of call – you should ask them for information on and referrals for non-interventionist options (see below). Good books to read include *Endometriosis* by Dian Mills (Element) and *Natural Progesterone* by Anna Rushton and Dr Shirley Bond (Harper Collins). Another condition which interferes with normal menstruation is polycystic ovarian syndrome, which is explored in depth in *PCOS* by Colette Harris (Harper Collins).

■ A number of other factors can be associated with absent or irregular periods including low body weight, anorexia nervosa, overtraining at sports, the contraceptive pill and extreme stress.

■ Severe PMS is called Premenstrual Dysphoric Disorder (PMDD) and anti-depressants are now licensed for use for PMDD. It might be that while you are trying to make positive changes to other aspects of your diet and lifestyle that a short course is of help.

■ Many period problems can be helped by using *Natural Progesterone* cream. You can buy it for your own use by contacting **Higher Nature** on 01435 882 880 or send an SAE to NPIS, PO Box 24, Buxton, Derbyshire SK17 9FB. It is permitted to be imported for individual use though it is a prescription item if you get it through your doctor (very few doctors have experience of its use).

Holistic Help – Diet

■ A sensitivity to wheat very commonly manifests in pre-menstrual discomfort and swelling. A trial period of one month avoiding bread, pasta, biscuits, cakes and other foods made from wheat should give you a clear idea if you are affected. Substitute rice, oats, corn, quinoa, buckwheat and other foods made from non-wheat grains.

■ Sugar and carbohydrate binges are common pre-menstrually as blood sugar hormones go a bit wild. Make a point of satisfying your sweet tooth with fruit (fresh or dried) and make sure that any grains you eat are whole grains (such as brown rice, rye crackers, oatcakes, etc) instead of white bread, white rice, etc. Eat a little protein, such as egg, nuts, cheese, yoghurt, lean meats, with the carbohydrates to further reduce their effect on blood sugar levels.

■ Stimulants prompt sugar cravings, use up B-vitamins, decrease potassium, zinc and magnesium levels. Give coffee, strong tea and alcohol a miss for a while. Substitute coffees made from other substances such as barley, chicory and dandelion root. Caffeinated drinks and alcohol can worsen period cramps. There is also a strong link between coffee, and other sources of caffeine (including some painkillers and cold remedies), with pre-menstrual breast tenderness and lumpiness.

■ Soya foods help to balance female hormones as they are rich in a type of plant hormone called phytoestrogens. Introduce a glass of soya milk or 50g of tofu into your diet daily. You can make fruity milk shakes with these for ease.

- Fibre is also important for balancing female hormones: too much progesterone can cause constipation. Add one tablespoon of ground linseeds to your diet daily. Add it to yoghurt, cereals, stews or just mix with juice and drink – you'll also never be constipated again! Linseeds are rich in lignans which help hormone balance.

- Other foods which help female hormone balance are the fibre- and phytoestrogen-rich beans, lentils and pulses. Enjoy four or five portions weekly.

- Potassium-rich foods can help to alleviate PMS. Bananas, potatoes (in their skins), tomatoes, watermelon (including crunchy seeds) are all particularly potassium rich, though all fruits and vegetables offer a good amount.

- Some foods have a diuretic action and are helpful if you have water retention. Up your intake of artichokes, watercress, asparagus and parsley, and drink camomile tea. Avoid salt which worsens water retention.

- For advice on how foods affect mood swings (which includes pre-menstrual mood swings) see the chapter on Mood Swings (page 160).

- Helpful organizations include, the Women's Nutritional Advisory Service which specializes in PMS/PMT problems (01273 487 366 or www.wnas.org.uk). Sue Penbrey, a retired nurse, holds workshops in the Oxford area called Balancing Hormones Naturally (01865 514 988).

Holistic Help – Supplements

- *Magnesium* helps to maintain normal brain chemical metabolism and hormone balance, and yet it is deficient in around 50 per cent of women with PMS. Take 400mg daily for two months and then cut back to 250 mg daily as a maintenance dose.

- *....min B6* can help pre-menstrually and 50–100mg *B-complex* can go a long way to alleviating pre-menstrual problems. It may be necessary to take the *B6* level up to 200 mg in the two weeks before your period. *B3* is needed to regulate blood sugar levels and is involved in the 'mood brain chemical' serotonin. B6 and B3 are valuable to help relieve depression, sleep disturbances and headaches, all of which can be worse pre-menstrually.

- GLA is the active compound in *evening primrose oil* which helps so many women with swollen breasts before their periods. It has a strong anti-inflammatory action. Your doctor may be willing to prescribe it to you, though prescribed levels are often a bit too low and you may need to buy some extra to bump up the dose to 500mg. *Borage (starflower) oil* is a more concentrated source of GLA meaning you can take fewer capsules: aim for 100–200 mg GLA daily.

- Iron levels are often low as a result of heavy blood flow and if you are feeling tired and have pale skin, then it is wise to have your iron levels checked by your doctor. If you then need to take an iron supplement, you may find that the type offered by your doctor (ferric iron) has a constipating effect. Ways to boost iron levels include eating beetroot, drinking nettle tea (or using nettle supplements) and taking chlorophyll supplements. Iron rich foods include red meat, dark poultry meat, oysters (a particularly rich source), nuts and seeds. Iron supplements that are less likely to cause constipation are ferrous sulphate or iron ascorbate.

Biocare make a good supplement called *EPA Iron* and also *beetroot extract*. Tannins in tea lower iron absorption from foods and supplements by up to two-thirds and phosphates in colas and other fizzy drinks also interfere.

- *Vitamin C*, together with *bioflavonoids*, can help to control heavy periods. Eat a wide variety of fruits and vegetables, at least five portions daily, and if necessary use 1g vitamin C supplement that is formulated with bioflavonoids. Vitamin C also increases the absorption of iron from plant foods such as wholegrains, dried fruit and spinach, so a small glass of orange juice with a meal can significantly help iron levels.

- Several herbal remedies are potent relievers of hormone imbalance and so help to abate period problems. *Dong quai (Chinese angelica)* taken from day 14 of your cycle can help to relieve painful periods and other PMS symptoms.

- *Agnus castus (chasteberry)* is a powerful modulator of female hormones and helps to raise progesterone levels (and so can also help slowly reduce fibroids).

- *Black cohosh* can help to relieve PMS, painful periods, breast tenderness and reduce fibroids. It is mainly used as a menopausal herb, but has uses for period problems.

- For moodiness and monthly weepiness take the herb *pulsatilla*.

- You can get combined remedies. One of my favourites is *PMS Formula*, available from **Herbalforce**.

- Experiment with homeopathic **Australian Bush Flower Remedy** *Woman Essence* (see Useful Resources page 235).

RECOVERING FROM ILLNESS

If you are indisposed because you have been in an accident, have had surgery or have a long-term illness, you may experience a range of stressful effects. Even if you are physically on the road to recovery, you may feel emotionally low. There are many things you can do to reduce the impact of negative feelings and stress.

Top Tips

- At the time, your world may seem to have fallen apart, but many people gain tremendous strength from their experience of illness. Believing in what is good in the world can help you to pull through.

- You may be experiencing feelings of helplessness. If you feel up to it, you can regain some control by taking measures to understand your condition and researching ways to improve your health. Get books from the library or, if you have access to the Internet, you can search for information about your condition.

- A powerful healing meditation is the 'mountain top meditation'. Visualize yourself at the top of a mountain, where the air is clean, you are surrounded by blue sky and there is a breeze and the warmth of the sun on your face. You are surrounded by other mountains covered with forests and with ribbons of rivers and pools of lakes in the valleys. Concentrating on your breathing see a bright white channel of light and energy flowing from the sky into your crown chakra (at the top of your head). The light flows through your body and limbs, energizing you and flowing through your feet into the mountain connecting you to both the sky and the earth. Let the light channel healing energy from the sky and the earth as it flows through your body.

■ As your condition improves, take pride in small victories as you gradually manage to do things that you were not capable of previously.

■ When you are on the mend, pace yourself to avoid a relapse. Don't do too much too quickly. Certainly do not consider returning to work until you feel up to it.

■ One strategy to resist feelings of depression is to remember that you, that is the inner you, are a distinct and powerful person. See your body as simply a vessel for the individual that you are. You have not changed, though your body has. This may be a difficult concept to grasp initially. Some remarkable people have had terrible things happen to them and gone towards their future with just as much energy and enthusiasm as previously.

■ The theory is sometimes put forward that anger can be a positive force in healing. It is said that the enemy of recovery from a serious illness is apathy and a sense of inevitability. By getting angry (not bitter) about the situation, in a constructive way ('I'm not going to let this beat me') you can muster your energy and force into healing. If you are feeling too exhausted to get angry, this might be a moot point, but it might make you feel better if you are currently feeling rage at the situation you are in.

More Hints

■ Use the time to do other things. Plan your future, take up a restful hobby, or what about all those books you've been meaning to read for years?

■ If you are in a facility with others who are more unwell than you, it can raise your morale if you form friendships and have people to play games with or chat to. If you are able, see if you can help others – you may be able to read to someone who cannot, or teach someone to play chess.

■ See the information covered in Infections on page 102.

■ The Speedwell Trust helps people by giving information, advice and hope for those with serious illness (www.speedwell-trust.net)

Holistic Help – Diet

■ Now, more than ever, you need food which is packed with nutrients to help recovery. Although it may be easier to eat convenience foods, especially if you live alone, try to introduce as much fresh food as you can. If someone is doing your shopping for you, ask them to buy ready washed and prepared vegetables and salads, as well as plenty of fresh fruit. Remember that dried fruit, nuts and seeds such as sunflower make great nutrient-rich snacks. Follow the advice in Healthy Eating (page 98).

- If your appetite is poor, there are some easy ways to improve nutrient intake without forcing down a lot of food. Here are some ideas.
  - Juices: you can create varied and delicious juices from a range of fruits and vegetables with the help of a juicing machine. They are full of energy-giving and tissue-repairing nutrients.
  - Soups and broths: these can be comforting and easy to digest.
  - Stews: these are more substantial but still easy to eat.
  - Fruit salads: get adventurous and use tropical fruit, chopped dried fruit and sprinkle on some coconut flakes and a little orange juice.
  - Yoghurts: live yoghurt is delicious with some fruit purée or a little honey and chopped nuts.
  - Fortified drinks: these are available to 'build you up' but often contain a lot of sugar. You can make your own with milk or soya milk, blended with fruit and some protein powder and liquid vitamins and minerals.
- Make sure that small platters are used if you have a poor appetite but that the food is beautifully presented. Sometimes strong tastes will be welcomed if the palate is a little jaded, though they might cause nausea.
- Hospital food can be dire and do nothing to help recovery. Make sure you line up someone who can bring you nourishing meals and snacks (you may need small frequent amounts if your appetite is poor).

Holistic Help – Supplements

- Always take a *multi-vitamin and mineral* to aid recovery. Avoid doses over 100iu of vitamin E, or too much garlic or fish oil supplements if about to undergo an operation as these have a blood thinning effect – you can start them again immediately afterwards. (Garlic and oily fish in the diet are fine.)
- Be cautious about taking herbal supplements if you are about to have an operation or on medication as they might interfere.
- Take homeopathic *arnica* six times daily to reduce bruising when you have an operation or if you have had an accident or sprained/torn a ligament or muscle.
- Use *MSM cream* directly on any tender area to aid healing. You can get this from **Higher Nature**.
- If you are plagued by wounds that won't heal, such as after surgery, bedsores or ulcers, make a point of taking 3g of *vitamin C with bioflavonoids* daily (in three divided doses) and drink 1.5 litres of water daily. High grade *Manuka honey* is an aid to healing, put it directly on the wound, under a dressing, to keep it clear of infections and aid healing. High-grade Manuka honey is available from **Comvita** 020 8961 4410 www.comvita.com

SEASONAL AFFECTIVE DISORDER (SAD)

As the winter months draw in and daylight hours eventually dwindle from around 18 hours to 9 hours, many people feel their moods, energy levels and, in fact, their whole metabolism are adversely affected. In some people, instead of this being an almost natural adjustment to the seasons, the changes can interfere quite dramatically with their everyday lives at home and at work and be a significant source of stress. If your energy levels are noticeably lower in the winter months it is always possible that you are experiencing Seasonal Affective Disorder (SAD). SAD can be distinguished from other conditions, such as chronic fatigue or depression, because its symptoms are only present in autumn and winter, and go away completely in the spring and summer. It is estimated that around five per cent of people in Northern hemisphere countries are affected by SAD, though many more than this may complain of feeling 'out of sorts' in the winter months and may have a milder form. In countries which are below the equator few incidences of SAD are found.

There are four major symptoms experienced by those with SAD. These are an increased desire to sleep, extreme lethargy, depression and an increased appetite (which often leads to weight gain). It is quite common for the need to withdraw to become quite incapacitating. Other secondary symptoms might accompany these such as loss of libido, mood swings, phobias and an inability to cope with stress. The most useful time to start measures to combat this effect is in early autumn before the days have shortened too much.

Top Tips

■ Light therapy during winter months, using a special light-box for up to a couple of hours a day, is a tried and tested way of helping to relieve SAD, and improves the situation for around 70 per cent of people. The light which is needed to offset SAD is full-spectrum light, sufficiently strong for us to manufacture vitamin D in our skin (half-an-hour daily sun exposure in the spring or summer for a light-skinned person and a bit longer for darker skins). Indoor lighting at home and in offices does not accomplish this. Full-spectrum light affects the hormone melatonin which is made in the pineal gland in the brain, and is responsible for setting our 'body-clock'. Insufficient activity of the pineal gland in winter is thought to contribute to SAD. You can rent before you buy – details are available from the SAD Association (see page 123).

■ Being cooped up indoors throughout winter will make the symptoms worse. Take every opportunity to get out even in the thinnest winter sunshine. Brisk walking will boost endorphin levels and improve symptoms.

■ A factor which seems to be important in understanding SAD is low levels of the brain chemical serotonin. This is often called our 'satisfaction' brain chemical and low levels are linked to depression and overeating. In people with SAD, levels may plummet with shorter days. Antidepressants which affect serotonin levels are sometimes prescribed, but foods can also have an impact (see Holistic Help – Diet below).

More Hints

■ If you are able to, take your holidays in the winter time when you need them most and find a sunny location you can afford to go to.

■ For more information read *Seasonal Affective Disorder* by Angela Smyth (Thorsons).

■ Contact the SAD Association on 01903 814 942 www.sada.org.uk

Holistic Help – Diet

■ Foods which contain the 'pre-cursor' for serotonin, called tryptophan, include meat, fish, eggs, cheese, milk, yoghurt, nuts and legumes such as peas, beans and lentils. Particularly good sources are turkey, cottage cheese, pheasant and partridge. Carbohydrates (crackers, bread, pasta, cereals – preferably wholegrain) also help the body's ability to use tryptophan.

■ In winter, those with SAD tend to eat more and their food choices may change. Often food is being used to seek comfort from tension and fatigue. Satisfying the need for comfort foods by eating thick bean soups or home made casseroles helps to avoid the perceived need to eat refined carbohydrates, such as white bread, white rice and sugary foods which are followed by dips in serotonin levels soon afterwards.

■ Be aware that cravings for coffee, alcohol, sugar and chocolates are also triggered by lowered serotonin levels and can also help to make the urge to binge worse.

■ Many people find relief by following a 'food combining' programme to find out which foods make their SAD better. Principally, food combining means making sure that you do not eat protein foods (such as meat, fish, eggs, cheese, milk) at the same meal as carbohydrate foods (bread, rice, pasta, potatoes). This means having a meal of, say, chicken with salad and vegetables, or a baked potato with salad and vegetables, but not chicken AND baked potato.

■ Eat protein-based meals on one day, and carbohydrate based meals on another day. Alternate, and keep this up for a week. At the same time, keep a detailed diary of what you eat, why you are eating (hunger, energy pick-you-ups, mood enhancers), when you are eating, and what your energy levels were at the time of eating, as well as an hour or so after the meals. Meals may make you feel:

– alert, relaxed, calm, refreshed, energetic, able to concentrate, enthusiastic or

– lethargic, 'woolly brained', agitated, anxious, tired, depressed, tearful.

■ At the end of the week you will have a much clearer idea of how foods make you feel. You can then use this to your advantage. For example, you could eat protein-based meals in the daytime when you need to feel more lively, and carbohydrate meals in the evening to bring on a soporific state ready for bedtime.

- Eating lots of fruits and vegetables, which are rich in antioxidants, has been shown to improve melatonin levels. You can simulate a summer diet, and prepare for winter by freezing large quantities of berries, using autumnal blackberries, blackcurrants and elderberries in recipes, or buying frozen or canned berries (in their natural juice) as they are high in phytonutrients called proanthocyanidins which are strong antioxidants.

Holistic Help – Supplements

- Natural supplements which help to normalize serotonin levels are the herb *rhodiola* and a plant extract called *5-HTP (5-hydroxy-tryptophan)*. 50-100 mg of 5HTP is usually enough for most people (but more can lead to sleep disturbance due to too much serotonin). Rhodiola is available from **Solgar** (see Supplements page 233) and is stocked by independent health food shops, and 5-HTP is available from several of the supplement companies mentioned.

- Herbal help can also be found by taking *St John's wort* which is an effective antidepressant for mild to moderate depression, with fewer side effects than the pharmaceutical antidepressant options. Avoid using this herb with a light-box as it can increase photosensitivity (see other comments about St John's wort in Supplements page234). The SAD Association has recently conducted a study amongst its members regarding St John's wort and has chosen to not endorse it as they feel that light-box therapy is more likely to be of use and they should not be used together. However of the respondents to their survey, 40 per cent found the herb helpful, 60 per cent would use it again and 30 per cent had some adverse effects, though a percentage of these had used it with the light-boxes or with antidepressants both of which are contraindicated.

- Do not use all these supplements at the same time, but see which one works for you.

SKIN AGEING AND STRESS

Internal worries and stress show fastest of all in posture (see Muscle Tension page 109) and in the skin. Apart from the obvious – frowns and wrinkles – stress increases damage to the very fabric of your skin. Looking after your skin can reduce this damage.

Top Tips

- Smile! You might as well have laughter lines as worry lines. Smiling will also trigger endorphins, making you feel better, and reducing your stress levels – so you win all round.

- Smoking wrecks skin and eye health faster than anything else, apart from excessive sun exposure. If you smoke, stop (see Giving Up Smoking page 94). If you really can't manage to give up, eat 7–10 portions of fruit and vegetables daily and take 1000mg of vitamin C with bioflavonoids.

- Some sun exposure is healthy and helps to make vitamin D in the skin, reduce breast cancer and prostate cancer risk and dispel depression. However, exposure to sun without doubt ages skin and leads to cataracts. Use a sun block SPF 15 each morning, even in winter, and wear a hat (so chic!) and cover up with a T-shirt in strong sun. Preferably use a non-chemical sunblock such as that available from **Green People** (01444 401 444 or www.greenpeople.co.uk).

- Pollution irritates the skin and adds to its ageing. Make sure your skin creams have good levels of antioxidants in them. They are effectively absorbed through the skin and can reduce some of the effects of ageing. **Pharmanord** (0800 591 756) have a cream with Co-Q10, vitamin E and picnogenol.

More Hints

- Practice face exercises to keep the muscles supporting the skin toned up. Best not to do this on the underground however as they might think you need to be locked away! To do face exercises, imagine you are a chimpanzee pulling all sorts of faces — pushing out your lips, grinning, widening eyes, and stretching face and neck muscles in every direction.

- The backs of the hands are just as affected (and often more so) than the face and show ageing dramatically. When you apply sunblock to your face, apply it to the back of your hands and your neck as well.

- **Dr Hauschka** (01386 7992 622) make lovely skin products from biodynamically grown flowers and other plants.

Holistic Help – Diet

- Probably the most important measure for skin health is to eat a diet rich in antioxidants. Aim to eat 7–10 portions of fruits and vegetables daily (if this sounds like a lot start with less and build up slowly – see Healthy Eating page 98). Carotene/vitamin A rich foods include orange fruits and vegetables such as cantaloupes, apricots, winter squash and carrots and dark green leafy vegetables such as spinach, cabbage and kale.

- There are other antioxidant-rich foods and drinks which might surprise you. You can drink moderate amounts of tea (caffeine-free is best) and redbush tea, use olive oil instead of other cooking oils, use herbs liberally in cooking, drink a little red wine and even enjoy some very dark chocolate (70 per cent cocoa solids is best) to get even more antioxidants.

- Drinking water and eating foods which are water rich (such as fruits and vegetables) stops skin from getting dehydrated. The healing process of skin is most inefficient when it is dehydrated. Attractive skin really does come from within. Drink 1.5–2 litres of water daily. Other liquids count, but not coffee or alcohol (and keep caffeinated tea to moderate amounts).

- Unsaturated fats in the diet from oily fish, nuts, seeds, vegetables and cold pressed oils are the best way to keep skin supple and reduce the effects of ageing. Stock up on foods such as salmon, tuna and sardines, unroasted nuts such as brazil nuts and walnuts, pumpkin and sunflower seeds, and flax oil and walnut oil for salads.

■ A fibre-rich diet translates into healthy looking skin as more toxins are eliminated via the bowels and less need to be eliminated via the skin (this may sound disgusting but the skin is the largest organ of elimination the body has). Boosting your intake of fibre from oats, wholewheat, brown rice, pulses and beans, fruits, vegetables, nuts and seeds really improves skin health.

Holistic Help – Supplements

■ Vitamin C is used to build collagen (which glues skin cells together) and if you follow the advice above you should get a lot from your diet. If you wish to take a supplement to boost this, use a buffered form, such as *magnesium ascorbate* or *Ester-C with bioflavonoids*.

■ Taking a daily antioxidant supplement with C and also E (*tocotrienol E* is most potent) will help to prevent damage to your skin.

■ A *Co-Q10* supplement, 50–100mg daily, is also great for skin. Levels are depleted by pollution and sun and it helps to protect cell membranes.

■ *Vitamin C* supplements have also been pretty convincingly shown to dramatically reduce the formation of cataracts (an age-related condition) when taken at the level of 500mg daily for at least five years – and this works even better when combined with *vitamin E*. *Bilberry (blueberry)* is a potent antioxidant-rich food, or supplement, which seems to have a specific role in helping to maintain eyesight by preventing age-related macular degeneration.

■ No skin care kit would be complete without a small bottle of *tea tree oil*. Its strong antibacterial properties make it ideal if you get a blemish or abrasion. Use a good quality brand such as **Thursday Plantation**.

■ *Rosa mosqueta oil (extract of wild Andean rose)* is fabulous for smoothing on the skin daily. It is particularly rich in essential fatty acids, such as GLA, and is great for maintenance as well as preventing scarring. Contact **Rio Trading** (01273 570 987).

■ If your hair and nails are going through a bad patch take *extract of horsetail* for two or three months to see if it helps. One brand is *Kervans Silica*.

SLEEP QUALITY

Sleep deprivation is known to be one of the most effective torture methods, and yet one-third of people suffer this ghastly imposition on daily life at some time or other. Lack of sleep destroys co-ordination and affects concentration. But it is not just the absence of sleep that affects us. Sleep quality is important because when we sleep we repair our bodies and make up for the stresses of the day. Sleep improves immune function, relaxes digestion and dreams are thought to play an important beneficial psychological role.

People's sleeping patterns are affected differently by different forms of stress. Some may find they become depressed and tend to want to sleep all the time though the quality of the sleep is poor, frequently with early waking, and leaving them still feeling tired. Others find that worry keeps them tossing and turning all night and unable to get to the deep level of dreaming sleep needed to feel refreshed and raring to go in the morning. Some people are not consciously feeling stressed but because of irregular habits – such as working shifts, burning the candle at both ends or simply consuming the wrong foods – find that their sleep quality is poor.

Sleep is governed by cycles and going through all the stages of sleep from the lightest (stage 1) through to the deepest (stage 4 and REM sleep) is necessary. Rising levels of the hormone melatonin, released by the pineal gland, together with lowering levels of the stress hormones cortisol and adrenaline, govern when we feel sleepy, while the opposite patterns, triggered in part by daylight in the morning, wakes us up.

Top Tips

■ Your circadian rhythms (body cycles), controlled by hormones, govern when you sleep. Establish regular routines to allow these rhythms to work properly. If, for example, you work shifts keep the pattern going at weekends if you can and talk to your bosses about always working the same shifts instead of altering them frequently.

■ Keep a pen and paper on your bedside table. If worry is keeping you awake, write down the worry and some quick thoughts about solutions and then lie down again. By transferring the worry to paper, you can banish it from your mind and have something positive to work with in the morning. You can also use Post-it-Notes for 'things to do' that you can then attach to the relevant place first thing in the morning.

■ If you have got out of a routine of going to bed at the same time, avoid lying-in in the morning even if you feel the need to catch up. You can't always control when you fall asleep but you can control when you wake up. If you always wake at the same time (even at weekends) your bed-time should sort itself out.

■ If you occasionally miss a full night of sleep to have fun that is one thing. But if you regularly miss out on sleep to meet deadlines and work harder you will cheat your health in the long run – you probably need to work on Time Management (see page 65), such as imposing working hours and sticking to them or learning to say no to work.

■ Snoring often induces wakefulness in both the snorer and their partner. (The loudest snore on record peaked at an astounding 93 decibels – louder than a passing underground train.) It is a sign of partially blocked airways and can lead to sleep apnoea where breathing is suspended for a few seconds. This can wake you up during the night. Several sprays, based on mint-flavoured natural oils, which lubricate the palate and back of the mouth are available and can be exceedingly helpful. Brands to experiment with include *Snorenz* (0800 096 1121 or www.passionforlife.com) or *GoodNightStopSnore* (0870 842 0870). (See also Holistic Help, page 130 for more snoring solutions.)

■ Combating insomnia with sleep inducing hypnotherapy tapes can work well. I have never yet been able to stay awake for the whole of Paul McKenna's tape, it is so effective. Contact 01455 852 233 or www.mckenna-breen.com for more information.

More Hints

■ Check your bedroom is well ventilated, though not draughty. Change your bedding according to the season to avoid becoming too hot or too cold.

■ Darkness is needed to raise melatonin levels. Consider having your curtains interlined.

■ Give yourself time to wind down. Find an activity that induces sleep such as taking a book to bed (not a high-tension one) or a warm bath. Some stretching and relaxing exercises may also help.

■ Save vigorous exercise for earlier in the day. Exercising within three or four hours of bedtime will boost your metabolism and make it difficult to sleep.

■ If you find yourself lying awake, it can be better to get up and do something low key, such as reading, in a chair – if you do this in bed it becomes a reminder of not being able to sleep.

■ There are two schools of thought on the napping question. Some say that a ten-minute nap is refreshing and a useful stress buster. Others say that getting into the habit of napping is counterproductive. Experiment to see which might help you. Certainly, if you are unable to nap, a period of quiet repose, and possibly meditation can be beneficial. Some famous nappers were highly productive people – Winston Churchill, J. F. Kennedy and Napoleon Bonapart. For more information and the latest research on the subject see www.napping.com

■ If you regularly wake up worrying about irrelevancies such as shopping lists and whether you changed the cat litter, set aside time earlier in the day to make lists of these things to get rid of the need in the middle of the night.

■ Avoid television late at night. If there's something you really want to watch set your video tape recorder.

■ Some medications such as decongestants or asthma treatments can stop you getting to sleep. Check with your doctor about any possible side effects to drugs you are taking (do not stop prescribed medication without your doctor's say so).

■ If you find yourself counting the minutes and hours you will find it even harder to sleep. Stop any chiming clocks and remove your alarm clock to a place where you can't see it.

■ If you are having trouble getting your children into a healthy sleep routine – which inevitably means that your sleep is being disrupted – read *Solve Your Child's Sleep Problems* by Dr Richard Ferber (Dorling Kindersley).

■ If you are finding it difficult to solve your sleep problems, keep a sleep diary, noting what happens and when, including what you eat, do, and what food/medication you consume. You will get a truer picture if you keep the diary for a period of 3 to 4 weeks, and will be able to see common threads and recurring behaviours that can be modified to break bad sleep patterns.

■ Read *The Healing Power of Sleep* by Sheila Lavery (Gaia Books).

Holistic Help – Diet

■ Eating late at night stimulates digestion and metabolism and can keep you awake, particularly if the meal is heavy or fatty. Normally our metabolism drops by around 20 per cent and eating late prevents this initially.

■ Caffeine is a strong stimulant which can keep some hypersensitive people awake even if they drink only one cup a day. Even decaffeinated coffee has similar stimulants, theobromine and theophyline – which may cause people sleep problems. Caffeine is found in coffee, tea, colas, chocolate, pain killers, cold remedies, the herb guarana and some 'energy' supplements. Substitute decaffeinated tea, herb or fruit teas, hot oat drinks and hot toddies made with a little cordial.

■ Avoid alcohol, especially late at night, as it can interfere with the ability to reach deep, restful sleep, even if it initially induces sleepiness. The result is fitful and restless sleep. Nicotine can also interfere with sleep.

■ Serotonin is a brain chemical, low levels of which are linked to sleeplessness. An amino acid (protein link) called tryptophan is made into 5HTP, which in turn makes serotonin. Tryptophan-rich foods include fish, turkey, chicken, cottage cheese, beef, eggs, bananas, oats, avocados, milk, cheese, nuts, peanuts, soya and other foods, but eating carbohydrates helps to selectively take up the tryptophan. Vitamin B6 is also needed to help this process. Eating protein-based meals earlier in the day and carbohydrate-rich meals based on rice, bread, pasta and potatoes at night is likely to help to induce sleep. Oats are particularly soporific so a small bowl of porridge might do the trick.

■ A nightcap of a sleep-inducing herb drink can help enormously. Camomile, vervain, peppermint, lemon balm, hops, rose hips, dill and fennel – either used singly or in blends – have a calming effect.

■ Calcium is a sleep inducer which is why a glass of warm milk at night helps some people. Combine the milk (or calcium-enriched soya milk) with oats and you have the classic night-time drink. It can also help if you take any daily calcium supplement you are using at night-time. Magnesium is also a relaxant and helps calcium to work more effectively. Take a supplement that combines the two with your evening meal – at a ratio of 2:1 calcium to magnesium – so 500mg calcium to 250mg magnesium. You might think that as milk is a good source of soporific calcium that cheese would also do, and yet another compound in cheese, tyramine, is thought to be behind its nightmare-inducing talents.
■ Blood sugar lows in the middle of the night can wake you up and make it difficult to get back to sleep. Combat this by eating mainly complex carbohydrates during the day time, such as brown rice, wholemeal bread, rye bread and whole porridge oats, and keeping a small snack such as a banana or a couple of oatcakes on your bedside table to snack on just before you drop off.

■ Snoring is more likely if you are bunged up with mucus. For some people avoiding milk or all dairy products can help. However, while using soya products instead will help quite a lot of dairy-intolerant people, soya can also increase mucus levels in others – it is question of experimenting with all the options – goat or sheep products may work, as might rice milk or coconut milk. Snoring may also be due to obesity, alcohol intake or smoking.

Holistic Help – Supplements

■ Natural sleep is always preferable to drug-induced sleep. Even with herbal sleep inducers it is best to view them as a short-term measure, while you establish a healthy sleeping routine.

■ Take one capsule of *valerian* half-an-hour before bedtime to help promote deeper sleep in the long term but be patient as it does take a month or so to kick in. Valerian also works very well with Kava kava but see warning on page 234.

■ To boost levels of serotonin (see above) you can take 50–100mg of *5HTP*, which is the precursor (step before) from which the brain naturally makes serotonin.

■ Very low doses of the hormone melatonin can be used to adjust sleeping routines. Melatonin levels dip as we age. It is illegal to sell melatonin over-the-counter in the UK, so most people buy it from the USA and it is legal to bring it back for personal use. Very low doses are used, about 0.3mg, and it is only advised to use it for a week or two to re-establish sleep patterns. Take it half an hour before bedtime. Melatonin is also used to help jet lag.

■ Herbal combinations including hops, lemon balm, valerian, passiflora, wild lettuce, skullcap and other sleep inducing herbs are readily available in different combinations. Buy from a reputable company and follow the instructions.

■ **Higher Nature's** *NeverSnore* contains enzymes which help to break down mucus and also contains decongestant herbs. In a trial, 86 per cent of those who used it long term said their snoring was cut by 75 per cent. Call 01435 882 880.

■ Early waking, where you cannot get back to sleep again, is a common sign of depression – seek counselling and also see Cognitive Thinking, page 219. Your doctor will prescribe a short course of antidepressants if you need them which can help your sleeping cycle as well. For mild-to-moderate depression the herb *St John's wort* is as effective as an antidepressant but without similar side effects. St John's wort is fine used on its own, or with complementary herbs, but must not be used alongside other prescribed medication, including the contraceptive pill, without checking with your doctor or a medical herbalist.

CHAPTER 4

EMOTIONS

Understanding your emotions can be a painful process, and most of us will do anything to avoid pain. Emotional stress may be caused by long-buried feelings about childhood, as well as ongoing anxieties about our personalities. People spend years burying their feelings, and the revelations that come from digging up old emotions can be difficult. While some people find it useful to examine past events or behaviour, it can lead others to live too much in the past, apportioning blame, rather than getting on with building an emotionally stable future.

If we are going to build firm foundations for the future, we need to know what we are feeling and what our needs are. This may sound incredibly obvious when put this way, but often we don't have a clue what we really want in life – which can be highly stressful. We can exist for many years on the cusp of anxiety until our health suffers or we find we start behaving irrationally. Now is the time to step out of that chaos, and to start feeling good about yourself. The tips in this section use accessible techniques, which will yield tangible results, enabling you to set your future on course.

ANGER AND TEMPER

Anger is a powerful force, and as such needs to be contained and expressed in appropriate ways. If you allow anger to persist, it will have a detrimental effect by keeping you in a state of physical readiness that is tiring and may fog your thought processes. Anger is often the only possible reaction in certain contexts. But if you find you are enraged by such everyday annoyances as a slow checkout counter at the supermarket, you may be living in a 'state of anger' which can have serious emotional and health consequences.

Top Tips

■ It is OK to feel anger when appropriate. There is no rule that says that you have to feel sublimely calm if your child is picked on at school or when you read news about some terrible injustice in the world. It is this anger, and the accompanying adrenaline rush, that spurs many of us on to make changes in the world and to make it a better place.

- There is a lot of sense in the well-worn advice to take a step back from whatever it is that has set you off, take a deep breath, and work out a rational way forward. There is a time to act, and a time to sleep on the situation. The next day you may feel completely different about it.

- Inappropriate anger, such as losing your temper when the photocopier jams or the driver ahead goes at a crawl, will only wear you down. It is also a sure sign that you are not able to get things into perspective. Each time you get angry about something (and this may be several times a day) make a note about what sets you off and what your thoughts are. Grade your anger on a scale of 1–10 about how angry you are. Use the techniques covered in Cognitive Thinking (page 219) to find more appropriate responses. Re-grade how angry you are after you have changed your statement. For instance: change 'How dare he criticize me and get so personal' (graded 8) to 'He's allowed his views of me and I don't have to agree with them. I think I am an OK person, though I might take note of the last thing he said' (graded 2). Another example: change 'I hate being kept waiting, perhaps I've been stood up' (graded 7) to ' A chance for a break, and maybe she's caught in traffic. If I have been stood up, it's her loss, not mine. I'll give it 15 more minutes and then get some exercise walking home as I'll have the spare time' (graded 1).

- It is not events that make you angry but your responses to them. The meaning you attach to events dictates your emotional responses. You can change your view of these events. You might get angry because you take something as a personal slight. Why do you care so much and does it really matter? You might feel helpless about something, but switch to a resourceful 'can-do' frame of mind, see what you can do to influence the situation and see how you feel better. You can nearly always change your reaction.

- Change your thinking from 'You are making me angry' to 'I am making myself angry about something you are doing or saying'.

- Change the way you feel about these things by changing the way you talk to yourself about them. Instead of saying 'I am furious' or 'I am so angry I could scream' change this to 'I feel annoyed' or 'I am irritated'.

- Figure your triggers. If you know that a certain situation is likely to make you angry, you can do several things. You could avoid the situation, though this might not always be practical. You can change the way you think about it (see above). You can stop it happening again by taking action.

- The person on the receiving end of your anger probably won't feel they deserve it. Rage will just serve to polarize you both and make the other person defensive. You might get a short-term gain if they give in, but this will be followed by hostility and resentment, the disadvantages of which greatly outweigh the advantage of the short-term gain.

- If you lose your temper with someone else, say sorry later. This is not always easy to do, but will heal both the situation and your own feelings. Say sorry unequivocally. You don't have to say sorry for what you said, if you feel you were right, but you can say sorry for the way it was said. You can say sorry for having a row instead of a discussion, or for any possible damage to the relationship.

- If you are on the receiving end of criticism which makes you angry, this is an indication of lack of self-esteem. If your self-esteem was intact you would feel confident about taking the criticism, evaluating it and even, if appropriate, using it to learn from.

- Here is probably the most important tip in the whole book: if you have long-term anger, leave it behind. If you are angry with your parents for the way they brought you up, angry because something bad happened to you or your family, angry because of a divorce or financial problems, angry because of anything – it is time to let it go. You cannot grow, develop, learn or prosper emotionally if you hang on to old resentments. You cannot change the past at all. But you can change your future. If you are hanging on to your past, you will find it difficult to create your future, and today, and each today that follows, will be less rewarding and happy.

More Hints

- Anger is one of the consequences of city life where proximity and impotence swiftly translates into rage (see also Urban Living page 217). We are now seeing road rage, office rage and even trolley rage (in the supermarket!). Even the most even-tempered people have lashed out verbally at someone in a traffic jam. The biggest problem is when it escalates. Changing your reaction is the only thing you have control over. If you tend to get uptight, get into the habit of preparing yourself in advance. In the car, have some good music to hand and spend the time planning for something nice. In the checkout queue spend your time people watching and noticing what other people buy (always interesting, this) – anything rather than getting irritable and angry because the checkout person is on the slow side.

- If you are talking to an apparently unhelpful complaints department or service engineer it will do no good to rant – they get difficult customers all the time. Be polite and pleasant, always take a name and reference number so they know you can get back to them, be firm and state when you will call back. If they know you are going to call back and be a pest your file will go to the top of the pile – guaranteed.

- The most idiotic saying ever has to be 'Don't get mad, get even'. I would change it to 'Don't get mad, find a solution'.

- Anger distorts logical thought processes. Remember if you are going to get mad, make sure it is with the right person. If you are taking it out on someone, such as a clerk, who hasn't the power to resolve the problem, this is not logical.

- You might be setting goals that are unrealistic and then getting angry when they are not met. Reassess your goals.

- Your expectations of others also might be setting yourself up for anger 'Other people should measure up to my standards', 'I should get promoted if I put in more overtime', 'Other people should act the way I do'. Who says any of these 'shoulds'? If you hear yourself saying the word 'should' frequently, then you are having inappropriate expectations and it is you who will be disappointed.

■ Children are experts at making parents lose their tempers. But remember that if they see you lose your temper regularly, they will have your example before them. If they then lose their temper with their schoolmates or teachers or family, they are following your lead. It is common for parents to yell at their kids 'Don't you dare speak to me like that', and 'How dare you hit little Johnny'. But often they are only copying what they are seeing.

■ Losing your temper really doesn't solve problems. Promise yourself that from now on you will take a constructive approach to dealing with 'challenges'.

■ Practice safe stress. If you are feeling like you just have to let rip, use the tried and tested method of beating up or screaming into a pillow!

■ Dealing with anger in other people is an art. Here are some possibilities.

– Diffusing the situation with humour is a valuable tool, but be very careful to laugh with the other person and not at them.

– Talk calmly and slowly to stop the disagreement escalating.

– Empathize with the other person's feelings before stating your point of view. 'I understand that this situation has made you angry. My take on the situation is …' By using empathy you can take some of the heat out of the confrontation. Notice the lack of the word 'but' in between the two sentences. The minute you insert the word 'but' you have changed the whole meaning from one of understanding to actually rubbishing the whole of the previous sentiment in favour of your point of view in the second statement. Say the sentence both ways out loud and see the difference this small word makes.

– If you refuse to respond, this can make some people get even more hot tempered (this is inappropriate, but a reality). Better to say you want time to think about their viewpoint, walk away and come back to the situation when everything has settled down a bit.

■ Your anger might just be an automatically triggered 'Pavlovian' response when faced with disagreement. Disagreement is just a divergence of opinion, and do you really need to make the other person see your point of view? Ask yourself why? There may be a good reason (in which case act on it) but if it really doesn't matter why wind yourself up?

■ Some people argue 'below the belt'. Anything you say will be turned against you, and old grievances are often dragged up. It can work very well to put your point of view in a note or letter. Because it is in black and white the meaning can't be twisted. However, take great care about what you write!

■ Some people are just bullies and use their anger as a weapon – they lose their temper at the smallest opportunity – steer clear of these people and if you are in a relationship with someone like this, you may have some serious thinking to do.

Holistic Help

■ You have two choices – you can spread happiness or unhappiness. We have all experienced anger as a chain reaction. Someone loses their cool with you, so you go home and take it out on someone else, resulting in misery all round. A smile and a friendly word will do the opposite and create a chain reaction of joy.

ANXIETY

The white rabbit in Alice in Wonderland, repeatedly squinting at his watch and muttering to himself as he scurries along, epitomizes what many believe anxiety looks like. Sadly, such manifestations of anxiety do not always elicit a sympathetic reaction, as people are often told 'pull yourself together'. It is easy to say 'Don't worry, be happy' but breaking the habit of worry can need a bit more than this.

Anxiety is heightened worry. Research has shown that there are chemical changes in the brain, in those beset by anxiety, that can lead to depression. There are times when it is appropriate to be worried or anxious, for instance if your child is playing near the traffic then it is fair enough. But if anxiety is breaking your spirit and ruining your enjoyment of life because you fret about things on a daily basis, then it is well worth addressing. Something needs to change, and you can change it.

Top Tips

■ You may feel that you are coping despite your anxiety, but 'coping' is not thriving, developing or enjoying life. Coping is getting by and making the best of a bad situation. Don't cope – deal with things. Enjoy the process of making things happen and to enjoy the here and now. Remind yourself of these positive thoughts regularly to help refocus your thinking.

■ Anxious people are adept at 'What if ...' thought patterns. They can't relax about a situation because they are always worrying about what might happen. Counteract your anxieties about a situation by writing down your worries. Rate, on a scale of 1–10 just how anxious you feel. Write down what your projected feelings are 'I will probably forget everything I have learned', 'I will probably make a fool of myself', 'The traffic will probably be bad and make me late and I will make everyone angry with me as a result'. Rate these projected thoughts as well. After the event, itemize how many of these things actually happened. Did they happen at all? If they did happen did they have as bad an outcome as you imagined? Did you deal with them if they did happen? Did you come out of it unscathed? What lessons can you apply to the next time you are in the same situation? Get into the habit of doing this exercise daily if you are feeling perpetually anxious.

■ Worry and anxiety felt for other people is common. It is different to deal with because the anxiety is one person removed. Parents will often feel anxious for their children (even grown up children), a person might feel anxious for their partner until they arrive at their destination, or worry about a friend they have not heard from for a while. Go through the same exercise as above. Recognize the fact that because it is one person removed you can do nothing at the time about it – you can't sit the exam for your child and you can't take the plane for your loved one. It is also important to work on your anxiety for others because there is every chance that you will transfer your anxiety to them and trigger worry in them – a counter-productive chain reaction for the most part. You can turn such anxieties into positive actions – when, for instance, teenagers are hiking through a far-flung country, pack them a medical kit, take out insurance and remind them to e-mail back frequently.

■ Take a hike. Research has shown that brisk walking, or moderate exercise of any sort, improves anxiety levels as well as, or better than, tranquillizers.

■ Breathing exercises are a tried and tested way to moderate anxiety and tension. Do the following deep breathing exercise. (If you are hyperventilating or anywhere near a panic attack do not do this, but see a different breathing technique described under Panic Attacks page 164).

– Get your posture right, which affects your diaphragm. Stand with your feet a shoulder-width apart. Relax your shoulders (no tension in your neck, no rounded back and shoulders not thrown back in a military stance).

– Immediately after you exhale through your mouth, use your lower ribs to force the remaining air out of your lungs (we normally exhale about 500 cubic centimetres and leave a further 1000 cubic centimetres in our lungs). By forcibly exhaling this you create the space for a deep breath to follow.

– Expanding your rib cage breath in a long slow deep breath (to a count of five) through your nose. Your shoulders need to stay still and not rise (if they do you are filling only the top of your lungs). This may take practice.

– Breathe out through your mouth.

– Repeat the whole procedure five to ten times.

■ There are many other forms of yogic breathing which can help to reduce anxiety. Read *Breathe Stress Away* by David Brookes (Hollanden Publishing).

■ Behaviour therapy, counselling, and hypnotherapy can all make a huge difference to anxiety disorders (see Useful Resources page 235).

■ Relaxation therapies such as yoga, meditation and autogenic training have a proven track record with eliminating anxiety (see Useful Resources page 235 and Holistic Help in Depression for autogenic training, page 140).

More Hints

■ Thoughts come and go. You have the choice about whether to hang on to them or to let them go. If you dwell on a thought that is making you anxious you will get all the associated physical symptoms. Work on letting the thought go. Replace it in your mind with a specific time when you were anxiety free, peaceful and happy. You may find it easier to do this as a meditation exercise. You can recapture feelings in a highly effective way by reconnecting to a time when you felt them in the past. If you felt like this once, you can feel like this again. (See Creative Visualization page 222).

■ A powerful visualization is to actually stand outside when it is warm enough to do so with your eyes closed and spend a few moments getting centred (you obviously need to do this on a safe balcony, in a garden, park or the countryside — a shopping district is not ideal!). See in your mind's eye, depending on the weather, the wind blowing your cares away, the sun evaporating them or the rain washing them away.

■ Loosen up and make yourself free again. Find something to smile and laugh about each day and practice, practice, practice. There are lots of things to smile about – a child's antics, a shared joke, a hug, a lovely vista, a quirky cartoon, a funny film, a compliment (not brushed off), an old love letter.

■ Read *Laughter Is The Best Medicine* by Robert Holden (Thorsens).

■ Spend time with small children you know (borrow nieces and nephews, or children of friends if you don't have your own) getting down on all fours and messing about. Lose yourself in play and see things the way they see them – children have an amazingly clear and uncomplicated view of life.

■ For more ideas see Overwhelmed? (page 162).

Holistic Help

■ Habitual coffee drinking is linked to anxiety disorders, and it actually increases stress hormone levels over and above those that would normally be registered in anxious people. Substitute chicory, barley or dandelion coffee which are caffeine free and provide nourishment.

■ The herb *kava kava* has been dubbed 'natural Valium' but see warning on page 234. It is one of the best-studied herbs in relation to anxiety and has quite a fast-acting effect. It works on the same centre of the brain as do tranquillizer medicines and can be taken to quell rising anxiety and panic as it is happening. Kava is even more effective if taken with *valerian* (for sleeplessness) or with *St John's wort* (for depression) as appropriate. You can take these combinations for a few months and not develop dependency as happens with anti-anxiety pharmaceutical preparations. Avoid using kava with prescribed anti-anxiety medication or with alcohol. Kava also combines well with herbal 'nervine tonics' such as *skullcap* or *vervain*. *Avena sativa* is a, mild herb which is very suitable for long-term use.

■ *Lavender* is an anti-anxiety herb. Add a few drops of essential oil to your bath or to a burner. Alternatively, place a drop on each temple. Other anti-anxiety aromatherapy oils are cedarwood, camomile, clary sage, frankincense, geranium, juniper, marjoram, rosewood, sandalwood or tangerine.

DEPRESSION

Depression is more than 'the blues'. We all get down from time to time and this is normal. It is also obviously normal to feel depressed for a while during times of difficulty such as bereavement. However, depression goes beyond this and can involve feelings of not being able to cope with everyday life.

Depression and anxiety together make up about four-fifths of GPs' mental health workload. The two overlap considerably and those who are depressed can also be anxious, while anxiety can also mask depression. To understand more about how to deal with anxiety see page 135.

Top Tips

■ The first step in dealing with depression is to recognize you are affected by it, so that you can do something about it. Typical symptoms can include: feeling inadequate, loss of self-confidence, loss of enjoyment of life, lack of motivation, avoiding people, withdrawing, agitation, change in appetite, changes in sleep patterns, loss of interest in sex.

■ Life doesn't have to be obviously problematic for depression to strike. You may have what seems to be a terrific job, a lovely family and a nice home. But even with these assets you might be finding it difficult to cope with pressures, feeling that expectations of you can't be met and that the burden of responsibility is too great. It is common for those around a person who is afflicted to be surprised when they find out about the depression. They may not see more than skin deep, and a good job might be being done of hiding the depression while underneath that person is crumbling.

■ People can be thoughtless in their communication and make crushing remarks to others as a matter of course. We particularly tend to do this to children for some reason ('Don't be stupid', 'Why are you so bad?'), and teasing at school, ribbing at work and cajoling by friends all can erode self-worth. Add to this some devastating events such as job loss or marriage breakdown and it is not surprising that most of us are affected by at least one bout of depression at some time or other. The point is, if you are feeling depressed, to realize that you are not a freak case and that you are not alone.

■ Depression can be left undiagnosed because it is often not seen as a 'real illness' and so help is not sought. There is a perception that one just has to carry on and muddle through. It is important to speak to your GP if you are depressed.

■ You might not feel like it but get out and about. Allowing yourself to sit and brood will worsen how you feel. See Lethargy and Apathy page 156.

■ Social support is vital to help you through times of depression. Don't hope to wing it on your own. Let those closest to you know what you are going through and what they can do to help.

■ Talking is also vital. Sometimes a friendly ear is enough for you to express your pain and fear. Crying can be a tremendous pressure release. If you need counselling – seek it.

- Cognitive Thinking, which is the art of turning a negative thought into a more useful or even a positive one, is probably the most useful tool for working through depressive thought patterns and correcting them. See page 219 and make a point of working through the exercises there. If you find them helpful, investigate the further information given.

- A sense of helplessness in the face of perceived problems is one of the most crushing and debilitating aspect of depression. To work on empowering yourself and giving yourself options and choices, see Self-esteem page 169.

More Hints

- Early morning waking is a feature of depression, though it can also involve excessive sleepiness. Follow the advice in Sleep Quality, page 126.

- You may not feel like eating anything but junk food, but this is a time to nurture yourself with healthy food which can help to balance brain chemistry. Concentrate on eating foods rich in zinc and the right type of unsaturated fatty acids such as nuts and seeds (preferably unroasted), oily fish such as mackerel, fresh tuna, sardines and salmon, a little lean red meat (game is particularly good), oysters and other shellfish, beans and pulses (see Chapter 3, Health).

- Alcohol will worsen depression and is not the relief you might think it is. It is very important to avoid alcohol if you are depressed.

- Working though depression might seem, initially, like pushing a peanut up a hill with your nose, but if you persevere a lot of good can come out of it. Not only can you ditch your depression but you may even find a whole new take on life.

- Sometimes depression is diagnosed when the problem is really chronic fatigue or ME (which can certainly include depression amongst their symptoms). See Low Energy, page 105.

- Depression causes changes in brain chemistry and righting these might be an important feature of treating those with depression. If you are offered antidepressant medication by your doctor you can get a good rundown of the pros and cons by reading the back section of *Feeling Good: the New Mood Therapy* by David Burns (Quill, Harper Collins). The book is mainly focused on cognitive therapy solutions for depression (see Cognitive Thinking page 219) but as a psychiatrist he also discusses the pros and cons of medication. Medication, if it is deemed necessary, is not an admission of failure. A short course for a few months can help to overcome acute symptoms of depression while working on the underlying problems for the longer term.

- For mild to moderate depression the herb *St John's wort* has been shown to be as effective as antidepressant medication but with fewer side effects (see Herbal Preparations page 233 for more).

- Some organizations can help with specific problems, for instance Relate for marital problems or Compassionate Friends and Cruse for bereavement. Other helpful organizations include MIND, and Depression Alliance. See Useful Resources (page 234) for details.

■ If you have severe depression, and particularly if you have any thoughts of suicide, you must seek your doctor's help or the help of an organization such as The Samaritans 0345 909090 (Helpline) or www.samaritans.org.uk

Holistic Help

■ Autogenic training is a powerful way to help reduce depression. You have to make time to do the basic ten minute exercise three times daily for the first three or four weeks (the best times might be on first waking, just before sleeping and at some other time during the day when it is possible). After this you can cut back to once or twice daily. The basic exercise is deceptively simple, though you might find it better to sign up for training for the self-discipline, to really explore its uses and to deal with the 'discharge of stress' that can happen (sometimes making you feel worse for a short while before you feel better). To find out about autogenic training see Useful Resources page 234. The following is the basic exercise.

– Lie on your back (in bed if you wish) and get comfortable. Close your eyes. Take a deep, slow breath and pause for just a moment. Exhale fully. Throughout the session continue to breathe slowly, naturally and easily.

– Feel your body sinking into the bed or floor. Repeat each sentence that you are going to say three times (three times is important). As you repeat the sentences feel and acknowledge the corresponding feelings in your limbs and other areas. These are the phrases:

> My left arm is heavy… (three times)
> My right arm is heavy (three times, and so on for all of them)
> Both arms are heavy
> My left leg is heavy
> My right leg is heavy
> Both legs are heavy
> All my limbs are heavy
> My left arm is warm
> My right arm is warm
> Both arms are warm
> My left leg is warm
> My right leg is warm
> Both legs are warm
> All my limbs are warm and heavy
> My breathing is calm and easy
> My heartbeat is calm and easy
> My solar plexus is warm (your solar plexus is the area more or
>   less just behind your navel)
> My forehead is cool and clear
> I am at peace

– Now you are ready for the return which brings you back to normal consciousness.

Quickly clench both fists

Take in a deep breath

Stretch both arms upwards

Breath out slowly

Return your arms to your side with unclenched fists

Open your eyes

Lie for a moment taking in your surroundings and just 'being'.

■ Aromatherapy oils that help to combat depression include camomile, clary sage, frankincense, geranium, lavender, orange, sandalwood, tangerine or ylang ylang.

FEARS AND PHOBIAS

So many people walk around being fearful for much of their life. They spend a lot of their time thinking 'What if it all goes wrong'. Fear is one of the most stultifying emotions. It stops us dead in our tracks and stops us from progressing, or panics us into avoidance. In evolutionary terms these are perfectly valid reactions as fear is an appropriate reaction to real danger, and retreating is an appropriate way of dealing with threats. But when the fear is of commonplace activities or objects then it is misplaced and will disempower you faster than anything else can.

Top Tips

■ First of all, understand what it is exactly that you are fearful of. For instance, if your fear is of speaking in public, break down your concerns until you get to the root cause of your reaction and confront it. Your fear could be of looking out at the sea of faces, making a fool of yourself, forgetting the points you want to make, questions you are unable to answer or that you are a boring speaker.

■ Diffuse the feeling of fear by altering your description of it. Instead of saying 'I get rigid with fear when I …', say to yourself 'I am concerned about…' or 'I am worried about…' We programme our minds with the words we use and if we repeat the disempowering ones often enough they have a suitably negative effect, but if we use the modified versions they lessen the fear. If you use empowering terminology, you are on the way to working through your fears. You might say 'I enjoy the challenge' or 'This is a growing experience for me'.

■ This is probably the most important and empowering question in the whole book: ask yourself in any given situation 'What would I do if I were not afraid?'

■ It is often the case that the major stumbling block to realizing our ambitions is actually a fear of success. 'If I succeed, I won't be able to sustain it and then the truth will be out when I am recognized for the failure I really am' or 'If I succeed, I will have so much more to lose, so it's better not to succeed in the first place'. If this is you, work on positive affirmations such as 'Success breeds success'.

■ Fear of failure is particularly paralysing. If you are thinking 'If I fail at this, I am no good which means I will fail at everything'. This is, of course, a huge over-generalization to make, yet many people think in this way. It is impossible to fail at everything and we all (and this includes even the most successful people) have our share of successes and defeats.

More Hints

■ Your fears and inhibitions are probably compounded by the fact that you are focusing on the end result alone, which is daunting for you. Taking small, measured steps towards expanding your operating boundaries is a tested means of dealing with some phobias. If you are frightened of spiders, you might initially look at a drawing of a spider, then a photograph, than a video clip, then a full TV programme, then look at a small real spider in a glass jar, then a larger one in a glass jar, then a few spiders in a glass jar, then a loose spider at the far end of the room, then a little closer and so on.

■ You may have a stoic approach to dealing with your fears: 'Just get on with it no matter what cost to myself' and in this way you suppress your fear. But in the meantime you may live with constant anxiety and dread. It is better to ultimately confront your fears (though obviously not with anything dangerous).

■ Phobias are irrational and involve all sorts of knee-jerk reactions. The adrenaline begins to flow, your hands become clammy and you just want to run away. They are sometimes linked to compulsive behaviour ('If I flick the light switch on and off ten times going into the room won't be dangerous'). Most simple phobias in children (involving reacting to a single thing) tend to disappear without treatment. Phobias that persist, which come on in adulthood, and which are compound or social phobias usually need treatment through counselling.

■ Cognitive thinking (see page 219) allows the phobic person to see what is actually going on rather than what they perceive is happening. For instance if you are excruciatingly shy and are phobic about going into a room full of people, you might believe that you are sweating profusely and flushing. However, if you are shown a video of yourself in a social situation, you will probably observe that in fact you are not sweating or behaving oddly in any way. Seeing it for yourself rather than being told by someone else can have a strong impact.

■ You might get help from the National Phobics Society 0161 881 1937 www.phobics-society.org.uk or Triumph Over Phobia 01225 330 353 www.triumphoverphobia.com

Holistic Help

■ If you know you are going to be in a situation where you will be confronted with your fear take the herb *Kava kava* which is calming (see warning page 234).

■ Many people swear by **Bach** *Flower Rescue Remedy* for fears and phobias and the **Australian Bush Flower Essences's** *Confid* can be used for boosting confidence in the face of fear.

■ Aromatherapy oils that can help in the face of fear include camomile, cypress, frankincense, geranium, lavender, marjoram, sandalwood or tangerine.

FEELING GOOD: TEN EASY WAYS TO CHANGE YOUR EMOTIONAL STATE

Daily struggles, petty problems, sensory overload, other people's moods, stuff to do – all these conspire to make even the most positive people feel deflated. Even if you are confronted with more challenging events, you can change your emotional state almost immediately in few simple ways. Get into the habit of reading, and putting into practice, the list on a regular basis. You are a resourceful person and these tools, when used regularly, will hone feelings of calm confidence.

■ Get into the habit of believing – really believing – that today is a once-in-a-lifetime opportunity. The present is all we have. As the saying goes 'Yesterday is history, tomorrow is a mystery'. What are you going to do with the gift of today?

■ Pay yourself a compliment each day. And while you are at it, pay someone else a heartfelt and genuine compliment. Their pleasure will make you feel great.

■ When faced with any challenge that tugs at your self-belief and you wonder 'could I?', 'can I?', 'should I?' – empower yourself by asking 'If I were not afraid, what would I do?' You have your answer.

■ Flirt. This does not have to be in an overtly sexual way (though it could be!). You can flirt with men and women of any age – it means getting a buzzy feeling going, where humour is bubbling under the surface and there is a sense of fun and appreciation. You can flirt with people and you can flirt with life. You don't have to play the fool, just find what is good about a situation, appreciate it and communicate it to others.

■ Walk like a person who is enthused about life and happy. If you throw your shoulders back, look at eye contact level rather than the ground, put a spring in your step and greet people, it is virtually impossible to feel down.

■ Programme your brain to feel happiness. As a specific exercise read Creative Visualization page 222 and create a vivid and totally real picture of a time when you were happy, powerful, relaxed, confident, calm and balanced. Capture that feeling in every fibre of your body, in every pore, in every neurone of your brain. When you have achieved this, anchor it. You do this by making a small, discreet, movement you associate with this feeling. For instance brush your finger against your palm or rub two fingers together. Having anchored the feeling, make a point of using this 'signal' a few times each day to recall this feeling. At first, it might be felt only weakly, but as you practice and get in touch with this feeling regularly you will improve and hone your ability to get there almost immediately, whatever else is going on around you.

■ Any time you make a self-deprecating remark, check yourself and counter it with a more realistic and preferably an empowering statement. Do the same when other people talk down to you.

■ When you feel cowed by other people (either because they are overbearing or because you somehow feel inferior) remember they have to go to the loo as well! They are human as well, with all the frailties that go with that condition.

■ Write out a mission statement for yourself. A mission statement focuses on the essence of who you are and what you want for yourself. Complete the following statements.

– The person I chose to be from this moment on is someone who is …

– The qualities I am emphasizing and am enjoying in myself are …

– Now add: I absolutely commit myself to these qualities being the essence of who I am and am reinforcing them until they are deeply ingrained in my being.

– Sign and date your mission statement and look at it regularly.

■ Do something completely irrelevant to your everyday life. Decide that this is the day you are going to: learn to juggle, balance a ball on your nose, rollerblade or skateboard in the park or knit a tea cosy.

FOOD AND MOOD

We all know that the mood we are in affects the type and amount of food we eat. If you are even-tempered and happy, the chances are that you are choosing foods which nourish you and make you feel good. But if you are feeling the pressure mount, you may be indulging in 'comfort eating', or you might be the sort of person who loses their appetite until happier times.

But food and mood have another intimate relationship. The types of foods we eat and drink have an effect on balancing our moods and so affecting emotional state and self-esteem.

Top Tips

■ The more you feel stressed, the more disordered your eating can become, and the more your moods can be adversely affected. On the other hand, if you motivate yourself to eat in a balanced way, it will help to even out your moods. For basic guidelines see Healthy Eating (page 98).

■ We crave certain foods for a variety of reasons.

– Foods affect serotonin levels in the brain which are involved in moods (Prozac and other similar anti-depressants work by changing serotonin levels in the brain.)

– Stimulants in particular, but also carbohydrates such as bread and sugar, trigger a short-term release of stress hormones which raise blood sugar levels and make you feel better in the short term, long term they can adversely affect energy levels.

- – Compounds such as caffeine (and other methylxanthines) have a direct effect on brain chemistry, but one that is short lived and needs to be repeated shortly afterwards.

- – Some foods such as chocolate have compounds in them which trigger pleasure-giving endorphins in the brain.

- – Fat is recognized by the brain as necessary for energy stores in times of stress, but the desire to eat it does not switch off if stress levels do not come down.

■ It is a general rule that the foods we are addicted to are those we eat most frequently, and find it hardest to go without. Such foods are also the ones most likely to adversely affect both our moods and our general health. Keep a food diary for a week, writing down which foods you crave most and how eating them affects your mood.

■ We self-medicate with alcohol, coffee, strong tea (weak tea is fine), colas and sugar to make us feel good in the short term. It will come as no surprise then that when this wears off we want more. One or two coffees in the morning to help shake you awake ends up with you topping up with caffeine all day, which can cause tension and depression. Use your food diary to help you cut down on such stimulants. Start by restricting yourself to two coffees in the morning then reduce to one.

■ Analyse the feelings that your particular food or drink craving represents. These could run the gamut of comfort, mood calmer, self-loathing, creative energy, pleasure, dealing with fear and so on. Writing these sentiments down will help you gain objectivity about the feeling and therefore to resist a compulsion to consume those foods. For information on making healthy substitutions for stimulants in your diet read Disordered Eating (page 88) and Addictions (page 77).

■ The most important area to focus on is how you eat carbohydrates which affect the production of serotonin in the brain. Serotonin plays a large part in our mood swings, and their relationship with the foods we eat – affecting how alert we feel, the urge to binge and the craving for stimulants. For instance, eating bread or pasta at midday could make you drowsy for the rest of the afternoon (if you are susceptible to being affected by carbohydrates in this way) and you might do better with a meal of chicken and vegetables. Save the pasta for the evening when you don't mind feeling sleepy.

■ Replacing the typical afternoon snack of cake or chocolate biscuits with a yoghurt and piece of fruit, nuts and dried fruit, or oatcakes with a little cottage cheese, will help to maintain you on an even keel. By making better food choices you can encourage equilibrium in your brain chemicals, avoiding the mid-afternoon dip in levels of the hormone cortisol, which lead to tiredness and sugar cravings.

More Hints

■ If you are going to indulge in your particular mood-bending substance (I am talking food and drink here) at least be aware that it will rob you of essential nutrients – B vitamins, antioxidants (vitamins A, C, E), magnesium, chromium and calcium. Make sure that you take a daily multi-vitamin and mineral supplement to replace some of these. A bowl of cereal before you go out can help to slow down alcohol absorption and nourish you with some B vitamins.

- Drink long drinks made up with juices if you can, for example: a bloody Mary, a vodka and orange, or a white wine spritzer.

- Give yourself some alcohol-free days each week.

- If you need an excuse for avoiding alcohol when in a social situation you could tell a little white lie – say you are doing a detox, are on antibiotics or you are driving.

- If you just have to have that chocolate or sticky bun, eat a large piece of fruit first and then indulge if you still want to.

- If you take sugar in your drinks, reduce it slowly over time until you no longer need it.

- The action of putting on the kettle is often as important as drinking the coffee. Indulge in hot water with lemon, some grated ginger for zest and a little honey.

- Read *The Food and Mood Handbook* by Amanda Geary (Thorsons) or *Potatoes Not Prozac* by Kathleen des Maisons (Simon & Schuster).

Holistic Help

- Eat foods rich in tryptophan (essential to the production of serotonin) such as fish, poultry, beans, avocados and bananas, to balance your mood.

- Centre your creative visualization (see page 222) exercises on serenity featuring the calm choice of nurturing, mood-balancing foods when in situations of food choice.

GENEROSITY

Despite the fact that it seems as if we live in a 'me' society based on consumerism and greed, there is a gratifying amount of fair-mindedness around and surprising numbers of people are generally willing to help others. Kindness and generosity spread good feelings around cancelling out the negative stresses of modern living.

Top Tips

- Giving can be many things – a helping hand, a kind word, time, expertise, money. What can you give, and to whom? There is a time to give and a time to receive. You may be feeling stressed at the moment and not able to give anything and you may feel bad about this, but eventually you will be able to give of yourself.

- When you give to others make sure you do not expect anything in return. First of all, this is because it taints the act of giving. Secondly, if you expect something back, you might well be disappointed. Finally, if you don't expect anything back, you will be pleasantly surprised when the boomerang effect happens and you do receive something back.

- The boomerang effect of generosity is obvious to all who have experienced it. When you give (in the right spirit), you definitely receive. Though it may not be in any way you expect.

It is quite surprising what opportunities open up, how friendships are made and how emotional and financial riches are bestowed on those who give.

■ If you are asked to give (of yourself, money, time, love) always take time to consider if you are really willing to do so. When you give, you must give without any feeling of resentment.

■ The problems of the world are too great for anyone to tackle on their own. Start in your own community. We can all make a difference – you can make a difference. What a powerful statement!

More Hints

■ Don't give from a sense of guilt ('I ought to', 'I should', 'It is expected of me') as this will only wear your down. Sort out your feelings of guilt first (see page 148).

■ You may find it difficult to receive other people's generosity – compliments or gifts. Instead of stammering that you are unworthy or that they are too generous – just say 'Thank you'! And enjoy it.

■ Don't assume that a gift is covering up guilt (say a bunch of flowers when your partner is back late from the office). This suspicion will taint the relationship and gives off the subliminal message that you are untrusting. Even if it is guilt, by giving off the message of undiluted appreciation you strengthen the relationship instead of weakening it.

■ People may not always be willing to ask. Without imposing your belief of what they need on them, you might want to ask if they could do with help. An elderly neighbour might welcome a few items when you go to the supermarket, a friend might be grateful for a few hours of child minding, a colleague might find your professional experience of help.

■ Be cautious when lending money and always take the view that you might not get it back again. Better to give money, rather than lend, and hope that the boomerang effect happens. If you do lend money, draw up a repayment and interest agreement so there are no misunderstandings later (if your friend gets shirty about this you probably ought to consider just how good a friend they are and if you are really likely to see the money again. You have a right to be businesslike about your money and emotional issues need not cloud the transaction). Many a friendship is lost over money.

■ While the ability to give is to be admired, some people become professional givers and do so with the expectation that it somehow puts them in a position of power. They start organizing all around them, dragging people in (willing or not), bulldozing people's needs to fulfil their own and generally behaving as if their view is the only one to take on. Be careful of other people's sensibilities if you have a 'cause'.

Holistic Help

■ Enjoying other people's achievements involves generosity of spirit.

■ If you find yourself alone one Christmas, there are many charities who could use help at this time.

GUILT

If you are not careful, you can find yourself feeling guilty for the whole human condition! Feeling responsible for everything, from leaving the milk out in the sun to guilt about a family bereavement, is a debilitating emotion that can deplete your energy and health. Assessing if it is appropriate to feel guilty is all about gaining perspective. The suggestions below will help you to deal with overwhelming guilty feelings, as well as to grade the degree of emotional responsibility that is appropriate to the 'crime'. Taking action and sorting out your guilty feelings will liberate you from this stultifying and useless emotion (by now you should already be feeling guilty about feeling guilty!). Read on...

Top Tips

■ The guilt cycle goes something like this:

– I feel guilty.

– Therefore I am worthy of condemnation.

– This must mean I have been bad.

– Since I am bad I deserve to suffer.

■ You are reasoning to yourself that since you feel bad you must be bad. With this cycle we end up punishing ourselves in a number of ways. We work harder, we berate ourselves, we overcompensate. If we chose to numb the guilt by overeating, drinking or worse, we may then use such reactions as further confirmation of what bad people we are. Thus we feel more guilt and the whole cycle perpetuates.

■ Break the cycle by finding more rational responses to your automatic thoughts. Take responsibility for your actions but refuse to take responsibility for those that are not attributable to you. This will take practice, take time out each day to give any processes and actions that are provoking guilt a cool appraisal. The more you do this, the more objectivity you will achieve, enabling you to deal with any guilty feelings.

■ Misplaced guilt is a strong sign of poor self-esteem. Some people feel responsible for the happiness of everyone else. They feel guilt for everything that goes wrong around them. If you are one of those people, then you are placing a massive burden of guilt on yourself, wearing yourself out trying to please others. This is a no-win situation. Cognitive Thinking (see page 219) is one of the best therapies for helping you see a situation differently. For instance, if you think a fellow member of the PTA committee is critical of everything you propose, and this makes you feel as if all your ideas are rubbish and so you volunteer guiltily for even more tasks, you need to think of other reasons for that person's behaviour. They could be coming down with flu, they could simply have an aggressive tone – thinking of alternative views on the same incident will help you to realize that you are not 'bad' and that, in most circumstances, you are not responsible for other people.

■ Have you noticed how there is an epidemic of apologizing? Apologizing has its place, but don't apologize for breathing. The habit of saying sorry for everything undermines self-esteem and soon enough you find yourself saying sorry when someone else bumps into you! If you are a child, you might think it is your fault that you are being bullied or abused. As an employee you might think it normal that you cover for your boss's inadequacies, or at another extreme accept being a victim of domestic violence.

■ When you take responsibility for your actions, you will be responsible for the outcome. Then you will know if you really need to apologize for something or if you are expressing misplaced guilt.

More Hints

■ You are not responsible for other people's happiness – they are. While you may empathize with their situation, feeling guilty for what they are experiencing only undermines yourself. To take a simple example, you might have chosen the restaurant to go to, but your companion elected to go with you and presumably they chose what to eat. If they did not enjoy the experience it is not your 'fault'. It is fine to empathize with the fact that the evening was not enjoyable, but to feel guilty about it is misplaced. Instead of feeling guilty for choosing the restaurant in the first place, laugh about it together, learn from the experience (you won't be going back again!), and move on.

■ Inappropriate 'should' statements, such as 'I should be grateful for what I've got', 'I should want to be with my family', 'I should be happy I have a good job' – are a guaranteed way to make yourself feel guilty. 'Should' statements are the domain of the perfectionist and very few people can live up to that. These statements also assume that you are omnipotent and always have to have a perfect response to a situation. Nobody can be grateful, happy and sociable all the time, and there is no reason to feel guilty when you aren't. This is an example of misplaced guilt and just serves to make you feel bad.

■ Religious faith can be a source of guilty feelings for some people, particularly those religions (Christianity, Judaism) which say that we are all sinners from birth. If you are a believer but feel dominated by guilt, then look for more positive messages within your particular faith. A tolerant, ecumenical approach will also enable you to borrow kinder ideas from other faiths such as Buddhism and Hinduism which view people as being intrinsically divine.

■ Once you have dealt with your own mantle of guilt, be wary of loading guilt onto others. In particular, you have influence over your children and their self-esteem. Pile them up with guilt and you perpetuate the cycle. Focus on what their responsibilities are, and not on imagined linked guilt associations. 'It is your responsibility to clear up your mess just as it is my responsibility to do the cooking – we each have our responsibilities' and not 'If you don't clear up your mess you will give me a headache'.

- We need to be aware when we are reproducing unhealthy relationships from our past. We all carry aspects of both parent/child behaviours into adult life and some of us find it hard to shake it off. We might view ourselves as the child, while seeing our partner/boss/flatmate as the parent, reproducing the same dynamic of guilt that we grew up with over and over again. Do say 'It is your responsibility to make sure you do not overspend so that the joint bank account does not get overdrawn because it then costs us a fortune in interest' and not 'If you get us overdrawn again it is going to make me have a nervous breakdown'.

- The opposite of guilt is denial. Denial is a refusal to accept responsibility for a situation. Just to prove how convoluted and creative the human mind is, both denial and feelings of guilt can easily co-exist. Where this has implications for the other person is when the denial takes the form of projecting the guilt or weakness onto the other person. This can take the form of nagging to correct a fault that the person needs to address themselves, or becoming a martyr to sorting out something in the person's life when not sorting out the mess in our own.

Holistic Help
- The **Bach Flower Remedy** *Pine* is for those who feel guilty and who tend to take the blame for others.

- Use meditation and visualize yourself as nurturing an animal – any type that comes to mind (a kitten, a rabbit, a dog, a dolphin, a bird). This animal represents your 'higher' self. Feed, stroke and care for this animal. Radiate warmth and love. You couldn't punish this lovely creature and also could not punish yourself. Practice this regularly and bring the creature to mind when feelings of guilt arise.

HAPPINESS

Realistically you can't live on the edge of joy all the time – it would be a little manic! But you can express your gratitude for having a fulfilling life by focusing on the happy aspects of your existence.

Top Tips
- There is a place for unhappiness and it is there to tell you that you need to change something about your life. Seen in this way it becomes a positive tool for change.

- Happiness is likely to follow when you lead a fulfilled life according to your standards and not according to the standards of others.

- Don't look to others for your happiness. Happiness has more staying power if it comes from within.

- If you are going through an unhappy phase of your life, it will pass. Remember to think of it as a transitional phase and not the milestone by which you will measure the future. For instance, people do adapt even to serious problems such as serious illness or injury.

■ Practising having a happy personality can pay dividends in so many areas of life. If you are cheerful and outgoing your marriage and relationships are more likely to last and you will have a stronger immune system and you might even live longer. So it really does pay to find things to be happy about and grateful for. If you are uncertain of what these are make a list (or mind map it, see page 226). No matter how small something is, put it in. Keep the list to hand and build on it daily.

More Hints

■ Finances are not altogether irrelevant to happiness – at least in the society in which we live. Research does show that happiness is, to a degree, linked to income, but it is relative. You need to be relatively poor to start off with to appreciate money and for it to make you happy. Very few people in our society are really poor financially (most people have fridges, TVs, videos and other symbols of an affluent society) and feeling you are poor is not the same as being poor (not enough food on the table, not able to afford heating, finding it difficult to provide for your children).

■ Success (whatever your definition of this is) does not necessarily guarantee happiness. Constantly maintaining that success and fear of losing it can dampen your enjoyment. In chasing success it is easy to lose sight of what really might confer happiness such as a good relationship with your partner and children or the time to pursue other interests. (See Success Brings New Challenges page 63.)

■ How you view life determines how readily you feel happiness. Do you look at the glass and say it is half-empty (you have a pessimistic tendency) or is it half-full (you have an optimistic tendency). Or would you say that you have more in the glass than you actually need (you are a realist!). Think how you apply this general principle to your life.

■ If you have been knocked sideways by something, give yourself time to bounce back. Recognize that it is normal to grieve for a while about something, but there comes a time when looking back and having regrets will not serve you. You have to throw off the mantle of the past and look to your future happiness.

■ Being happy does not mean putting on a brave face. This will not change or solve anything. If you find that you are being brave on the outside and everyone thinks you are doing fine, when you are unhappy inside, you need to find someone to whom you can talk and unburden yourself.

Holistic Help

■ Spreading a little happiness leads to more happiness. Say a kind word and it will be reflected.

INSPIRATION AND MOTIVATION

Few things make a person more interesting, happy and forward looking than if they are inspired by life. How do you find this inspiration?

Top Tips

■ Get inspired by really focusing on something. If you have many theoretical interests but never do anything about them, then you are fogging your potential with too many options and not enough action (see Overwhelmed? page 162). Take one activity, which you really want to tackle, and make a plan, now, to do something about it. Book classes, buy equipment or books, set aside time in your diary, talk to some experts, encourage a friend to come along for company – get inspired to take action.

■ Get curious. If you ever wonder why or what something is, find out. You never know where it will lead.

■ An optimistic approach to life comes naturally to some people, while others may need to practice a little. Optimists usually expect the best from people and situations, view mistakes as learning experiences, safely release their frustrations, and are likely to talk about the future with excitement.

■ If you are still left feeling that optimists are a little irritating and unrealistic, take the middle course and head for realism. It is the optimists in this world who see obstacles as mere hurdles, and view problems as interesting challenges and who achieve their aims most easily – in part by being flexible in their aims and avoiding rigid attitudes.

■ Getting inspired about something is a terrific way to empower yourself and to start an upward spiral of satisfying emotions leading to a happier life. As you get inspired just watch your problems fall by the wayside.

■ Take yourself out of situations where others squash inspiration and positive thinking with their negativity, or worse, with put-downs. By all means listen to good advice, but also learn to listen to your inner wisdom.

■ When you are inspired you set a wonderful example for your children. It helps them to become resourceful and to follow their own inspirations. A child's enthusiasm can be an inspiration to you.

■ Be inspired by those who are around you and who you admire. Understand how they view the world and what they find rewarding. This can give you ideas to mould for your own use.

■ Talk to people every day. Get curious about other lives and experiences. Instead of pigeonholing others find out what has inspired them and what they have learned. Your grandfather, neighbour or friend of a friend might have a whole dimension to them you never thought to ask about beforehand.

More Hints

- If you do feel inspired, avoid preaching to others. In any event, they will notice that you are happy, more fulfilled and active and, if interested, they will seek out your views, but they do not need unasked-for information pushed at them. You will win more fans and converts this way!

- Take chances. This does not mean being reckless or dangerous, but does mean expanding your boundaries. Unless you take a chance, you will never know if it was to be. Never let fear of taking chances get in your way. Always ask yourself 'What is the worst thing that could happen if I do take the risk'. Even if the worst does happen, it is usually not that bad!

- Rejection can often have a dampening effect on inspiration. Work on seeing rejection as an opportunity to change your approach. Remember that one rejection does not mean more will follow.

- Stay on track. The beginnings of a new project can be very inspiring, but lack of consistency of action or stumbling blocks can soon erode this. Is your enthusiasm enough to carry you through? Where and how else can you renew your motivation? Take regular stock checks to evaluate these feelings.

- Being motivated by negatives never really works that well. Think about it. Wanting to leave a relationship because you don't find your mate attractive any more, find habits irritating or are no longer in love often means a long drawn out process until you finally can't stand it any longer. Being in a job you would like to leave because you don't like your colleagues, you are underused or the travel is too difficult is not likely to be the most forceful way of helping you to make up your mind about what to do. On the other hand, fall madly in love with someone, or be inspired by a terrific job opportunity and you are out of there without a backwards glance. Whether it is right or appropriate to leave is a different question, and needs to be balanced against other issues. but what we are talking about here is inspiration and motivation. Finding positive reasons to make changes are powerful motivators.

Holistic Help

- You can enhance your motivation for something if you associate it with pleasure, rather than with pain. Visualize yourself succeeding at whatever it is you are motivating yourself to do, and get firmly in touch with the pleasure this engenders.

JEALOUSY AND NEEDINESS

The 'green-eyed monster' of jealousy is a destructive force, yet many people succumb to it at some time or other. Perhaps jealousy it is a natural urge to protect what is ours from rivals and to acquire what we think we need for survival. But as with many natural survival instincts it can be distorted by modern living, and lead to expressions of neediness that only serve to alienate possible sources of help and comfort. In any event, these emotions are guaranteed to be a waste of energy, to lower self-esteem further and possibly to destroy relationships.

Top Tips

■ If you are jealous, it is your behaviour that needs to change and not the behaviour of the person who is the target of your jealousy (their behaviour is a different issue).

■ Much jealousy can be avoided if you manage, early on enough in a relationship, to set the ground rules for future behaviour. Do you mind, in theory, if your partner has affairs? What would you do about it? Do you think you could work through it, or that it would mean instant separation. Establish your views early on so that you have a framework to operate within, even if the reality is that your feelings change if you find yourself in such a situation. You might think this is unromantic, like a prenuptial agreement, but, by talking openly about it, you reduce the potential for ambiguities. Another strategy is to agree with your partner to have an annual review of where you are emotionally in the relationship.

■ If something is bothering you, talk about it instead of resorting to supposition and spying.

■ Jealousy and neediness have broken up many a relationship without real cause. It can take the form of a self-fulfilling prophesy along the lines of – 'I feel insecure and so I don't trust you, therefore you must be guilty of something, therefore our relationship is rubbish, and if our relationship is rubbish why are we together at all?' Even a saint would leave in the face of this.

■ Neediness is oppressive and is not a way of showing how much you care. 'Why are you home late from work?' 'Why don't you want to spend more time with me at the weekends?' 'Why don't we do more together?' These are questions that will exhaust both you and your partner. Improving your self-esteem (see page 169) will help you to feel happier in your own company and able to do things without needing your partner always by your side.

■ Jealousy is not a more intense form of love. Jealousy of a lover or partner leads to strange behaviour – listening in on phone calls, getting friends to spy, sifting through pockets, mail and wallets, stalking. This behaviour is more common than we might think. If you find yourself doing any of this, you might justify it to yourself if you believe you are being 'cheated on'. But no amount of justification can get away from the fact that the need to creep around like this is demeaning and smacks of low self-esteem. But if your partner is cheating, you almost definitely do not need to go to these lengths. If they believe they can get away with it, the chances are that they will get careless in their subterfuge eventually and you will know anyway, without putting yourself through this behaviour. Then you have the difficult decision of what you are going to do about it.

■ Why are you jealous and what are you jealous about? Are you protecting what you believe is rightfully yours? (We don't own other people.) Do you have particular moral standards which, if transgressed, mean a particular course of action? If you really love yourself do you need to seek the love of other people, even your partner, to the exclusion of others? There is absolutely no right or wrong answer to these questions and we all feel differently about them. However, asking yourself these questions can help to sort out your own feelings about yourself and the relationship.

- Being content to pursue your own interests and develop your own friendships will lead to a mature and contented relationship. This may take courage initially, especially if you have been in a cycle of neediness, but is vital to achieve balance in life. If you elevate your partner, lover, boyfriend/girlfriend onto a pedestal, then no activity will be enjoyable without that person. It can be a tremendous burden for that person to bear, and also means that you will not feel as satisfied as you could in that relationship. Having your own interests means that you will have more to talk about and, therefore, a richer relationship. Work on other interests at a pace that allows you to expand your comfort zones. Instead of dragging an unwilling partner on a shopping trip, go shopping on your own and have a coffee on your own. Eventually you may be happy to join a theatre group or a gym on your own. If your partner wants to join you, it is done voluntarily and not because it is 'expected'.

More Hints

- No matter how good a friend may be, if they succeed where you might have stumbled in the past you may find a fleeting emotion of jealousy. Acknowledging this is not shameful. You can work on seeing your friends as allies rather than rivals. You will be a richer person emotionally if you can enjoy your friends' successes and triumphs unconditionally. Use the following affirmation to promote this feeling 'I enjoy [name]'s wins as if they were my own and support [her/him] unconditionally in [his/her] achievements. 'I can learn from [name]'s successes.' Repeat this often (see Creative Visualization page 222).

- Gossip is a damaging tool that is often used to further the aims of jealousy. If you find that you are drawn into gossiping by another person, avoid doing so as it is often malicious.

- Get yourself out of the jealousy mentality by refusing to read the gossip pages in newspapers and magazines which often take the line of 'how the mighty have fallen'. This breeds a culture in which we enjoy watching the failures of those who have done well in the past, and inevitably leads to a jealous, miserable society.

- If your jealousy is focused on other people having what you feel you do not, remember there is always going to be someone richer, thinner, cleverer than you. This is a train of thought that creates only negative feelings and leads to unhappiness, so it is best to forget it.

- The most important competition is with yourself. You can't always be first or best so aim to better your own score each time and you will always be ahead of the game.

- For a useful questionnaire which helps you to evaluate your feelings of jealousy log on to www.psychologyhelp.com/emotquiz.htm

Holistic Help

- *Holly* is the **Bach Flower Remedy** to help eliminate feelings of envy, jealousy and suspicion.

LETHARGY AND APATHY

Feeling lethargic and apathetic can affect even the most positive of people and it is a natural part of the waxing and waning of moods. But if it is a regular occurrence then it may be a sign of lack of motivation or depression. It is common to experience weekend lethargy as a reaction to the structure of the working week. Apathy often plagues single people who find they mope around when on their own. Lying around staring at the ceiling and channel hopping between equally dreary TV channels while subsisting on cheese sandwiches and instant coffee is bound to make you feel depressed, with time to think about all that is not right in your life.

Top Tips

- Lethargy might be simply mistaken for boredom. If you find that you are bored by what you are doing, it is no surprise that you are unenthusiastic about life. Ask yourself why you are you bored. You may be bored because your job is too repetitive, you feel undervalued, or your finances keep you from having interests. If any of this rings a bell, you have to fall back on your resourcefulness and create an action plan (see below).

- At weekends, you might feel that you just want to slump in front of the telly to unwind. But those who remain moderately active tend to be less depressed, while those who crash on the sofa tend towards lethargy and depression. If you let the weekend creep up on you unplanned, it is more likely that you will fall into this trap. On Wednesday each week, plan at least a couple of things you can look forward to at the weekend.

- There is a simple and effective way of lifting yourself out of an apathetic state, by creating a Daily Activity Plan each day for a week. You then have a tool with which to focus yourself in on satisfying and pleasurable activities. Take a sheet of paper and put a line down the middle to create two wide columns. On the far left hand side write time slots, in a narrow column, by the hour from 7 or 8 am to 11 pm or 12 am (whatever your normal day is). Date your sheet. Now plan your activities (these need not be elaborate) for the day on an hourly basis and write these in the left-hand column and head them up 'Anticipated'. You may not carry out the whole of your daily plan, but by simply creating one you give yourself a structure to work towards. You might simply write 'dress', 'eat breakfast', 'take a walk', 'write letter', 'make lunch', etc.

- Aim to make a balanced action plan which combines activity and rest, mental challenge and calm, work and play, achievement and indulgence. In the right-hand column you will write, at the end of the day, what activities you actually did, and head this up 'Actual'. Write down everything even if it was just lying in bed. Next to each actual activity add either an 'A' for achievement and 'P' for pleasure. 'A' represents activities that actually achieve something such as taking a shower, preparing a meal, commuting to work or doing the laundry. 'P' denotes the pleasure you receive from doing something. It may be that you enjoy the activity or the satisfaction of having completed a necessary task. Rate each 'A' and 'P' according to how you feel from 1 to 10. A simple task such as brushing your teeth might warrant A3 P1. Cooking a meal might be A5 P2 or if you enjoy it A5 P7. If you are feeling depressed even going to see a movie you would normally enjoy might only rate P1. You might dread seeing someone or going somewhere, but it turns out to be an unexpected pleasure – P9. Keep this chart going for a week. It will stop you procrastinating, give you some structure, make you think about what you can do and go a long way to helping you understand what you wish to do. It is a first step to self-reliance in the face of lethargy and apathy. You can now use this weeks-worth of information to help plan more enjoyable and satisfying activities in the future.

More Hints

■ If you are short on cash, work out what you can do that does not cost money. Here are some options to consider: join a reading group and take books out from the library, start jogging, do crossword puzzles, turn a hobby into a money-making scheme, go to a museum or exhibition at times when they allow free entrance. If you are short on ideas get hold of a magazine of local activities from your library – they are usually stuffed full with events.

■ If you feel 'flat' and uninspired, a short boost of activity can act as a pick you up. Go for a swim, visit a friend, go to the cinema (to see something cheerful not something depressing!), visit an uplifting exhibition, treat yourself to tea in a nice place.

■ If your apathy takes the form of procrastinating about a task (sometimes for weeks or even months!), break it down into bite-size chunks. If you need to write a letter, for instance, break the job down into Outline, Draft, Final Draft and Send. Grade from 1 to 10 with the anticipated difficulty and satisfaction of each stage. By writing this breakdown you will find it less daunting to start the job. At the end of each stage, grade the actual difficulty and satisfaction. You will probably find that you were projecting more difficulty and less satisfaction than you actually felt in the end. This approach is highly effective for stopping yourself from projecting difficulties and putting off doing things.

Holistic Help

■ You need to eat healthily and regularly to keep your energy levels up. Blood sugar balance is particularly important if you suffer from energy dips in the afternoon or if you just want to snooze on the couch after a couple of glasses of wine in the evening. See Healthy Eating page 98 for more information.

■ Brain chemical balance is affected by food choices and eating a little protein with each meal can help. Healthy snacks are also important so focus on yoghurt and fresh fruit, nuts and dried fruit, oatcakes and cottage cheese (all of these have a little protein in them).

■ Raw juices can give you a mental energy boost just when you need it. This is especially useful if you are feeling apathetic at weekends when you do have the time to make a fresh juice. A 'Carrot Zinger' combines carrots, apple and a 2.5cm cube of ginger (you will need a juicer to do this).

LOVE

My six-year-old son asked me thoughtfully the other day 'Mummy why are so many songs about love?' This is a very good question. Love remains one of the most potent yet indefinable feelings that humans are capable of. This is probably why so many poems, stories, books, plays and films centre on the subject and why love can be a metaphor for hope, peace, passion and brotherhood. Yet, whatever type of love we are thinking about, many of us seem to find it hard to express. Perhaps this is why there are so many love songs – an expression of the feelings we find it difficult to acknowledge.

Top Tips

■ Learn to love yourself. Love of self is the essential first step in improving self-esteem, and in being able to experience loving relationships with other people. Most people need convincing that it's OK to love themselves. Try this exercise. First of all write down at least ten ways, and preferably more, that demonstrate that you are capable of showing yourself love. This might involve changing how you talk to yourself, such as not apologizing for your failings or beating yourself up for not being 'good enough', taking time out to give yourself treats, countering destructive comments from other people with life-enhancing thoughts, and saying 'no' when you want to. I am sure you can think of many others.

■ Don't confuse self-love with selfishness or arrogance.

■ We all want to be loved or at least liked – it is a fundamental need from childhood. Of course it is not always possible to be loved or liked by everyone all the time. Seeking popularity because of a basic need to be loved can wear you out in the long run as you try to please everyone. We seek approval all the time and getting out of an addiction to people-pleasing habits can take time to master. Acknowledging that you can't always be popular is a sign of maturity. Ultimately you need to approve of yourself and be able to live with the decisions you make on a daily basis.

■ We have different capacities to love and receive love at different times in our lives. In a loving relationship it is ideally one of give and take, but the balance might vary at different times because each person feels stronger at different times. Understanding this can reduce the scope for unhelpful conflict and unhappiness in a relationship.

■ Many people give only conditional love. It goes like this: 'If you behave in a particular way, or give me something I want, then I will love you'. This is a travesty of love and is the height of manipulation. Above all, it is a form of emotional blackmail that damages the self-esteem of the person on the receiving end. If you are subject to this from another person, you need to find the tools to work out what you want, and to find your satisfaction from within yourself.

■ Regularly tell those who are close to you that you love them. Your children will feel secure, your partner will reflect it, your friends will be warmed, your grandparents will feel appreciated and your parents will think it was all worth it after all!

Holistic Help

■ Nurture your love for another person by doing small and thoughtful things for them. Romance often goes out of a relationship unless it is nurtured with loving thoughts, nice little surprises and caring actions.

MINDSET/FLEXIBILITY

A rigid mindset is a guaranteed way to stay stuck in the same repetitive patterns in life. Flexibility means not being wedded to your own ways and thoughts to the exclusion of alternatives. If you find that you are incapable of cooking a meal with a friend because you can't bear the way she chops the carrots then you need to loosen up. Appreciating help and friendship will ensure that you always have both assistance when you need it and friends to provide it. Even if you are currently happy with everything around you and do not feel the need for anything to change, it is still wise to adopt a flexible approach to life. Nothing stays the same and if you can be adaptable then the stresses and strains that life throws up will not seem like overwhelming crises.

Top Tips

■ Get into the habit of looking to see how many paths you have open to you (it may take some practice to see these paths). A rigid approach will say 'This is what I have to do', 'This is the only option' or 'This is just the way it is'. Whereas a flexible approach will say 'These are the options I have' or 'I will seek options'. How many possibilities have you missed in the past because you were not allowing yourself to see alternative paths?

■ You may be flexible enough to deal with events around you, but how flexible are you towards yourself? Work out what your core beliefs are in life and challenge them, which will test their validity. Do they work for you, or do they work against you? You might be surprised by some of the negative core beliefs you have which are limiting your ability to be flexible. Core beliefs you will definitely want to work on and change (see Cognitive Thinking page 219) might sound a little like some of the following.

– Life is difficult and requires hard work and hard work is not meant to be fun.

– I am not worthy of reward (this could be in a particular situation rather than in general).

– I have to work harder than I already am and I am still not worthy of reward.

– I am unattractive and am therefore worth less than someone who is attractive.

– There is something wrong with me.

– Love is painful and I might get hurt.

– The world is becoming a more precarious place all the time.

- If you want to guarantee success in just about all aspects of your life, remain flexible. The reality is that in life you will encounter situations when you are not in control. Remain flexible in the rules you use to govern your thinking, the meaning you attach to things and your approach to meeting challenges and you will win through.

- Read *Who Moved My Cheese?* by Dr Spencer Johnson (Vermilion) – this book takes only about half an hour to read and is probably the most important book recommendation I can make.

More Hints

- Stability in all areas of life is the key to a worry-free existence. We have moments in our life when suddenly everything is calm and balanced and we can heave a sigh of relief. However, the minute one area of life becomes unbalanced, it is a flexible approach that will restore stability. If you stay rigid, the situation will get more unbalanced and can eventually overwhelm you.

- Treat changes as challenges to overcome rather than as upsets to your perceived order of things.

- Lack of flexibility breeds resentment and discontent. If, for example, you are moved sideways or are even demoted in your job, you have two choices. You can feel bad about it, moan, get depressed and feel that your world has been threatened. Or you can take it as a wake up call to change how you operate at work, use the opportunity to learn something in the new position, or find something else more challenging to put your mind to.

- If you made a bad decision, say you lost money on an investment, don't worry about what might have been – because there is nothing you can do about something that has already happened! Being flexible will allow you to get on with the next option – which might work to your advantage.

Holistic Help

- The rigid tree breaks in the wind, while the flexible one bends with the wind and springs back. This is an image that works well as a visualization designed to create a flexible approach.

MOOD SWINGS

Common causes of mood swings are hormone imbalances, for instance in pre-menstrual women and teenagers, and low-blood sugar due to irregular or unhealthy eating. However, mood swings can also be an effect of stress and feelings of anxiety. The feeling that you cannot seem to control your moods – one minute you're happy the next you are going off the deep end at someone – can further deepen that stress and anxiety. There are a number of steps you can take to regain a sense of balance.

Top Tips

■ Mood swings can be an indication that you do not know your own mind and that you need to sort out what the problem is. Work on setting your priorities so that you are more comfortable about the demands that are being made on you or that you are making of yourself. You might be reacting, in a seemingly irrational way, because you are resentful of how you are having to spend your time. You might not be brave enough to state this to others, or to yourself, and so your resentment comes out as moodiness. Once you isolate the problem, you will be well on the way to stabilizing your moodiness.

■ Beware of using moodiness as a tool such as to avoid unpleasant tasks. 'I am in a mood so don't even think of asking me to ...' If this becomes a habit, it will cause long-term communication problems and may become an unwelcome facet of your personality. If there are things you do not wish to do, it is better to get into the habit of saying it straight 'I don't want to ... because ... ' or simply 'I am busy right now'. Clear communication will cut across the frustrations caused by mere moodiness.

■ If you find that mood swings come with alarming regularity when you are pre-menstrual, then they are linked to your monthly hormonal cycles (see Pre-menstrual Health page 116). Regular exercise will release a steady stream of endorphins to calm moods, and supplements such as the herb *Agnus Castus* and *B6* and *magnesium* are renowned for restoring calm feelings pre-menstrually.

■ Dependency on any substance can worsen mood swings. If you drink alcohol regularly, take drugs, or even consume large amounts of caffeine, this may affect your moods adversely. Reduce your intake of these stimulants gradually.

More Hints

■ If you are the parent of a teenager then you will know that mood swings in teenagers go with the territory. But be aware that mood swings are not simply physiological and might indicate an urgent need to talk. Although teenagers often find it difficult to ask for help, they still need to talk through problems. Be prepared for subjects that you don't feel comfortable with such as experimentation with drugs, eating disorders or uncertainties about sexuality. Or it may be more mundane (but important to the teenager) and involve acne, exams or the course of true love.

■ Mood swings in an adult can be just as much a message for a need to communicate. Lend a friendly ear.

■ Times of transition can lead to a roller-coaster of moods even when you think you are of an age to be over them. Divorce, mid-life crisis, menopause and retirement are all potential triggers for mood swings that can take you by surprise. See Stages of Life page 205.

Holistic Help

■ The brain needs a steady supply of glucose and nutrients and, if it does not get these, it responds with unpredictable behaviour. Your mood swings could easily be linked to an irregular diet which is producing unfavourable blood sugar control. Eating a wholefood diet and reducing dependency on sugary foods, stimulants, such as coffee, colas, and alcohol, as well as refined carbohydrates such as white bread and rice, can have a dramatically positive effect on mood swings (see Food and Mood page 144).

- Important nutrients for brain health and balancing moods come from a healthy diet, but you may want to boost with supplements. The most useful are the B-complex vitamins (50 mg daily), the mineral selenium (200mcg), zinc (25mg), magnesium (250mg) and the fatty acids found in fish oils (take sufficient supplements to achieve 1–1.5 grams of EPA daily).

OVERWHELMED?

If you have a sinking feeling that you have just too much to do and can't cope, then you need to take some time to find the source of such overwhelming feelings. Once you know what is causing this feeling you can change things around in a short time.

Top Tips

- The first step is to work out if your sense of being overwhelmed is actual or perceived. In a quiet place where you will not be interrupted, commit to paper all the things you are feeling overwhelmed by. Concentrate on detail and put everything down as you think of it. You can put it in some sort of order later. Put a number from 1 to 10 next to each item to grade the degree of overwhelm you are feeling.

- Concentrate on the items you have scored 6 and above. Ask yourself if they are principally things you have to do or scheduling problems (such as reports to finish, getting across town in time to pick up the children from school) or are they emotional issues (such as how you can communicate with a parent). Some of these may be both emotional and practical, such as an impending divorce.

- Work out how you can resolve these challenges using the relevant sections of this book. Remember to set aside sufficient time to work through each item. You may find it easier to work on the practical issues first using a logical step-by-step approach. This can give you a much-needed sense of achievement. Or you may find that you need to address the emotional issues before you are freed up mentally to deal with the practical. Either way you can make a plan.

- Tell those who need to know that you are feeling overwhelmed and that you need to work it through. Your partner, boss and close friends may be supportive and instinctively back off until you are feeling better about things, or they may be a part of the problem and you need to explain to them how they can help.

- If you perceive that you just don't have the mental or physical stamina to address the items on your list, your sense of overwhelm might be coming from a degree of depression. Turn to page 138 for information about this (but also read on in this section for more hints).

- To reduce the possibility of overwhelm in the future, work out if you habitually set yourself unrealistic targets in terms of practical tasks and goals, and in your relationships with other people. Are you setting yourself up to be overwhelmed and for disappointment and failure? Are you able to say 'no', not just to other people but also to yourself? (You may be your own hardest taskmaster!)

More Hints

- Your sense of overwhelm may be coming from stimulus fatigue. For instance, if you are the sort of person who has stacks of journals to read through for work, but never get to them, or your heart sinks when you switch on your e-mails and are accosted by the list, you might need to do something about this. Become rigorous about binning junk mail, asking people who send round-robin e-mails not to do so, cancelling subscriptions to magazines you don't read and so on. You can also cancel your daily paper, lose the TV and turn off your mobile phone for a while. You'll be amazed by how little you really miss them and by how much this can simplify your life.

- Clear the decks. All the items on the list you created (in the first point in Top Tips) with a rating of 5 and below might not be the most important contributors to your sense of being overwhelmed but they will certainly slow your progress. If you are able to set aside a couple of days (take time off work if necessary) to systematically work through them, using the principles in Order Out Of Chaos, page 29, or Communication Skills, page 181, you will feel better and be able to focus on the big issues. With many of these items you will just have to steam through them and not be a perfectionist about how you achieve them. If you have five thank you letters to write, don't do that but pick up the phone and say thanks. If you are committed to doing some things but need the spare time, and in any case you are not in the mood for them, cancel (clearing time in your diary can be a huge help).

- Even if depression is a feature of your sense of being overwhelmed, you can still work through the practical, rather than emotional, aspects of the feeling. By doing small things to help, you can slowly gain a sense of control and remotivate yourself.

- Read *Life Was Never Meant To Be A Struggle* by Stuart Wilde (Hay House, Australia www.hayhouse.com) – this is a small book, with some tough talking and home truths, but it gets straight to the point!

Holistic Help

- Nutmeg is a warming spice that is helpful for settling nerves. If you feel 'strung out' put ¼ teaspoon of the ground spice into warm water and drink down (do not use more than this because in high doses nutmeg has hallucinogenic qualities that can be unpleasant).

- Aromatherapy has several solutions to help you feel calmer – experiment with clary sage, frankincense, lavender and ylang ylang.

PANIC ATTACKS

Panic attacks are a severe form of anxiety and can come on without any warning. Symptoms can include palpitations, a pounding heart, restricted breathing, the shakes, nausea, sweating, confused thinking and feelings of terror. When they first come on, they can be so unsettling that the person thinks they are about to die. Some people will try to hide the fact that they are having a panic attack because they are embarrassed. Panic attacks can worsen problems with self-esteem as you feel out of control. If they continue, they can seriously interfere with daily life. There is a lot you can do to get yourself through a panic attack and to eliminate them in the long run.

Top Tips

■ Panic attacks can be a sign that the stress in your life is getting out of control. Use all the techniques in this book that seem relevant, but also seek counselling. Your doctor may be willing to prescribe counselling on the NHS.

■ Cognitive Thinking is particularly successful at treating those with panic attacks as it alters the way you handle a situation (see page 219).

■ Initially avoid situations you know are most likely to bring on a panic attack (say on the tube or a crowded room). However, by taking this approach alone you run the risk of creating a full-blown phobia, so eventually you will need to address this with counselling.

■ Relaxation classes can make all the difference to the frequency and severity of panic attacks as well as controlling them when they happen. Check out your local yoga, Pilates or autogenic training facilities.

More Hints

■ If you are over-breathing (hyperventilating) emergency measures include breathing into a paper bag for only a few minutes or, more discretely, into your hands. You can also exercise the major muscle groups by, for instance, pacing up and down.

■ In the longer term, practice steady breathing on a regular basis so you know what it feels like. Slowly inhale though your nose, low down into your tummy (without lifting your chest), easily and regularly. Exhale. Avoid holding your breath and sighing. Do not do deep breathing exercises if you are in danger of over-breathing.

■ If you find that you get palpitations, your *magnesium* levels might be on the low side. Take 400mg daily for two months and then cut back to 250mg with 250mg of *calcium* daily thereafter. Also take 100mg of CoQ10. See if this makes a difference after four months.

■ Contact HOPE (Help Overcome Panic Effects) 020 7729 9418 or www.support4hope.com

Holistic Help

- **Bach Flower** *Rescue Remedy* has a good track record with helping at the moment a panic attack is about come on. Keep some with you all the time.

- The aromatherapy oils most useful for quelling panic attacks are clary sage, frankincense, lavender and ylang ylang.

POSTNATAL DEPRESSION

Postnatal depression can cover anything from feeling weepy to severe depression. The more serious forms are fairly rare, but the milder forms are fairly common and between five to ten per cent of new mothers are affected. Because this comes at a time when they are expected to be feeling boundless joy at having a new baby, this is also usually bound up with tremendous feelings of guilt. The causes of having the 'baby blues' are unknown but could be tied into hormonal shifts, a difficult birth, fears surrounding having a baby, the structure at home and nutritional status. One of the concerns surrounding postnatal depression is that it might have a knock-on effect by reducing the ability of the mother to bond with her baby. It is also inevitably an additional stress for partners and other family members.

Top Tips

- Having good support at home lowers the chance of experiencing postnatal depression. If you can say 'I'd like to take a bath now or have a break for an hour, please take the baby for a while' there is obviously less pressure on you.

- You need to do your best to get at least one proper rest each day, during the daytime, in the week after the birth.

- If you feel like crying, let yourself. You will have to explain this to your partner, but the first few days after birth are a roller coaster of emotions and hormones that can make women weepy.

- Crying babies and sleeplessness are difficult at the best of times, but when affected by postnatal depression it can just be that extra pressure that makes it seem unbearable. Finding ways to minimize crying and to get your baby into a regular sleeping pattern can be an enormous boon. If you can, get your partner or a close friend to take over one night feed. Read *Solve Your Child's Sleep Problems* by Dr Richard Ferber (Dorling Kindersley). For help when babies cry excessively, contact **Cry-Sis**, 020 7404 5011.

- Baby massage has an excellent track record for relieving the effects of postnatal depression, as a more relaxed baby will cause you less stress. Baby massage also helps babies with trapped wind and colic. You can find out more from the International Association of Infant Massage on 020 8591 1399 or www.iaim.org.uk or ask your health visitor for local classes or check out *Baby Massage: The Calming Power of Touch* by Dr Alan Bainbridge (Dorling Kindersley).

More Hints

■ Don't make the situation harder for yourself by thinking that you have to be the perfect mother. There is no such thing.

■ Some babies just cry more than others. Conventional wisdom seems to be that if you run to the baby all the time it sets up a pattern of reward for crying which perpetuates the cycle. But if you don't have the mental resources to work on establishing a new pattern, it might be simplest to keep the baby happy with close contact. You could invest in a sling and keep your baby close to you most of the time. (Everyone around you will have opinions about this but there is no right or wrong, just what feels best to you.)

■ Work on understanding your baby and his or her needs by observation. Focus particularly on the communication between the two of you. Avoid using terms like 'he's a difficult baby' or 'I can't seem to get to grips with what she wants' in order that you don't attach a 'tag' that self-perpetuates to become a fact. To help you understand your baby, read *The Social Baby* by Lynne Murray and Liz Andrews (The Children's Project Ltd).

■ Single mothers coping on their own can find it particularly difficult to cope with postnatal depression. If you are in this situation, do your utmost to find someone who can help you out – a relative, a friend or a kindly neighbour. Some older people who are themselves living on their own might be happy to become surrogate grandparents and you can find out more via www.lamaze.com (though I would always advise you to be sensibly cautious about strangers).

■ Don't forget that you can speak to your midwife, district nurse or health visitor about how you are feeling. They should also be able to tell you about support groups in your area. Contact your local branch of the NCT (National Childbirth Trust) who usually run social get-togethers for new mothers. Sharing problems with others in the same boat can bring relief.

■ When breastfeeding, it may not be possible to take antidepressant or sleeping medication which means that using diet might be a more valuable way forward (see below). If you have severe postnatal depression, it may be suggested that you switch from breast to bottle in order to take medication.

■ You can find out about postnatal depression by sending a large SAE marked 'PD' to **WellBeing**, 27 Sussex Place, London NW1 4SP , www.allaboutparents.com

■ At all times remember that postnatal depression does not go on for ever and you will recover.

■ See Baby Boom page 173.

Holistic Help – Diet

■ Well nourished mothers are less likely to be affected by postnatal depression than those who are less well nourished. The time to really think about this is during pregnancy. However, if you are in the throws of depression, it is not too late to start nurturing yourself with a healthy diet (see Healthy Eating page 98). Simply changing the way you eat will make you feel that you are doing something positive and make you feel better about yourself.

■ If your baby is particularly irritable and colicky, you might find that he or she is reacting to substances in your breast milk or in bottle milk. Commonly, babies react to garlic and onions in the mother's diet, and also to undigested wheat proteins and milk proteins. It can be worth a two week period of avoiding these to see if it makes a difference. Another possibility is lactose intolerance and you can add lactase (milk sugar digesting enzymes) to made up formula milk or to expressed breast milk. You can get these enzymes from **Colief** (0800 028 1187 or www.colief.com) or **Biocare** (see Useful Resources page 235). A baby who is less windy will make for a much happier mother!

■ If you are breast-feeding a colicky baby, space out the feeds as 'feeding on demand' might worsen colic. Also feed from just one breast each time.

Holistic Help – Supplements

■ *Zinc* is an important nutrient to help normalize mood and depression, including postnatally. In the last trimester, the baby uses up large amounts, and maternal reserves of this essential mineral can plummet. Take 25mg daily.

■ Take a 50mg *B-vitamin complex* to help to improve brain function, and also to help the zinc work efficiently. There is some concern about B6 during breast-feeding but this is at a much larger dose.

■ The fatty acids found in fish oils are vital for proper brain function and help to reduce depression. If you are not eating much oily fish make sure you take 2g of *fish oil supplements* daily.

■ The vitamin and mineral supplements suggested here are safe to use when breast-feeding but avoid herbal supplements at this time. If you are bottle-feeding, you can go ahead and use herbal supplements suitable for depression such as *St John's wort* or *Kava kava* (see warning page 234).

RESTLESSNESS AND HYPERACTIVITY

Finding it difficult to relax can pervade every area of life. If you are keyed up and always on the go, you may find that even during your down time, you are living on adrenaline. You may feel that you are not happy unless you are doing something, feel guilty about resting and even be a bit manic on holidays. Your restlessness might be a creative force for good and many people will undoubtedly envy your apparent energy levels. However, if you are wearing yourself out, take heed and actively learn to relax so that you can slow down from time to time. If you are twitchy and find it difficult to rest, here are some ways to help.

Top Tips

■ Work consciously at slowing down your speech. Talking more slowly slows down your breathing and heart rate and allows you to think more clearly.

■ Do at least one thing each day in slow motion and really savour the experience. In doing this, you will learn to focus and appreciate things more. See mindfulness in Meditation page 224.

■ You might be doing a lot, but are you enjoying what you do? Ask yourself this question at regular intervals. It is often easy to be busy for busy's sake. Cut out activities that do not gratify you.

■ Categorically avoid doing more than one thing at a time.

■ Ask others who are close to you to tell you every time they see you fidgeting, your eyes wandering off to the next thing you are thinking of, or if you are pacing the room. Awareness will help you to relax more easily.

More Hints

■ Focus your energy on finding out how to relax. This may seem a contradiction in terms but you can divert your restlessness wherever you please. Check out relaxation classes and exercise classes such as yoga and Pilates, which have a calming effect (see Useful Resources page 234).

■ Make a strict cut off time beyond which you will not do anything more active than take a warm bath or read a book. Restlessness can be a habit that needs to be broken and by making firm rules you can reset your habits.

■ If your brain is always buzzing with the next job to do you might not be able to focus on what you are doing at the moment. This can lead to errors and not enjoying the moment. People around you might be irritated because you are not really participating in your time with them. See the tips under Concentration and Memory page 85.

■ Your restlessness may be linked to Anxiety (see page 135) and Guilt (see page 148). You might be overcompensating for low self-esteem (see page 169) by doing more than others around you. This never quite works because if you don't deal with the underlying self-esteem, no amount of activity will satisfy you.

■ Drugs such as amphetamines (speed), appetite suppressants, and cocaine have the effect of increasing restlessness. You may think that you are doing fine and appearing normal while able to cope with more things in your life, but in the end drugs do not solve the problem of having too much to do or overcoming obstacles in your life.

Holistic Help – Diet

■ You may be hyped up by too many sugary foods in your diet, or by ingesting too much caffeine from coffee or colas. Reducing your intake of these will combat that buzzy, distracted feeling.

- A high percentage of children who are hyperactive and who are diagnosed with attention deficit disorder (ADD or ADHD) can be very successfully treated with diet and nutritional intervention. There may be many factors to treating ADD/ADHD but the triggers are often dietary and involve poor nutrient status (zinc and essential fatty acids particularly), caffeine, sugar, food colourings and other additives, and food sensitivities. It is best to get specialist advice on this to ensure a balanced diet and safe use of any supplements. Contact the Hyperactive Children's Support Group 01903 725 182 or www.hacsg.org.uk

- Drink calming herbal teas such as camomile, vervain or lemon balm.

Holistic Help – Supplements

- Toxicity from lead can interfere with normal nerve functioning and is sufficiently bad to affect one in ten children (and therefore probably adults). Have your water pipes checked by your local water board to see if they are lead and need changing. To help detoxify lead and other heavy metals such as cadmium take a supplement containing 25mg *zinc*, 200mg *magnesium*, 400mg *calcium* (this advice is for adults). Also take *pectin* (fruit fibre) and add *seaweed seasoning* to your food (for alginic acid) both available from health food shops. Cigarette smoke is a significant source of heavy metals.

- Essential fatty acids are vital for normalizing brain function and have a good track record with hyperactive children. Adults also need these essential fats. Taking a high dosage of *EPA*, say 2g a day over at least three months may have a calming effect. EPA is found is *fish oil supplements*.

- Restless leg syndrome (Ekbom's syndrome) can involve involuntary twitching of the legs and make you seem hyper. Caffeine is a major culprit, and too much sugar and alcohol can contribute. Eating a good quality diet, with at least five helpings of fresh fruit and vegetables a day can be a tremendous help (see Healthy Eating page 98). *Magnesium* is vital for proper nerve function and works well for involuntary muscle twitches. Take 400mg daily for three months and then reduce to 250mg daily. A 50mg *B-complex* and 800ius of *vitamin E (d-alpha tocopherol)* daily will support this regime (do not take high doses of vitamin E if you are on blood thinning medication). If you are anaemic, you will need iron which also helps. Magnets worn in socks at night can help reduce twitching. (These are available from www.homediscsuk.com or 0161 798 5885.)

SELF-ESTEEM

Feeling good about who we are is the key to dealing with many aspects of stress, yet low self-esteem is a widespread feeling. Self-esteem is the subject of many books and some people find that spending time on researching and assessing their self-esteem is a great help towards understanding themselves both emotionally and behaviourally. Throughout this book, there is much discussion on why we end up short changing ourselves, as well as a variety of suggestions aimed at improving self-esteem. Knowing who you are is a fundamental aspect of stress busting – raising your self awareness about how much you like yourself and why you are doing what you are doing will help you to work on your self-esteem. In this section I have concentrated on offering quick-fix advice that can place you firmly on the road to improving your sense of worth.

Top Tips

- If you are in the habit of criticizing yourself, change this by getting into the habit of congratulating yourself instead.

- When you are telling yourself off ('I'm so hopeless,' 'Why am I so thick?') the easiest way to correct yourself is to imagine how it would sound to you if you heard someone else saying this about themselves. You would probably think 'He's being a bit hard on himself' and might even say to that person 'Of course you are not hopeless, thick, etc'. Do this every time you start to do yourself down.

- Other people can whittle away at your self-esteem if you let them. They will be one of the following:

  - of a negative mindset ('I wouldn't do that because the chances of failure are high', 'Don't be surprised if you are disappointed', 'Do you really think that's possible?')

  - predators disguised as friends (for example, your mother saying 'I'm only saying it for your own good dear but don't you think you need to lose a few kilos' or a friend who eggs you on to 'go on have a drink, just one, otherwise you won't enjoy yourself' when you are hoping to have a booze-free week.)

  - bullies.

- You can be firm in your convictions and not swayed by others if you work out in advance why you are doing something, what it means to you to succeed and why you believe it is the right course of action for you to follow. Then negative and tricky people can't trip you up so easily.

- When faced with criticism, say from your boss, there are three likely responses. The low self-esteem response is 'I'm no good and always making a mess of things'. You then feel sad and anxious and react by moping and getting depressed. The denial response is 'He's a pain and always bugging me.' This then makes you angry and frustrated, and openly hostile which then damages your relationship with your boss even further. The positive self-esteem response is 'Here's a chance to learn something'. From a position of security you discuss the issues with your boss, define the problem and find a solution. Your boss is suitably impressed.

- Don't highlight your weaknesses to others, especially if they are likely to remind you of them later. Replace:

  - 'I know I shouldn't be eating this' with 'I'm enjoying this'

– 'Don't mind me banging on about it, sorry if it's boring' with 'I feel strongly about it so I tend to take every opportunity to do something about it'

– 'I'm so disorganized I'll probably drive you crazy' with 'My organizational skill could use a little work, but I do get things done'

– 'OK I'll go on the sailing course though I may sink the boat' with 'Yes, I'd love to learn something new – a real adventure'.

■ Life is a series of lessons. If you don't succeed at something avoid (like the plague) berating yourself for what has happened. Instead do the following.

– Work out what you have learned from the experience (write it down methodically).

– Apply what you have learned and change your tactics if necessary. Keep focusing on your aims.

– Do something about your body language. If you walk around looking defeated, guess what image you will project?

– Just because it doesn't work out it might be nothing to do with you and everything to do with timing – you might call someone just at the point when their dog died and their wife has left them. Does this mean your idea is not good?

– Remember that countless successful people were turned down at some time or other (Fred Astaire, The Beatles). You can gain self-esteem just from the process of having a go at something. Any success you gain is a bonus.

■ People with low self-esteem are often drawn like magnets to partners who will compound the problem. And sometimes people who start off with fairly good self-esteem will find that they are dragged down during the course of a relationship into low self-esteem. Getting back to a state of self-belief is made doubly difficult if someone is always pointing out your faults and making irrational accusations and demands. If you find yourself always subjugating your needs to that of your partner, remind yourself of your own desires and goals. Seek responses that give you respect, autonomy, freedom of thought, mental and physical health, safety, an emotionally stable home for your children. Give yourself small, manageable steps and goals along the way and you will get your self-esteem back in stronger and better shape than ever before.

More Hints

■ Invest in yourself – you are worth it. Don't ask yourself the question 'Can I afford it?' Ask yourself 'Can I afford not to?' At a most basic level, this could mean treating yourself to a beauty treatment. You might buy time by hiring some home help. You could sign up for something that interests you. Pay for someone to promote your business.

■ Take pleasure in small victories and do not belittle their importance.

■ If someone says something to you which stings and tugs at your self-esteem, instead of going home and diving into the ice cream tub (and further punishing yourself) work out, in your own time, your response and let them know in what way they were hurtful. If you are too shy to confront them, write a small note. Avoid recrimination but let them know how they can avoid hurting you in future (in other words a positive outcome).

■ In addition to doing the above, work out why you have been upset by their words or actions and what you can learn from it. You might have interpreted an innocent comment as a poisonous one. Yet you might think of this as confirmation of any self-loathing you feel. Work with cognitive thinking (see page 219) to find more appropriate ways of interpreting seemingly negative comments.

■ There are times when we all respond more acutely to hurts. If you're already feeling low, because a series of things has gone wrong recently, then a comment that would have been water off a duck's back at some other time, might really hurt. Use this knowledge to balance your reaction and acknowledge that you need to get through this current phase intact. This can help to put the 'hurt' into perspective.

■ Avoid regrets and wishful thinking ' If only I had...', 'Why did it have to happen to me? ...', 'I wish I was able to...'

■ It is easy to numb the pain of low self-esteem with drink or drugs, by focusing all available emotional energy into others (such as your children), or throwing yourself into non-stop activity. If you are doing any of these, stop, take a deep breath and start at the top of this section again.

■ Read *Self Esteem* by Gael Lindenfield (Thorsons).

Holistic Help
■ Allow miracles into your life.

CHAPTER 5

RELATIONSHIPS

Relationships can be a source of empowerment, comfort and joy when all is going well, but at times they can also be the cause of stress and conflict in our lives. Today, the wider family such as parents, grandparents or cousins, the people who often know you best, may live far away. Friends may be so busy with their own lives that they don't have time for you when you need them. Daily routines are as much dictated by our working lives as by the needs of our personal relationships leaving us with a feeling that there is not enough time to simply enjoy each other's company. Finding ways to take time out to listen to others, spend time with them and to enjoy spontaneous pleasures as they happen enhances and enriches our relationships.

BABY BOOM

Babies can be a source of great joy, but they can also turn their unsuspecting parents' world upside down. How much trouble can a baby be? They're little, they're cute and they sleep a lot. Of course they are lovely but nobody is ever fully prepared for the difference a baby will make to daily life. Babies are necessarily selfish and utterly dependent on you. This means that your needs go out of the window for quite a while, and making this adjustment can be stressful for modern parents. It helps if you can acknowledge the difficulties you are experiencing which doesn't make you any less loving or devoted a parent. Simply recognizing that you will be able, as the baby grows, to get a little balance back into your life can go a long way to reducing the tensions you might be feeling.

Top Tips

- No one can be a perfect parent at all times. Babies don't require perfection, they require love.

- Before you had a baby, you and your partner enjoyed each other's company as adults without any distractions. Having a baby enhances the relationship for many parents, but for some they begin to forget why they originally enjoyed spending time together. Take time out at least once a week, by asking a grandparent to take over or booking a baby sitter, and go out together to do something you always enjoyed doing as a couple.

- Do not be afraid to ask others for help when you need it. In days of old, we had the luxury of extended families, but now it is no longer automatic that granny or older cousins stay home and look after the children. If you need advice, ask for it. If you need a few hours, ask if you can trade babysitting duties with a friend. Above all, if you are a single parent, either by design, by accident or because it has been thrust upon you, you will need time to yourself occasionally and the only way you are likely to get this is if you plan for it and seek help. If you have no immediate family, you might find suitable friends at playgroups.

■ When you are at the end of your tether with your child (it happens to us all), take a deep breath and remind yourself that children have not been specifically designed to drive you wild. Find something to divert you all away from the drama in hand. Rising tensions are often forgotten about quite quickly if you put a constructive spin on the situation by finding something else to think about (this is not the same as bribery or giving in). (See Kids-zone page 21 for more tips.)

■ Sleep deprivation has to be one of the most difficult things to deal with in the early years (at least it was for me!). If you have a partner, negotiate to have one or two nights a week where you each have a full night of sleep while the other is on duty. Work at establishing a good sleeping pattern in your baby (see helpful tips for both yourself and your baby in Sleep Quality page 126).

■ It is common for older siblings to feel put out when a new baby arrives and takes much of the attention. They may feel displaced as they are no longer the baby of the family. Prepare for the new baby's arrival by letting your older children know that it is THEIR baby as well, and involve them in some of the planning and decision making. Put some time aside for them and let them know that this is your special time together.

■ When you are ready to resume a sexual relationship with your partner, it can seem as if the baby times its crying just as passions are aroused. Rather than get frustrated about this, aim to retain a sense of humour. Sex does not always have to be involve penetration. Remember the pleasure of affectionate kissing, cuddling and massaging. There are other approaches you can try to re-establish intimacy. Make love in the afternoon, when baby is sleeping, or go out on a date where you dress up and set the scene for romance.

■ It is common for one parent (usually the father) to feel resentful of the amount of time lavished on the baby. While this may seem an irrational feeling, it is often a deeply felt one. Talking about these feelings can help to prevent resentments building up. Again, make time for your partner either by going out if you have a babysitter, or simply by cuddling up on the sofa during a lull.

■ Some new parents may experience the new baby as an added burden on already stretched finances. Remember that babies really do grow incredibly fast and most baby items only last for a very short while. Pick new items that will really last a long time, and for the rest you can get very good second hand items (as long as they are safe).

■ Many people agonize about the size of their families, worrying about which is the best number of children to have. You will find that everyone has an opinion – either urging you on to have more, or chastizing you for having too many. In truth all sizes of families have their benefits and disadvantages. The fewer children you have, the more time, energy and money you will have for them individually, the more children you have, the more they can support each other. The wellbeing of a family depends upon so many variables: love, money, extended family, and the number of children are only some factors of many. Don't feel pressurized either way and follow your own instincts.

■ The effect on the family of having a baby who has a disorder of some kind depends very much on the views of the family, the stability of the parents' relationship, and on the other children in the family. Do not struggle alone as there are so many support groups available. Initially your doctor will be able to direct you to appropriate health care, but you will also be able to find a lot of other information from relevant groups, libraries and on the Internet. Understanding the issues surrounding, say, the autistic spectrum or cystic fibrosis, will help you to manage the situation to the best advantage of your child and the rest of the family.

Holistic Help

■ *St John's wort* also helps with mild depression, but do not take this if you are breast-feeding. See Postnatal Depression page 165.

■ A few drops of *Lavender* essential oil in the bath helps with relaxation and tension, as well as making you feel that you are taking care of yourself.

■ If you are hoping for children, but have not yet been able to conceive, this may be a considerable source of anxiety. Once you have been checked medically to make sure there are no physical reasons, such as blocked fallopian tubes, advanced endometriosis or genetic disorders, you might benefit from contacting **Foresight** who can take you through a nutritional programme designed to increase fertility in both partners contact 01483 427839 or www.foresight-preconception.org.uk

BEREAVEMENT

The death of a partner, close relative or friend is one of the most traumatic events in our lives. The death of a parent can release a storm of emotions and guilt, regrets and anger which often need to find an outlet. Crying, talking to friends or a counsellor and keeping active are all good ways to deal with grief.

Top Tips

■ If the person has been ill for some time, some mourning may have been done during the illness. Although the death is still experienced as a hugely sad event, the sadness may be mingled with feelings of relief. This can then engender feelings of guilt. Think of all the positive moments in your relationship together and create a space in your mind to store all the happy memories you shared with that person.

■ The sheer volume of things to take care of after someone dies can delay the grieving period. Arranging funerals, death certificates, dealing with probate, cancelling and transferring health policies and bank accounts, disposing of property and notifying people is a lot of work. Be aware that when all the activity stops, grieving and depression often then set in. Stay moderately active, go back to work if you feel you can, instead of having to deal with the enormous contrast between having lots to do and then nothing.

■ Often people are very kind and are prepared to be called on and make this known to you. However, just a few short months later it can seem as if everyone thinks it is business as usual, when this may be a time when you need support. Don't be afraid to ask for help at this time.

■ Children can really help you to come through the process of grieving faster because of the need to keep their lives as normal as possible. However, if you feel that you are not coping well and that the children are affected, you must ask for help with activities and for some time out.

More Hints

■ Adjusting to the fact that someone has died can sometimes be helped by viewing the body. Sometimes people keep children from this as they worry that it is too macabre or insensitive, but it can be a great help if handled properly. It depends on the child and the circumstances, but it is an option to consider.

■ Children usually need special handling to help them through the experience of losing a loved one. If they have lost a parent or sibling it is obvious, to most people, that a child will need help through this, but they also need help if the deceased is more distant such as a grandparent or school friend. Not only do they need to deal with feelings about not seeing that person again and learning coping skills, but they also may have many questions around the whole issue of mortality and even their own mortality, which can be quite scary. They may not express their feelings and so it may need to be teased out of them. Always be willing to listen, and answer questions honestly at a level they can understand depending on their age. Keep the person's memory alive with framed photos, conversation and stories.

■ Contact Cruse Bereavement 0870 167 1677 (www.crusebereavementcare.org.uk).

■ Contact The Compassionate Friend 0117 953 9639 (www.tcf.org.uk).

Holistic Help

■ Many people gain great comfort from their spiritual advisors.

■ Thinking about death as a part of the cycle of life may help.

■ People often fall ill when bereaved. Now, more than ever, you need to look after yourself. Although you may not feel like it, remember to eat at least one meal daily with protein such as eggs, chicken or fish. You will need your strength to take you through this time.

■ Do not allow bitter feelings to take a hold, as this is always going to cost more emotionally than the spirit can deal with. Feeling sad and missing someone is appropriate, as are feelings of depression and anger for a while, but bitterness will just eat you up.

■ Homeopathic *Ignatia 30c* and **Bach Flower** *Star of Bethlehem remedy* are useful for reducing feelings of shock and grief.

BROKEN HEART

Your doctor may shoo you away if you say you have a broken heart or at best give you a course of antidepressants, but most people will at some time or other use the expression to define how they are feeling. A broken heart is a kind of shorthand for a host of stressful feelings, including hurt, severing of a relationship (even if contact is still maintained), great disappointment, and an emotional vacuum. Although a broken heart is most commonly associated with a broken romance, your heart could be just as easily be broken by a parent or step-parent who leaves the home, a friend who betrays the friendship, or any other significant person.

Top Tips

- There is a degree to which the afflicted person's self-esteem is bound up with the 'offending' person. The term 'broken heart' also implies a sense that there is an unfinished business and maybe a hope that love can be rekindled. This makes it hard to draw a line under the relationship but this is precisely what has to happen.

- Often the end of a relationship just leaves a vacuum of activity that needs to be filled. You might be reminded of the person all the time and feel that this is yet more evidence of your broken heart. However, it might be that you simply don't know how to keep yourself occupied in other ways. Concentrate on other activities, you need to focus on getting busy again.

- The most important long-term resolution to a broken heart is to deal with your self-esteem and to work out why your self-worth is bound up with this other person and why rejection cuts so deep. This is no quick-fix solution but it is a more lasting one. (See Self-Esteem page 169.)

More Hints

- The most straightforward resolution for a broken heart (but this is a bit of a cop out as it doesn't address the underlying issues) is another relationship. Time does heal and there truly are plenty more 'fish in the sea'. (See Finding a Mate page 186.)

- The quicker you let go of your old attachment, the sooner you will find someone else in your life.

- Avoid bitterness resulting from a broken heart – it will only eat you up. Bitterness is like an uncontrollable emotional cancer. Feel sorrow or even anger for a while, but then determine to move on.

Holistic Help

- Mending a broken heart is something most of us have to do at some time or other. Time is, indeed, a great healer, as is falling in love again! Until one of these two takes effect, you could experiment on some alternative therapies. At the top of the list is always the calming practices of yoga, t'ai chi or meditation, but there are others you could experiment with. Herbalists recommend hawthorn to open up the heart, lemon balm for its calming influence or St John's wort to head off mild to moderate depression. Aromatherapists will offer lavender or rose, colour therapists also rate the colour rose which softens pain, and will add in violet to restore self-respect while energy therapists will work on the heart chakra.

CELEBRATION TIMES

When families are thrown together, seemingly for joyous occasions, tensions and family dynamics can actually lead to quite a few stresses. Suicides and divorce rates are known to rise at Christmas more than at any other time of year. Among the many reasons for this is the fact that families are not used to being in close proximity to each other any more, and haven't acquired the skills to deal with the resentments and squabbles that are part of every day life. Christmas, like many other celebrations, is also a time when we are supposed to be happy, an expectation that we may feel we cannot meet, amplifying any feelings of depression. Christmas is also a time of financial stress.

■ If you know that a member of your family has a problem, then it might be advisable to pre-empt a worsening of relations by helping them to express their feelings before the holiday-time starts.

■ If you are the one that ends up doing all the catering at family gatherings, but you feel resentful about it, you can change this. Let everyone know, beforehand, what his or her responsibilities will be. They might be asked to bring a pre-cooked dish, to wash up, do the shopping or clear away at certain times.

■ At family gatherings such as Christmas and weddings everyone has an opinion about how things should be run, but not everyone pulls their weight. Decide in advance who the 'queen bee' is going to be, and who the 'worker bees' are going to be – you can take this in a rota basis if you wish. The one rule is that what the queen bee says goes, and the worker bees keep quiet with any comments and just help out. This saves a great deal of dissent.

■ Buying presents for someone should be a joy as you think about what that person would really enjoy receiving. Ideally it is a time when you show thoughtfulness and understanding of that person. But in reality we trawl around shops with a blank mind, wondering what on earth we can buy, end up buying something in desperation and spending more than we can afford. Here is a guide to pain-free present buying.

– Keep a list at the back of your diary or notebook with the names of those who are nearest and dearest to you. If they happen to mention something they need, you have a brainwave, or you see something ideal in the shops, make a note next to their name, so come birthdays, or other celebration times, you have a ready-made list.

– Keep a drawer of gifts. When you see something particularly nice or of good value, buy it and keep it in your stockpile. On birthdays and other occasions you can look through for something that person might like.

– If you have children, you will probably spend many weekends ferrying them to birthday parties, and they are usually all within the same age group which means they usually more or less like the same things. Buy presents for these, within your budget, in bulk and you won't have any last minute panics.

– Christmas can be extraordinarily expensive and, be honest, how many gifts do you remember as being things you really want? Why not draw up a present-exclusion-zone agreement? Only buy presents for children and ask everyone to only bring things that you can all enjoy together over the holiday period such as a game, some chocolates, wine or a cake. This will save everyone a fortune and a considerable amount of present-buying stress, and you can focus on seasonal fun instead of a consumer nightmare. Alternatively, make sure everyone has a stocking or pillow case and put an upper limit of, say, £5, on gifts and throw them all in the relevant stocking for a light-hearted, not too serious, present opening time.

CO-HABITING AND MARRIAGE

You've made that momentous decision to set up home together and possibly made the commitment of marriage. Making it work from the very beginning involves give and take, and respect for the other person. But as you each get caught up in busy lives, rushing around and getting things done, you can forget to stop and think about the relationship until it becomes a priority. It is so easy to take a partner for granted, and then find that the relationship has been damaged. Such simple things as cherishing those around us, listening to a partner's memories, saying 'I love you...' we can all do these things, and maybe then we would enjoy our relationships more.

Top Tips

■ At the stage in a relationship when you are wearing rose-tinted spectacles, it is easy to gloss over possible sources of difficulty, but it is as well to think about them before they become a source of dissent. You may not think this is very romantic, but it never hurts to sort out an agreement about the details of an arrangement. It is common to have a loose understanding of what the other person wants, but to sit down and talk about the specifics and to write them down is a useful approach. These are some of the things you could cover:

– money – who pays for what, how finances are to be organized (i.e. joint or separate or household bank accounts)

– work – who has what work ambitions and how much time you might actually be able to spend together

- kids – who will look after them if you have them, how many you want (or if you want them at all), when you want them. (It is even a good idea to discover each other's attitude to child rearing and issues such how you would handle a child with physical or mental challenges)

- social life – how much or how little you both enjoy going out, how you feel about time out with others (the regular Saturday football match or visiting in-laws)

- cooking and cleaning – who does what and how (you may want to hire a cleaner but your partner may think it an extravagance)

- minor details – not so much leaving the lid off the toothpaste or the loo lid up, but any niggles you both need to air (nagging, interfering in-laws, etc)

■ An agreement like this is even valid if you are getting married after having lived together for a while. It is amazing how the act of marriage changes the assumptions that people put on a relationship which, if not voiced, can lead to misunderstandings.

■ Agree between yourselves to take time out to monitor the health of your relationship on a regular basis. Get into the habit of saying what is on both of your minds and listen to each other.

■ If you suppress your emotions in a relationship, the relationship is more likely to suffer, but if you express your emotions in a relationship, the relationship is more likely to thrive.

■ Social and racial barriers are breaking down on all fronts (one statistic I read said that one in eight children under the age of 14 in the UK are mixed race – we have become a real melting pot of cultures, ideas and influences). Nevertheless, inter-racial, cross-faith and cross-cultural relationships can present particular challenges. Crossing social classes can also present hurdles.

- When you begin to think about long term commitment make sure that you both fully understand what you are entering in to.

- Talk to others who have converted to your partner's faith, or not (depending on what you are planning).

- Be as open as you can with family and friends. They might have genuine concerns, or even hidden prejudices, that may take you by surprise and which need talking through.

- Some practical issues may become more important as time progresses such as different dietary requirements and dress and behaviour codes, particularly if one partner becomes more embedded in their religion as the marriage progresses.

- Family gatherings may need special handling. Even if you are both content and at ease, members of extended families may not be welcoming. If you demonstrate that your relationship is an easy one and stand firm in your love and respect for each other they are most likely to be won round. (Remember you can't please all the people all the time)

- Religious holidays can highlight some of the differences – one way to deal with this is to celebrate those of all relevant faiths and enjoy the diversity.

The solution to all of these is good communication. Build a firm foundation of respect and understanding through mutual consent to bridge any differences which have been inculcated since childhood. Vive la difference!

■ For gay issues see Sexuality page 202.

More Hints

■ Working different shifts from your partner can easily lead to feelings of isolation, and increases the likelihood of a split. Couples that cope well with this will tend to make sure that the time they spend together is highly focused on their relationship, otherwise they just drift apart, having different interests and different social circles.

■ Very few people bat an eyelid these days about couples living together instead of marrying, or having children out of wedlock, but you may have parents who will disapprove. Explain your position to them calmly. You may not be able to win them round but do your best not to get cross – being of a different generation they may see things differently. If you keep the channels of communication open, the chances are high that they will eventually come round.

■ The seven-year-itch is not uncommon (though it could be three or ten years). The solution to this is to retain some romance in the relationship. Take time out for each other, do nice things for each other, court each other, take surprise romantic weekend breaks together, listen to, respect and appreciate each other. Passion may have mellowed, but romance can be kept alive with just a little input.

■ Second marriages often break down because one person is not really over the first one. Make sure you come to terms with the fact that your first marriage is over and that you have moved on.

Holistic Help

■ As music is the food of love, make a point of going to concerts (or operas or musical theatre) together. If this is not possible, spend the occasional evening together without the TV but with music you both enjoy and with the lights restfully dimmed while you just sit and chat.

COMMUNICATION SKILLS

If you are feeling misunderstood by others and can't quite seem to say what you really mean, work on some of these suggestions.

Top Tips

■ Send out clear signals that can't be confused. Being confident about your needs may feel awkward. You might worry that you are being selfish or too assertive, a word that can have negative as well as positive connotations. If you say 'Jane is really assertive' you might simply mean that Jane knows exactly what she wants and how to get it, but many will hear this as Jane is difficult, unyielding and bossy. But being assertive does not mean you do not take into account other people's feelings, rather it means saying what you want as clearly as possible without aggression. Certainly being assertive does not imply that you have to step over other people to get what you want. Bear this in mind when you read the following list.

– Clarify your understanding of the issues before you decide to make your statement (don't be goaded into making pressurized decisions).

– Stand your ground for what you believe in.

– Look for alternative solutions.

– You have the right to say 'no'.

– Say 'no' with conviction.

– Give reasons and not excuses.

– Don't apologize or agonize over refusing.

– Don't get sidetracked.

■ Teach your children the above and they will grow up to be happier, more confident adults and you will encourage clear communication between you as they mature.

■ If you have difficulty getting along with a colleague, friend or member of your family, work on a visualization exercise (see page 222). Spend a few minutes each day, in a quiet meditative state, imagining yourself with this person, and see yourself getting along with that person. Visualize relating to each other using good communication, being honest and harmonious. Really imagine yourself in this situation. Repeat the exercise at least a couple of times a day, and you will find that you slowly begin to improve the relationship. Be aware, however, that you cannot use this technique to control the behaviour of the other person, but are likely to move towards a better understanding by synchronization of thought patterns and body language.

■ Don't blot out communication problems by, say, drinking. Distancing yourself for a bit to get a perspective is fine, and taking time to find the right time to talk is fine, but don't miss the boat, and talk to friends and family about issues that bother you. Don't mind read what their reactions are going to be. Just get on with being honest, and not hurtful.

■ One of the reasons why conversations can escalate into disagreements is that one person feels as if they are being put under a spotlight and interrogated. This can lead to them clamming up. Peppering your conversation with such interrogative words as why, what, how, when, and where may well feel a little uncomfortable for the person on the receiving end. Experiment with the following and see the positive results you get. Wait until the other person has finished speaking (never interrupt). Instead of jumping in with your question say 'And?' instead. Avoid jumping in with a comment or opinion, just say 'And?' (or 'Because?' or 'And this meant?'). These are all leading questions rather than interrogative ones. You can repeat these whenever it seems appropriate in the conversation. You will find that you lead the other person to disclose more information and in a confident and comfortable manner. This is a basic approach used by therapists to encourage people to open up and come up with their own conclusions and answers. This simple way of improving communication is highly effective (it is also great for getting more information out of recalcitrant children).

More Hints

- Chameleon behaviour, changing your personality to please other people, is very draining and destroys self-esteem in the long run. However, mirroring (see page 205) is totally different and allows you to use empathy to tune into other people and build rapport with them. In one, you are out of control and cheat yourself, in the other, you remain in control and true to yourself.

- Show your appreciation of others. It is all too easy to take our nearest and dearest for granted, but small kindnesses will be repaid a hundred-fold. Remember to say thank you, and to tell people how you appreciate them. Do small, nice things for people, especially those you are close to. Send a card, buy some flowers, leave a note saying 'I miss you', run an errand, book some tickets to a concert, or make breakfast in bed.

- Keeping in touch gets more difficult in the busy world in which we live. You would think that with so many means of communication – phones, e-mails, planes – that it would get easier, but it does not seem that way. To make it easy on yourself, keep a stack of beautiful postcards that you can quickly jot a friendly note on and pop in the post. It is so nice to receive something that is not a bill, and lets your friends know you are thinking of them – and it only takes a minute.

- Set aside fifteen minutes to call friends and family. Concentrate on them during this time and free your mind of other tasks. Use the time to arrange your social life.

DIVORCE

Fifty per cent of marriages end in divorce. It is a social epidemic of our times. Given this high statistical probability – though the positive slant is that fifty per cent of marriages last – what can you do to increase the chances of a 'happy' divorce?

Top Tips

- The time leading up to the decision to divorce is often the most difficult. Lack of confidence, worries about what might happen afterwards and bitter arguments can stretch out the misery for ages. Once the decision has been arrived at it can, quite simply, come as a relief. It is often during this time that the real damage is done because then the actual process of divorce can become a way of seeking revenge for one or both partners.

- Before the relationship completely disintegrates, it might be helpful to seek couple or family counselling. These counsellors are adept at helping partners to find the nub of the problem and to guide them to the other end of the tunnel unscathed. Relate is worth contacting on 01788 573 241 or www.relate.org.uk or if alcohol or drugs are contributing to the break up seek out one of the relevant help organizations (see Addictions page 77).

■ Money and custody arrangements are the biggest bones of contention in any divorce – it is worth seriously working at reaching an agreement because otherwise it is the lawyers who clean up.

■ It takes time to get over a divorce – divorce can often be experienced in the same way as a bereavement (see page 175). Allow yourself time to come to terms with the change.

■ Do your best to avoid such destructive emotions as guilt, hate, bitterness, jealousy and blame. Don't spend time worrying about what your ex is getting up to. Work on the need to move on. Introduce some joy into your life on a daily basis, no matter how small or tentative. Re-establish your sense of identity outside the marriage. Plan and set goals (see page 16) to avoid wallowing in the past. Forget what might have been and concentrate on what can be.

■ There are many issues you may have to deal with in the aftermath of a divorce which can take time to work through – many of which are covered in this book such as Money Management page 52 and Loneliness page 192. You may also be facing being a single parent or dealing with being a remote parent.

More Hints

■ Stay hopeful for the future and learn from what went wrong in your previous relationship. Make lists of the lessons learned and what they mean to you.

■ A surprising number of couples who divorce end up getting back together again (viz Taylor and Burton). The divorce may have been too hasty or they might realize that the grass isn't actually greener or that it is easier to fall back into old patterns with someone who is used to them. It is also fairly common for divorcing partners to continue to sleep together through the divorce proceedings as they yo-yo between emotions and uncertainties. If you find yourself in these situations make sure you both consider the messages your children are receiving and that their needs are considered – you don't want to disappoint them.

■ Get in touch with Aquila whose aim it is to help divorced people to get back on their feet. 01892 665 524 or e-mail them – aquliatrust@aol.com

■ Contact the Gingerbread (Association For One Parent Families) 020 7336 8184 or www.gingerbread.org.uk

■ As a father, you might want to contact Families Need Fathers 020 8886 0970 or www.fnf.org.uk

Holistic Help

■ Buy a 'happy divorce' card or throw a party. This is not malicious but a way of expressing humour during a difficult time.

CHILDREN AND DIVORCE

- Helping your children through a divorce is essential and it is ideal if you and your ex-partner can present a united front on at least this score. It may be difficult if the years leading up to the divorce have been turbulent, but it is well worth agreeing on a joint strategy for dealing with the children.

- Ideally, you both need to stay involved in your children's lives. Agreeing on a rota of care and participation in activities helps. If you can provide a united front at events such as school plays or parent/teacher meetings your children will be much happier.

- Make sure that you stick to the same rules about routine, discipline and treats.

- Children will often feel confused, insecure and angry. Even if they feel relief that mummy and daddy are no longer arguing on a daily basis, it is still a time of huge change – one parent may move out and not see them as frequently or it may involve a change of home for them. Keep as many things as you can comforting and familiar. Children respond well to routine, so aim to keep these the same as far as you can.

- However tempted you might feel, do not gripe about your ex-partner to the children.

- If you have managed to keep the turmoil preceding the separation to a minimum and your children are not aware of the discord, it may come as a huge shock to them that the family is splitting up. You will both need to explain the situation to them as openly as possible, avoiding recrimination of each other if at all possible, and being patient about answering their questions.

- Children may not verbalize their confusion and frustration and react in other ways. They might become withdrawn or, at the other end of the scale, disruptive. See this for what it is, and give them every ounce of love you can. If they are, for instance, confused that they are not seeing the other parent for a while, but are not saying so you can suggest to them that they telephone your ex-partner.

- Children often blame themselves for their parents break-up 'If I had been good this would not have happened'. If they find it hard to talk to you about such feelings see if you can ask a relative or family friend whom they feel comfortable speaking to.

- Let the school know what is going on so they can be supportive and watch out for behaviour changes.

- Just because the parents are getting divorced doesn't mean that the children are divorcing half their family. Do everything you can to make sure they stay in contact with grandparents, cousins, aunts and uncles.

- Never involve the children in an emotional tug-of-war by asking them to take sides, you will live to regret it.

FINDING A MATE

The primal urge to pair up drives young and old alike to play the dating game. While many people are content to be single, the acres of print and the hours of prime time TV devoted to the issue of finding a mate and the astounding rise of the dating agency business attests to the fact that many singles are looking for their soulmates. If you find that being single or looking for a mate is stressful – read on!

Top Tips

■ This is most important: to find a companion with whom you can develop a satisfying relationship you need to be happy in your own company in the first place. If you are interested in life and are someone who explores and develops your interests, you will automatically be a more interesting person and more attractive to other people.

■ If you are in a emotional void that you just want to fill with the presence of another person, the search can be fruitless. Potential partners will often back off in the face of such neediness. Happiness through the presence of another person is valid, but it is not the be-all-and-end-all.

■ In the past, people did not need to travel very far to meet a mate, and would often marry someone from their own locality. Often marriages would be arranged by the family or a match maker – in a way this made the choice easier (the less you have to choose from, the easier the decision is!). But the fluid structure of our society means that in the face of overwhelming choice and opportunity many people flounder and there are no set expectations or rules any more. For this reason honesty is always the best policy. If you know what your expectations are, communicate them to the other person so that you can both know if you have common criteria.

■ If you think you have been unlucky in love so far, this is a big message. You have not been unlucky, you need to change your strategy. If you feel that you have a history of attracting the wrong sort of person or you change, chameleon-like, with each new mate who comes along, then you need to do at least one thing different in the future to improve your chances of finding Mr or Ms Right. Go to different places. Network with different people. Develop your interests. Change your criteria of what type of person you are seeking.

■ Ask yourself what you are seeking? If it is romance and commitment, then you are on the lookout for a mate. If it is companionship and someone to share a social life or holidays, perhaps you really need more good friends?

■ Would you know your potential mate when you clap eyes on him or her? You may be unsure of what are the most important qualities you are interested in. Make a list of the important features: intellect, humour, danger, fun, stability, looks, kindness, responsibility. Do you want to go out with drop-dead gorgeous types, but who have a cavalier attitude to life, when the plainer 'frog' down the road is responsible, stable, kind and bright and would be the ideal mate once kissed? The point I am making is that we often idealize our desires, but feel we have to compromise in reality. Once you write down what are truly the most important qualities, you may find that your ideals are different to what you have been attracted to or think you have been seeking. Knowing your most important expectations will help you to spot the right person when they come along.

More Hints

■ If you have broken up with someone, don't convince yourself that this was your one shot at happiness, and that the chances of finding another love are remote. There are millions of people on this planet and there is always going to be someone else out there for you.

■ If you have been in a relationship for a while and now find yourself 'on the market', the prospect of dating can seem quite daunting. When you are on a roll in the dating game, you take these things in your stride but, if you've been out of practice, just the thought of these can be enough to make you feel wobbly. You may have simply forgotten just how much fun it is to meet new people who like you and how good it can make you feel.

■ Go at it slowly, expanding your horizons, get a new haircut to make you feel attractive and sexy, comb through your wardrobe for new combinations of outfits, and enjoy yourself. Dress for yourself, and not for other people. If you are pleased with yourself so will others be.

■ Romance is often a question of timing. You might be ready to fall in love, but is the object of your dreams also ready? Or vice versa, of course. Because your romantic hopes have come to nothing so far, do not get despondent and let it damage your self-esteem, as the chances are it was just not the right moment, or the right person. On to the next one!

■ Dating agencies, singles clubs, singles holidays and lonely-heart columns can work. Stick to some simple rules however. Always meet in public places and keep safety to the forefront of your mind. Don't give out your last name or your address until you are certain that you are in company you want to continue to keep. You may not meet the person of your dreams, but you could well make some friends – treat it as fun and don't get too serious about whether this means of meeting people is going to work or not. Be cautious about parting with huge fees to introduction agencies before speaking to some people who have used the service and are happy with it.

■ It often pays to have some time on your own between relationships so that you can have a rest emotionally. Seen in this light, time spent on your own can be viewed positively.

Holistic Help

■ In feng shui, a rose quartz (the crystal associated with romance) placed in the south-west corner of your house, room, garden or workplace, is believed to enhance finding a new love. Paired items are believed to represent togetherness and romance.

FRIENDSHIP

You can have a bulging phone book, but how many really good friends do you have – ones you can really rely on?

Top Tips

- Friends provide our social support system, and when you have good friends they can be an important part of balancing out the stresses in our lives. As in any other area of life, it is usually a balance between give and take with friends, and lovers. Sometimes you may find yourself giving a little more and sometimes you are the taker. This is fine until it becomes imbalanced and you find yourself always giving, or always taking. The major source of resentment in friendships is the feeling that you are doing all the giving – even if the other person does not see the relationship this way. You need to be careful to distinguish between real giving, and giving in the hope that you will be given to. Use your judgement to interrogate this negative feeling – it may be that you are giving too much instead of communicating your needs to the other person.

- If you are having relationship problems, avoid compounding it by making other major changes in your life. Don't run away from the challenge of resolving conflicts with friends as it will only deplete your vital energy and become a burden for you to carry around. Take a deep breath and work out how to build a bridge.

- People change and this can test your friendship. You may think that everything is just so, and then your friend goes and finds religion, dates someone you don't especially like, or gets a high-powered job which allows them less time for the friendship. Do you ditch the friendship or do you move with it and still manage to appreciate each other with all the changes that have gone on? By embracing changes in relationships instead of opposing them, the friendships will become richer, more anchored and last a lifetime.

More Hints

- The real test of a friendship can be in extreme situations, when you are in trouble, or a friend of yours has a problem. However, there are certain common-sense rules. Don't expect too much. The other person will give what they are able and if you expect too much you could be disappointed. On the other hand don't be afraid to ask as long as they are allowed to say no without recrimination. Avoid thinking 'He owes me a favour'.

- If you invest too much importance in your social life, you could set yourself up for disappointment. Concentrate on quality rather than quantity.

- Your address book may be cluttered with 'friends' or acquaintances with whom you have little in common but you keep hanging onto the friendship because you just can't work out how to get out of it – and so you keep sending those Christmas cards year in year out. But sometimes you have to accept that the friendship just ain't going to work. There is a time and a place to de-clutter your friends, in the same way as your house or desk. Letting go of some 'friendships' will give you more time and energy to focus on people you really appreciate and enjoy. Be bold and rewrite your address book.

- But there may be people from your past who you would get on with if you only knew where they were. If you want to track down old school friends, log on to www.friendsreunited.com

Holistic Help
- Give without expecting to receive.

HOLIDAYS

We all need down time to unwind and de-stress, and in theory we take holidays for just this reason. However, there are many reasons why we sometimes find holidays less relaxing than expected. The destination may not be as idyllic as you imagined, your child may get sick, you may lose your luggage, or your expectations of the holiday may be unrealistically high. So if you have ever come back from your holiday more exhausted and frazzled than when you set off, it's time to think through your holiday plans!

Top Tips
- Keep holiday strains to a minimum when things go wrong. Make sure you have a photocopy of your passports, airline tickets and insurance documents. Divide cash and credit cards between you for safety. This way, if you do lose something, you can avoid the additional tension of finger-pointing and blame.

- It is well worth planning to get away, whether for a weekend or for a longer holiday, at a time when everyone else is not doing so. Travel can be the worst bit of a holiday so don't spend it stuck in bank-holiday traffic or hanging around at the airport at peak times.

- Holidaying with children can be a source of mixed feelings. You probably love being with your children and watching them enjoy themselves, but you may also need some time out for yourself. Most children love camping and caravanning, but on this type of holiday you are unlikely to get much peace yourself, unless you take it in turns with another adult to skip away for a couple of hours. Find a holiday company that specializes in family holidays, where there are activities, or even clubs, for children. Some holidays offer baby minding services, even villa rental agents usually know of at least one reliable babysitter. Taking a young friend along as company for your child could be another solution.

- Teenagers present particular challenges as they often want to break away from parents and do their own thing. While it is important to allow them some freedoms, you need to establish rules, covering safety in particular, before you go.

- Pick the friends you go away with carefully. Don't say yes just because you don't know how to say no. Do they have the same interests and expectations as you? Are their needs similar (the same age children for instance). Do they feel the same way about things like eating out and what to spend money on? Sorting these things out in advance can avoid strained relationships and broken friendships.

- On self-catering holidays make sure that you agree a division of labour beforehand. No one likes to feel that they are doing the lion's share of boring domestic chores, and this can be a principal cause of seething resentments.

More Hints

- A high percentage of people use their holidays to plan the rest of their lives. If you are spending all the time thinking about your career, or similar, this may not be restful. Set aside time before you go to deal with these issues, so you can really rest on holiday.

- If your idea of the perfect holiday is to get the adrenaline going with lots of high-energy activities that is fine as long as you don't also feel clapped-out when you get back. If you don't engage in such activities regularly, you could injure yourself. Prepare as necessary and make sure you pace yourself. Aim to have a more restful holiday next time.

Holistic Help

- Take *acidophilus* and *bifidobacteria*, and also ideally FOS (fructo-oligosaccharides) for at least two weeks before going on holiday to an exotic location to reduce the risk of picking up tummy trouble. My favourite product, which combines all three, is *Lepicol*, but many others are available.

- Other natural essentials for the traveller are *ginger* capsules (or crystallized ginger) for travel sickness, *neem* or *citronella* as insect repellents, *grapefruit seed extract* as an all purpose anti-bacterial agent and *tea tree oil* for cuts or burns.

- The recycled air on planes can mean that some bacteria and viruses on board gets spread to every passenger. Take *echinacea drops* daily one week before, throughout your holiday and for the first week back.

- Frequently people will become ill after a holiday as a result of post-holiday blues. There is an emotional cost to a holiday that is to do with facing the realities of daily life once more or simply the sharp contrast between the bright sunshine abroad and the UK's gloomy weather. Take the herb *St John's wort* to relieve mild depression (**Kira's** one-a-day monthly pack is excellent).

IMPOTENCE AND SEXUAL DYSFUNCTION

People often find it difficult to talk about their sexual problems and the subject of impotence seems to be particularly taboo and awkward for people to express their feelings about.

Top Tips

- Male impotence is called erectile dysfunction (the inability to maintain an erection) and is different from infertility (the inability to produce viable sperm to make a baby). There are many reasons why impotence may be a problem. About half of all men will experience erectile dysfunction at some time or other though only one in ten seek help.

- Male impotence may be linked to diabetes, hardening and furring of the arteries, prescription drugs, recreational drugs, leaky veins in the penis, hormone imbalance, previous surgery, spinal chord injury, epilepsy, Parkinson's and Alzheimer's. See your doctor to rule these out.

- One of the most common reasons for impotence in men aged 55+ is prostate problems, usually an enlarged prostate but also cancer. The prostate is a small gland located just below the bladder. The urethra, which transports urine out of the body, runs through the prostate gland. When the prostate becomes enlarged it puts pressure on the urethra. This results in incomplete emptying of the bladder which leads to a feeling of the need for frequent urination. A diet that helps to reduce prostate problems is rich in oily fish (at least three portions a week) high in fibre from beans and pulses and with at least five portions of fruit a vegetables daily. Soya can also be highly beneficial. It is necessary to drink 1.5–2 litres of water daily and avoid excessive consumption of dehydrating alcohol and caffeine. Take 300mg of the herb *saw palmetto* twice daily and 25mg of *zinc* daily.

- Performance anxiety can be a big issue for men and can worsen the erectile dysfunction. Tense groin muscles can impede the flow of blood to the penis, required for erection. Stroking, massage and caressing can often help to dispel anxiety and provide sufficient stimulation for erection.

- Premature ejaculation is also a common form of male sexual dysfunction and is defined as ejaculation which happens within a minute of, or before, penetration. Anxiety is a cause and may be linked to anxiety about a new partner. It can be helped by wearing a condom to reduce sensations or using a local anaesthetic cream for the same reason. Tensing your buttock muscles while thrusting blocks nerve signals and may delay ejaculation as will squeezing the penis firmly for five seconds between thumb and two fingers just below where the glans joins the shaft, and then waiting for a minute before resuming sex (repeat as necessary). If you experience premature ejaculation you can often have successful intercourse around an hour later.

- Psychosexual counselling can help with impotence, premature ejaculation and also with retarded ejaculation (difficulty in achieving orgasm and ejaculation).

- Couples often learn to live happily with male impotence and sex can involve closeness and many types of physical contact that does not require the man to have an erection.

- Cigarette smoking is linked to erectile dysfunction.

- Many drugs are linked to impotence including cannabis abuse. Cannabis is initially a stimulant but high doses over time can lead to erectile dysfunction.

- Not only men have impotence problems. There is also female sexual dysfunction, including finding it difficult to be aroused, not easy to reach orgasm or pain with sex. There are a number of possible causes including low sex drive or an unskilled lover.

- A woman who encounters pain with sex needs to rule out endometriosis, pelvic infection and thrush with her doctor. Other factors can be lubrication (many types of gel are available) and psychological causes including tension.

- It can be difficult to find information about psychosexual problems, especially if you are shy and don't have a sympathetic GP. Contact the Institute for Psychosexual Counselling 020 7580 0613.

- Contact Impotence Association helpline 020 8767 7791 or www.impotence.org.uk for factsheets about diverse conditions including premature ejaculation, prostate problems and impotence, sexual difficulties for gay men and female sexual dysfunction.

- www.newshe.com deals with issues of sexual dysfunction in women including low libido, dryness and pain on sex. *Read For Women Only* by Jennifer Berman MD and Laura Berman PhD (Virago Press).

- Try www.esda.eu.com European Sexual Dysfunction Alliance for a variety of support groups.

- Contact Brooks Advisory Centres 020 7713 9000 for sexual health and contraceptive advice for women under 25 or Marie Stopes 020 7388 0662 and www.mariestopes.org.uk

LONELINESS

Do you enjoy your own company? If so, you will rarely be lonely. Obviously we benefit from varied situations – time to be on our own, time spent one-to-one with a friend, or in a crowd. But if you only operate comfortably when you are with other people and feed off their presence, you might find it difficult to be on your own.

Top Tips

- We can be lonely even when surrounded by other people. Ultimately we have to be able to fall back on our own strengths. We have to like ourselves.

- Keep at the forefront of your mind that Alone Does Not Equal Lonely.

- Use mindfulness to enjoy experiences you have on your own (mindfulness means savouring the moment). You might also get pleasure from sharing these with other people, but don't feel they are less pleasurable for being experienced in solitude. Smelling a flower, watching a sunset, seeing a child play, enjoying a film, eating a slice of mouth-watering chocolate cake are all enjoyable to experience without others. We do not necessarily need other people to experience joy.

More Hints

- If you have been in a long-term relationship which has recently ended, or the children have just left home, you may find yourself feeling lonely as your routine has changed. This void needs to be filled with activities. Make a list of the things you enjoy and start to build a structure to your life again. (If you are feeling apathetic see Lethargy and Apathy page 156.)

- You might think that enjoying activities is not the true answer to loneliness and that they are temporary stop-gaps until you find the real answer to loneliness in the form of another person or people. But, trust me on this one (and I know I've already said this), if you enjoy your life, others will be irresistibly drawn to you.

- Do you short change yourself? If you are with someone else you might create a fancy meal and pull out all the stops, but on your own you heat up a TV dinner. You are signalling to yourself that you are not worth the trouble and time, but your time spent with other people has greater value. Even if you only eat a piece of cheese and an apple, make it look nice on the plate as a small signal to show you value your own company. If you do not make such small efforts you will create a self-fulfilling prophecy and, indeed, you will find it unpleasant to be on your own.

- Having decided that you enjoy life and you like your own company, you now need to do something about your social life, and get out there to meet more people. It is likely that your pursuits and interests will give you plenty of opportunity but if this is not enough you need to get organized. You could establish all sorts of clubs for activities (bridge, swimming, reading, walking). Join existing clubs and start to throw a few dinner parties.

Holistic Help

- As an experiment, the next Friday evening, plan to have a glass of wine with your meal, light a candle and set the table. Follow this with a scented bath and start reading a good book. After a leisurely breakfast, the next morning take yourself off to the park for a walk or to feed the ducks and then visit an art gallery. Sit in a coffee shop and watch the world go by for half an hour. When you get home, tidy out a drawer you have been meaning to do for ages. Then enjoy an attractively made sandwich with all the trimmings, and then continue reading your book. I'll bet that, by now, you are enjoying your own company.

LOW LIBIDO

If the statistics are to be believed, we think about sex almost all of the time. Whether this is true or not, if you believe that your sex life is less than ideal you could well be building up feelings of anxiety about it. The contemporary obsession with sex – particularly in the media – can make it seem as if everybody is enjoying sex except for you.

Top Tips

■ Up to 40 per cent of women and between 10–30 per cent of men are thought to have problems with loss of libido at some time or other, and obstacles to a satisfying love life can be many, including physical, psychological and social factors. Some of the more obvious include the following.

– Stress and low energy levels. If you have too much to do and are exhausted it is not surprising if you are also disinterested in sex. You must deal with the root causes. Decrease your commitments and make time for relaxation in your relationship.

– Too much alcohol and some recreational drugs interfere with sexual desire. A period of time off the booze might make a huge difference. If this is difficult to achieve you may have early problems with alcohol dependency.

– Relationship problems can be at the root of libido loss. If you are always rowing then you may not feel like having sex later. (Although some relationships resolve conflict with sex, this is not a long-term solution.) It is also common for withdrawal of sex to be used as a 'punishment' for relationship misdemeanours. You may need to seek relationship counselling from an organization such as Relate (see page 236).

– Menopause is a common cause of loss of libido as it can cause vaginal dryness and sometimes depression.

– One of the recognized symptoms of depression is a loss of interest in sex. Yet, while prescription antidepressants may help resolve the depression they, in turn, can have a devastating effect on libido and sexual function (see Holistic Help – Supplements page 196).

– Some types of contraceptive pill drain libido.

■ When working through solutions to enhancing libido, you need first of all to accept that some people are less interested in sex than others. This can help to relax you about the subject and help you to stop putting pressure on yourself to 'perform'. There can be great differences in the sexual needs of the partners making up a couple and this is best addressed by seeking psychosexual counselling.

■ Pay attention to your physical messages and you might find that there are times when you feel more like having sex. Note if there is a pattern to these times, for instance, a woman is most likely to be aroused around the time of ovulation.

■ One of the sexiest quotes I have heard was attributed to a major rock star who apparently said 'Tantric sex is about treating your partner as a goddess. Sex is a wonderful way of giving thanks'. If we all treated each other as gods and goddesses in bed, we might feel sexier more of the time. You don't have to learn tantric sex, simply bringing some romance back into your lives can raise sexual interest. If you have children, get them to bed early so you and your partner can have a candlelit bath together. Even turning off the TV and eating a delicious, candlelit meal together can create the right mood for sex.

■ A successful technique for restoring sexual interest is for the couple to concentrate on touch and massage instead of penetrative sex. This takes away a lot of the 'pressure' of sex, helps to rebuild sexual drive and improves confidence and body image. You need, as a couple, to set aside specific time for this and initially concentrate on simple stroking and massage while avoiding the genital areas. You may start off with massaging the neck and upper torso only. This goes on for several sessions. With mutual consent (this is always important) you slowly build up the variety and type of touch, and the areas of touch, over time. Eventually, if you both wish to, you can get to penetrative sex (though this is not essential).

- Sensuous exercise such as yoga, t'ai-chi, gymnastics or ballet can help to put you back in touch with your body and help to improve self-image and stimulate sexual feelings.

- Moderate exercise is linked to improved sex drive and if you increase your exercise out of bed, you are more likely to feel like exercise in bed. More intense exercise is even more likely to have a positive effect, possibly by improving blood flow around the body.

- Read *Increase Your Sex Drive* by Dr Sarah Brewer (HarperCollins) which concentrates on how to improve libido with nutritional help. Other good books, which might give you some ideas, are *How to Make Great Love to a Man* and *How to Make Great Love to a Woman* by Anne Hooper and Phillip Hodson (Robson).

- See Impotence and Sexual Dysfunction (page 190) for more specific information.

- For help organizations and psychosexual counselling, write to the British Association for Sexual and Marital Therapy, PO Box 13686, London SW20 9ZH or contact the British Association for Counselling 01788 578 328.

- If you have health problems such as Multiple Sclerosis or Parkinson's, this can obviously affect your sex life. Others will have gone through the same experience and there is sensitivity to the particular problems associated with these illnesses. Get in touch with the relevant help organizations. Very little is written about this that I am aware of but one book covers sexual issues for those with Parkinson's: *Parkinson's Disease – The Way Forward* by Dr Geoffrey & Lucille Leader (Denor Press). For those with disabilities, contact Sexual and Personal Relationships of People with a Disability (SPOD) 020 7607 8851.

Holistic Help – Diet

- Diet is known to play a major role in hormonal balance, for example in menopausal symptoms, so there is every reason to suspect it is also important for libido. Of particular importance are phytoestrogens found in foods such as soya (a very rich source), wholegrains, chick peas and lentils, as well as zinc (lean meat, nuts and seeds) and B-vitamin rich foods (wholegrains, liver and green leafy vegetables).

- Stress is also a major inhibitor of sexual feelings and when we are stressed it is common to crave fatty, stodgy foods or, at the other extreme, to stop eating regularly – and both can impact on libido.

- There is no doubt that a bottle of wine shared between a couple can help to set the mood making the situation more relaxed and lower inhibitions. However, alcohol can have a dual effect. In women, a moderate amount can increase testosterone levels making them feel sexier, but more than this has the opposite effect. Sadly, for men they do not enjoy the same benefits of increased testosterone levels, and we all know what too much alcohol can do.

■ Too much alcohol also severely depletes B-vitamin levels. We need B-vitamins for energy and to combat low moods and eating a diet rich in wholegrains and green leafy vegetables, and with the occasional serving of liver, helps to ensure a good supply. You could also take brewer's yeast or a B-complex supplement.

■ Some foods do have aphrodisiac qualities. The lips and tongue are packed with nerve endings and some foods, such as chocolate, can help trigger hormones and endorphins which lift mood. Chocolate contains a substance called phenyethylamine, the chemical we produce in our brains when we fall in love. The higher the cocoa content of the chocolate the better the effect, so stick to 60–70 per cent cocoa solid chocolate. Oysters are famous for their erotic appeal and are certainly reminiscent of the female sex organs. They contain more zinc than any other food, at 80mg per dozen molluscs. Zinc is needed for making sex hormones, and is also vital for seminal fluid in men. Around 3mg are lost with each ejaculation, against the recommended daily intakes of between 5.5 and 9.5mg, which means that men who are highly sexed may also be depleting essential nutrients. Potassium, a mineral which is terrific for boosting energy levels, is found at high levels in bananas, so perhaps these fruit merit all the innuendo. Selenium is another mineral vital for healthy sperm production and just a couple of Brazil nuts daily will keep levels topped up.

Holistic Help – Supplements

■ The most important nutrients for sexual function are the mineral zinc, the B-vitamins and essential fatty acids (as found in evening primrose oil, borage oil and fish oils).

■ *Niacin*, a form of vitamin B3, taken at around 100mg daily produces a non-harmful 'blushing' effect akin to a short menopausal hot flush (this effect reduces with regular daily use). B3 acts as a vasodilator (dilates blood vessels) and helps to release histamine which are factors in orgasm.

■ *Damiana*, a central American aphrodisiac herb, can be a successful remedy for low sex drive and works particularly well in combination with oats, or it can be taken as a herbal tincture.

■ For men, damiana has been combined with *gotu kola* and *saw palmetto* by herbalists for centuries to improve libido and balance testosterone.

■ *Kava kava* (see warning on page 234) reduces the anxiety often associated with impaired libido (do not use with alcohol).

■ *St John's wort* can be used for stress relief and alternative to antidepressants. (Do not stop medication without speaking to your doctor and see Herbal Preparations page 233 for more advice about St John's wort.)

■ *Ginkgo biloba*, a Chinese herb, is known to improve blood flow around the body, and that also means to the sex organs. One trial showed that gingko biloba effectively enhanced sex drive by up to 90 per cent, in both women and men whose libido had been knocked out by the antidepressants they were taking.

■ Another successful herb is *Muira puama*, (or potency wood), an Amazonian Indian herb. In a trial looking at the effects of a Muira puama and Ginkgo biloba mixture on libido, 63 per cent of the 200 women in the trial noted improvements. **Swiss Health's** *Herbal vX for Women* and *vY for Men*, are supplements containing Muira puama, and both are available from pharmacies and health food shops. Call 0870 841 0870 for stockists.

■ *Black cohosh* or *red clover* are herbs to use if there are problems of dryness for women as they have an oestrogenic effect.

■ **Napier's** herbalists mail order 0131 553 3500 or www.napiers.net can give advice on herb use for libido and menopause. They have a specially formulated *wild yam cream with marigold oil* that is effective for vaginal dryness in menopausal women.

■ In India, *jasmine oil* is thought of as a sexual stimulant. Massage some on your abdomen area or burn some in a burner. Drink *jasmine tea*.

THE MODERN FAMILY

Love them or hate them, your family are a part of you. Invest in your family whether nuclear (your immediate family), extended (your natural blood relatives across the generations and including cousins) or step-families (brought together by marriage). These people form a valuable support system and are a part of your identity.

Top Tips

■ Families are subject to changes and shifts in the way they relate. Just when you thought you knew everything there was to know about your family, they change. Remember that relationships are interesting precisely because they are complex. To use a great metaphor I once heard 'You've learned to ride the bicycle, but the road changes every day'. What this means is that there is no instruction manual. The vagaries of family relationships are as different as the people involved in them. One of the greatest challenges is redefining roles within the family, and adapting to the changes caused by divorce and remarriage, that create new step-, half- and in-law families.

■ If you are divorcing and kids are involved, it is best if you and your ex can manage to get on with each other. If your self-esteem is good, you will not be threatened if your ex finds a new partner, remarries or has more children. You don't have to like any of these, but for your children's sake it is usually best to get on with all concerned. Of course you can't be responsible for how your ex, or any new partner, might behave, but by being even-handed and non-judgmental you may be an influence for more positive behaviour.

■ After divorce or bereavement, you might have found happiness with a new partner, and yet your family seem determined to judge you and the relationship. There is no more harsh a critic than your own children (it's OK for them but not for you!). Don't expect your children to be happy for you (they will see it in very personal terms and how it affects them and they may still be mourning the passing of their parents' relationship). You may need to steer them towards a confidante to whom they can talk and complain – someone who is neutral such as a family friend or relative.

■ Don't feel guilty if you find a new romance 'too quickly'. If your family and friends don't approve, deal with their complaints objectively. You can't please everyone so you might as well please yourself (as long as your children are not neglected emotionally because of it). Only time will tell if they were right or not.

■ Taking on a new partner's children (either full or part-time) can be unfamiliar territory. While you can never be a replacement parent, you can be a 'significant other' and taking on the role of confidante is one way forward. Don't try to buy their love however – this will come out of respect and kindness. If you don't establish ground rules early on – preferably with all the adults concerned, including the ex and new partners, agreeing on the same tactics – children can become adept at exploiting conflicts and playing everybody off against each other.

■ Don't assume that step-children who are thrown together will get on – they may well be jealous of each other. This needs tact and careful handling. New half-siblings are also a milestone for older children which needs to be handled intelligently. Involve older children in planning for the arrival of a new sibling, generating excitement in the prospect. Do not make them feel in any way left out or usurped.

■ Financial stress is a common occurrence when a partner is having to support two families. Sorting out your money in a fair and equitable way will remove the blind panic this situation can induce. Also don't forget you will need to make new wills.

■ National Family Mediation 020 7383 5993 or www.nfm.u-net.com can help with a range of problems that come about as a result of marital discord and broken or complex family arrangements or alternatively look up the Institute for Family Therapy 020 7935 1651.

MONEY AFFECTING RELATIONSHIPS

Money is one of the major causes of stress in relationships. We live in a very materialistic world where, it seems, people are valued according to how much they have. This idea affects personal relationships, and money, with its ability to provide us with the 'right' house or look, has become bound up with issues of trust, self-esteem and pride. People also find it hard to discuss money, which only serves to add to its importance as a complex emotional issue rather than simply being currency.

Top Tips

■ It is as well to be aware that the idea of money plays a large part in your relationships, particularly for co-habiting couples. Distance your view of money from emotional issues and treat it as a form of currency. If you remain both impartial and open about money, it will help to keep issues of conflict separate, which then improves your chance to have productive discussions.

- Work out your financial arrangements before entering into a new phase of a relationship such as living together, marriage or setting up a business. Come to an agreement that ensures that bills and other costs will be shared fairly. This also goes for flat shares with people you don't know that well. Don't let previous assumptions about friendship or romance get in the way of a sensible discussion about money. If the other person is reluctant, or unwilling, to discuss these issues treat this as an early warning sign of potential problems. If you stand accused of not trusting their friendship or being unromantic or untrusting, be aware that this is an inappropriately emotional response to a practical concern.

- When one partner gives up work, leaving the other as the sole breadwinner, it often changes the relationship. It is an unfortunate truth that money is often used as a source of power within relationships and this causes a huge amount of dissent. Ask yourself if by giving up your financial independence are you going to get into conflict over spending? Again sit down and establish in advance what the issues are going to be. Who pays the bills, and decides what money needs to be spent on, how the money is to be divided, and so on. This can be a difficult process but may save you from arguments later on. Remember even those in long-term relationships are taken by surprise when the 'balance of power' shifts.

- Not having enough money is of course a source of stress in relationships. If unemployment hits or if you are on a low income, this can be very distressing. Resolve to tackle it together as a unit rather than letting one person shoulder the whole responsibility. Avoid pointing the finger of blame for the lack of money and take steps to find solutions together.

- If your partner is prone to sudden spending sprees on extravagant items, then you need to establish parameters. Agree a set of rules concerned with impetuous buys, such as consulting each other before buying anything over, say, £500. This strategy will help to minimize nasty surprises on the bank statement.

- Be absolutely open and clear when lending or borrowing money. Always treat these transactions as a business arrangement with a known repayment schedule, and put it in writing.

- Make a will. The number of people who die intestate is alarming. It is particularly vital to make a will if you have children to arrange guardianship. You need to change your will any time that your circumstances change, such as marriage, new children, divorce, new step-children, etc.

More Hints

- Deciding if you are going to have a joint bank account is a major decision when you set up home together. There is no right or wrong about this, it just depends on what you both feel most comfortable with. You may prefer one account for all activities, or you may prefer to each have your own account and any 'housekeeping' money to be transferred from one to the other. Another option is a joint account for household spending and separate accounts to retain autonomy for individual needs.

■ Teaching children about money is important. One day they will have to manage their own finances, understand about the value for money and earn their own money! If your partner has different views and, for instance, spoils them with gifts all the time, try to come to an agreement so that you can present a united front. Discuss such issues as pocket money, gift buying, earning money from odd-jobs and saving money. Once you agree as a couple, you can then instil your values in your children. Children as young as five years old are capable of understanding a regular sum put into a piggy bank. An added bonus is that counting their savings helps a child develop numeracy skills.

■ Who is in charge of choosing things in your household? Often one person will go to great lengths to do research on a particular item and go through the process of learning about and choosing something. The next thing that happens is that the partner comes along and criticizes the choice because they have not been through the same process. There may be criticisms of extravagance, taste or even the need to buy the item at all, and this can lead to a row. If this tends to happen, agree to discuss things at each stage, though this will mean pouring over technical brochures or sales literature, and investing time in visiting showrooms. Or make one person in sole charge and accept their decision.

■ Honesty is nearly always the best policy. Avoid hiding your spending from your partner or sneaking home with items you know your partner won't approve of. It may feel like a harmless white lie, but you are on the slippery slope to dishonesty in the relationship and this might not serve you well in the long term.

Holistic Tips

■ According to feng shui, the south-east area of a home or room is considered to be the area of prosperity. Placing a money plant in this area is believed to mirror your fortunes by how well it grows. A water feature such as a fish tank will similarly enhance your prosperity area. Ideally it should have an odd number of fish in it.

■ Don't go shopping if you don't need to and avoid thinking about buying things as a leisure activity. Instead, stay home and read a book, listen to music or cook a delicious meal.

NETWORKING

Networking is not a new concept. People have been making advantageous connections throughout history. However the term 'networking' was an innovation of the 1980s and this label made it a recognized activity that even has clubs devoted to its pursuit. The term, networking, has business connotations but can be applied to any area of interest where you use your social life, and keeping in touch, to deliberately further your interests.

Top Tips

- Networking is different from friendships, which have an emotional depth to them. Of course, one can come out of the other, but they usually have different starting points. Not confusing the two can reduce disappointments if networking relationships don't mature into deeper friendships.

- If you are keen to network, there are many avenues to explore. Your work environment is the obvious starting point. You can add to this professional bodies such as special interest clubs, networking groups, fund-raising activities for charities linked to your interests and others. Networking can happen on the level of organized meetings or you can further it by striking up closer relationships and socializing with individuals.

- Because we are thrown together with our workmates for so much of our time, it is only natural that we should spend some time socializing with them. But no matter how relaxed you feel, your office environment is still different from your personal and home environment. If your behaviour clouds the domains of your life, you may have to live with the consequences. Think carefully before you get completely plastered at the office party, or invite a workmate to your home

- The office party was obviously invented by a masochist. You have on offer the makings of a great evening with people you know well, good food and lots of free booze. But let it get out of hand and you might regret it if you are hoping to convince professional colleagues of your seriousness and commitment to an enterprise. Living down being caught with a colleague in a 'compromising' situation, telling the boss what you would do if you were running the company as your tongue is freed up by alcohol, falling down on the dance floor in your high heels or worse, is, there is no other way to put this, inappropriate. Your career will certainly not be helped.

- Office romances can be precarious at the best of times, and if it one does not work out, will you both be able to face each other across the office floor after the event? If the romance is successful, will you want to spend so much time together both in the office and outside? What happens if one person is promoted, or relocated? The heart often follows where the loins lead, but the practicalities of working together need to be addressed.

More Hints

- Avoid chasing up people with whom you are networking unless you are on very certain ground. They may have busy lives and a tenuous relationship might not be something they want to develop immediately. Instead, send them useful or appropriate information occasionally to keep your name in their awareness. This will allow you to have a stronger basis from which to develop the relationship next time you meet.

- Keep an e-mail, or Christmas card list, and keep in touch in this way with news of your relevant activities (you may decide this is a lot of extra, unnecessary work, or it may work for you. It is not an absolute rule of networking).

- If you are shy at meetings and find it difficult to strike up conversation, remember that other people may feel the same way and may not be aloof as they initially seem to be. Usually it is easier to talk to people at this sort of meeting because at least you know you have common interests and a starting point for conversation.

- If you spend a lot of time having drinks with your colleagues after hours, remember that this might be a source of concern for your partner. He or she might feel excluded, resentful or even jealous. Your partner may not even tell you about this but just internalize it until it blows up into a row. You can pre-empt the situation by explaining why you do it (to unwind, because you enjoy it, because it is good networking), and you could occasionally invite your partner along.

Holistic Help

- Respect for other people is important when networking. People don't always want to be viewed as 'useful'. When networking, remember to be interested in the other person for reasons other than just your immediate aims, learn something about them (while keeping a certain formal distance). Be genuinely interested and they will respond. Equally, don't cut dead those who are not of use to you. Treat everyone with respect, and they will respect you as well.

SEXUALITY

We learn about our sexuality in late childhood and adolescence, but it may take years for some people to come to terms with their sexuality.

Top Tips

- As parents, we have a tremendous effect on our children's view of sex and their ability to relax about the subject. How we discuss sex with them can affect them for life. It is true that they will find out a lot from classmates and other friends but a lot of this might be misinformation, so it is best if a parent can talk to them about sex. Many parents avoid the subject and leave it to school sex education classes. This is not necessarily a wise move as talking about sex will help to build a rapport with your child so that later, sex-related problems can be discussed openly and easily with you. For instance, at some point the child may raise issues such as pressure to have sex when not ready, pregnancy, sexually transmitted diseases and homosexuality.

- Many parents will disagree with the following advice believing that it is best to leave discussions about sex until the child is old enough and the need is presented such as when a girl starts menstruating (which can be alarmingly early these days). However, children are sexual in many ways from an early age and spend time touching their sex organs and thinking about 'where babies come from' sufficiently to ask questions. My view is that, when they ask, this is the time they are ready to be given selected information in a form they can cope with and which is suitable for their age. Don't give children misinformation such as babies are in your tummy – babies are in wombs and food is in stomachs. You do not have to tell them everything, but you can gently and accurately answer their questions as they crop up. If they need further information they will eventually ask. A three, four or five-year-old will not be embarrassed and can take on board simple facts, while a squirming ten-year-old might be mortified and start to clam up on the subject. There are many good books in your local library to help with the discussions.

■ Children experiment with sex, whether their parents wish to acknowledge it or not. It is very common for them to experiment with members of their own sex at an early age, but this does not imply any particular sexual orientation. Many children will feel 'guilty' about early experimentation with their own sex if there is an atmosphere of disapproval at home and this can contribute to lack of communication and confusion about sexuality later.

■ It can be hard deciding on how to express sexual orientation if you are bi-sexual. Homosexuality has, in many quarters, become acceptable and is no longer a cause for remark. However, living a bi-sexual life can be complicated and there are no obvious rules about how to deal with this. If you are not open about the situation you will cause difficulties in your relationships with both sexes. It takes a particular type of partner who is content for their other half to be having regular sorties with members of the other sex.

■ Bi-sexuality can lead to problems later on in a gay relationship when one partner decides they are not, after all, gay – it happens. If they can be honest about their bi-sexuality from the beginning this might be avoided.

■ Announcing you are homosexual to your family can meet a variety of responses, and not always the ones you think you are going to encounter.

– A well-known singer who has a large following among the gay community found herself inexplicably going absolutely ballistic when her daughter announced she was gay. She calmed down later, but the intensity and the type of her reaction was a surprise to both of them.

– On the other hand, you may be dreading telling your family, assuming that they will instantly disown you, only to find that they are unshocked and supportive.

– Some members of your family might even have guessed a long time ago, but did not have the nerve to bring the subject up.

– They may simply not understand what has lead to your conclusion and say things like 'This is a phase you are going though' or 'You just need to meet the right girl'.

– They might be genuinely worried for your wellbeing but express themselves in a way that is alienating and sounds judgmental. 'You'll be discriminated against', 'You'll regret not having a family', 'You'll get AIDS', 'You'll be beaten up in a gay bar', 'You'll have a horrible life'. Instead of taking affront you have to talk them through the realities of the situation.

■ Coming out about being gay is going to be easier if you are confident about your feelings. Some younger people are confident and have grown up in a culture where it is OK to be gay and the issues are not so overwhelming for them. But if as a youngster you are in the least uncertain, unconfident or anxious it can be a tremendously difficult thing to muster the courage to do. Dizzy is an organization set up to counsel young people age 14–19 about gay issues. Phone 01273 204 050 or e-mail them at dizzyyouth@yahoo.co.uk or visit www.switchboard.org.uk/brighton/ They can help to deal with such problems as how to tell parents, workmates and bosses, the Aids issue and social advice.

■ As an older person you may have been living in a way that does not suit you for quite a long time and it is quite a relief to be honest and open. Your true friends will stick around.

■ Many people choose to live split lives. At work and with their family they are thought of as straight, while those in their social and love lives know they are gay. This can be a complicated way to live life, but it works for some people. It is no good being purist and saying they must come out, when they are happy with the arrangement. For instance you may have divorced and come out as gay, but feel that this is not the time for your young teenage children, who are only just finding out about their own feelings and sexuality, to be affected by your decisions about your own sexual life. Life is complicated and finding solutions that work has to be very individual.

■ On the other hand, it could be doubly hurtful for a family member to find out you are gay from someone else. Better that it comes from you, no matter what the short-term consequences.

■ It is often helpful to speak to a counsellor or advice centre. You may be experiencing personal confusion, isolation, discrimination or prejudice. A lack of information only makes these situations worse and a list of helplines can be obtained from National Friend on 0121 684 1261 or www.friend.dircom.co.uk/index.html

■ Psychosexual counselling can help with coming to terms with your sexuality, for example if you are a transsexual or transvestite, or are transgender.

SHYNESS

Initially, you can work on the effects of shyness, and as this gives you more self-confidence you will, hopefully, find that your actual shyness slowly dissipates, at least to the point where it no longer interferes with your life.

Top Tips

■ Be who you are. You will be appreciated for this.

■ When you meet people, maintain eye contact with them. Avoid looking down at your feet, or over their shoulder at other people.

■ If you know you are going into a social situation where you will need to make conversation, but you regularly get tongue tied, work on a little planning. Think up five topics that you can use as conversation openers or to oil the wheels when the conversation dries up a little bit. You could pick headlines from the papers, something that highlights your interests, something about the event you are attending.

■ We tend to change our body language when we want to get on with someone. Apart from flirting in a potentially romantic situation, we also mirror other people's stance, actions and movements. 'Mirroring' is not sycophancy but a natural way of building rapport with other people, as is dressing to fit in and speaking at a volume that matches our surroundings. We are attracted to people who fit in with our social grouping. Watch two people who really get on and you will find that they adopt the same poses, walk at the same pace and even cross their legs at the same time when sitting. By being aware of this, you can use this to help build rapport. We pick up small clues from each other without even realizing it. By subtly mirroring and matching another person's movements (in a subtle way or it will just be artificial and irritating) you can leave someone with the impression that you are a really nice, interesting person – because you move and act just like them!

More Hints

■ Ask people about themselves when you meet them. This means you do not have to think of something to say. It also means that the emphasis is placed on them to talk instead of you, and just about everyone enjoys speaking about themselves. At the end of the conversation they will think that you are an interesting person to know!

■ If you think you are the only person who is shy when everyone else seems confident, this is not the case. Even the most accomplished stage performers can be excruciatingly shy – they are able to suppress their shyness when they take on another character. Personal contact is more difficult for these people than performing in front of hundreds of people!

Holistic Help

■ **The Bach Flower Remedy** *Larch* is for those who wish to restore confidence and remove hesitancy.

STAGES OF LIFE

Stress does not respect race, creed, social standing, or gender, but there are particular difficulties and challenges associated with each stage of life. By developing an understanding of these stages we are more able to appreciate what is happening to us, and therefore to ease the stress we are feeling or that of our loved ones.

CHILDHOOD

We have an idealized picture of childhood as being full of laughter and learning, but anxieties, emotional problems and even depression, sadly, often afflict children. In part, this awareness has come because we are better at recognizing when a child has been emotionally disturbed, but living in a fast-paced society and with changing family structures also takes its toll.

Top Tips

■ Whatever the problem is, remember first and foremost, that a lot of love and understanding will go a long way to helping resolve most problems. Instead of dictating to the child what the solution is or being tempted to tell them 'don't be so silly', listen to their viewpoint, their anxiety, their voice. So often children just want to be listened to and to express their fears.

■ If children are not able to express their anxieties, they may signal stress in other ways. If you notice a change in behaviour at school, a change in appetite, aggressive behaviour, sleep problems, temper tantrums, bedwetting, inhibitions or other unusual change, suspect an unvoiced anxiety.

■ Bedwetting is one of the most common childhood stress signals. By the age of five 85–90 per cent of children are dry, but bedwetting (nocturnal enuresis) can be the sign of something that the child is not able to express. It is not uncommon for it to come on when a new baby arrives in the family and is a form of regression. Bedwetting can cause the child distress and undermine their self-confidence. Make sure that you communicate nothing but understanding and reassurance. If you are cross or impatient this can further erode self-esteem. Around 70 per cent of older children with bedwetting problems manage to be dry within sixteen weeks with the use of an alarm (though some will relapse). Contact the Enuresis Resource and Information Centre 0117 926 4920 or www.gnfc.org.uk/bedwetg.html .

■ Children who have hearing problems (sometimes due to glue ear), who are dyslexic or dyspraxic, or who are at the very mild end of the autistic spectrum, are sometimes misunderstood and are believed to be inattentive or lazy. This is always something to watch out for because the child won't be able to tell you and carers, such as teachers, may miss it. Being misunderstood in this way can be very frustrating and demoralizing for the child.

■ Bullying is something that most children come across at some time or other. If your child is being bullied, he or she may be reluctant to talk about it. Do your best to persuade your child to speak about it because it can easily destroy your child's self-esteem and undermine their enjoyment of school, clubs or playing in the local playground. If you suspect it speak to the school at once, or parent of the child if you know them, and lodge your concern. You may find that the parent of the child or children, or even the school or club leader, are in denial about any trouble. Bullying can take a physical form with a bloodied nose, or a psychological form with teasing and stealing of personal belongings. Make sure that your child always knows that they will be supported if they come to you and reassure them that the situation will be dealt with. If necessary, join clubs further from home so that your child does not need to come into contact with bullies. Team up with other parents if there is a general problem (not a vigilante approach however), and teach your child about victim body language and remedy this by joining martial arts classes to build confidence. Information can be found on the Internet at www.pupiline.net/ or from Childline (page 208).

■ A child may be showing signs of stress because of marriage break-up or the death of a family member. In dealing with their own problems, adults may forget that their child needs all the support they can get. You need to be aware that a child's view of the situation may be completely different from the parents'. (See Divorce page 183 or Bereavement page 175 as appropriate.)

■ Children can lose confidence if they feel they are not doing well at school or that a teacher does not like them, but might not think they have the option to tell their parent. Try 'actively listening' to your child. Instead of asking 'what's wrong' as you distractedly make the tea, sit down and say something like 'you seem upset'. The child may walk off, refuse to answer or deny it, but after a while will begin to feel they can confide in you and that you are truly listening.

■ It can be easier for another close relative or friend to get close to a child than it is for the parent. Don't worry, or feel excluded, if this is the case, it is simply that a different ear and voice, away from the family home, seems easier for the child to unburden itself. Do ask for help from the 'significant others' (grandparents, uncles, godparents, etc.) in your child's life as this could be a way forward.

■ Hobbies for children are a great way of encouraging all sorts of skills. Even if it is something with no obvious educational merit, such as collecting cartoon cards, it still instils certain qualities such as organization, responsibility for keeping things, and knowing a subject well, which can foster a sense of pride. A hobby can also encourage the ability to research and plan, to be self-disciplined and patient. Helping your child to find a hobby they enjoy, or to look after a pet, can be a terrific way of supporting your child. However, it is their hobby not yours, so don't take over but support them. Remember to guide rather than instruct, to not make fun of it, show an interest (even if you find it boring) and to be ready with praise. You may, however, need to set a time limit on the activity to stop it impacting on homework and sleep hours.

■ Discipline is always a contentious issue. Some believe that smacking is fine while others abhor it. My personal belief is that, occasionally, any child can drive a parent to the edge of being tempted to smack, but ideally it should be resisted. The main reason for this is that it shows the child that physical intervention is an acceptable way to get a result. (Although in families that very rarely resort to smacking, the event is likely to be such a trauma for all concerned that it won't be seen as a useful strategy by the child.) Far better in my view to be firm about ground rules and to use deprivation (of treats, visits to friends, TV, computers, money), or being grounded, as chastisements. Using 'time out' (where the child has to leave the room and go to a designated, and dull, place such as sitting on the stairs for an agreed length of time, say a count of 20) can help to diffuse situations before they get to 'smacking point'.

■ It is an uncomfortable fact that a number of children become violent, even toward their parents. (This can involve psychological as well as physical abuse). Common contributing factors to this are absent fathers, learning difficulties, or witnessing violence regularly in the home, and can happen in families of all social classes. Giving in to violent children perpetuates the cycle. Set clear boundaries. Limit access to TV, computer and video games to which they are often addicted. Be assertive (say 'What needs to happen is…' rather than 'You shouldn't do…'). Punishment often leads to further rebellion and it is better to get them to think about what they are doing and the effects of their actions. Love them, value them, praise them (every small positive victory is an opportunity to build their self-esteem), talk to them. Helplines and professional help for a range of problems include Childline 0800 1111 or www.childline.org.uk Institute for Family Therapy 020 7935 1651.

TEENAGE YEARS

The teenage years can be quite a challenge as so many major issues come bubbling to the surface, compounded by the physical and hormonal changes experienced by the child. The first thing that any parent needs to do when there is a teenager around is to recall what they felt like in their own teen years!

Top Tips

■ Remember that teenagers need to work out many things at a time when they are still growing and hormones are often in flux. They have to work out how to deal with new responsibilities, independence, exams, finding employment, the temptation of drugs and their sexuality.

■ The parent of a teenager needs to get used to the idea that their child is now a young adult and treat them accordingly by talking calmly, seeking their opinion and not laying down the law in a heavy handed manner (though you have the right to be firm).

■ The most useful approach a parent can take at this time is to help their teenager to build their self-confidence and offer a friendly ear to discuss issues that are concerning them. Remember to pile on the compliments whenever you notice something praiseworthy, no matter how small, to help maintain self-esteem.

■ Deal with areas of conflict such as noise levels in the house, household duties and curfew times during school terms in a constructive manner – you may also have to be prepared to negotiate on some issues.

■ A major source of stress for teenagers are looming exams (see page 45). Keep a sense of perspective if your teenager is going through exams, and if results are not what you hoped for, remember that your teenager may well feel worse than you do and does need to have self-confidence undermined with criticism. Exams can always be re-sat. Offer constructive and practical help, but beware of nagging which is often a touch paper for another row.

■ Distressed adolescents can grow up in to distressed adults, so take note if your teenager is expressing angst.

■ Racism may become an issue in teenage years. While there may have been exposure to it at a younger age, it is likely that the parent would have dealt with the consequences. However, as an emerging adult, your teenager has more autonomy, has to start to make appropriate decisions about how to handle it and might make the wrong choices such as getting into fights. Educating your child to not get wound up is probably the only practical thing to do. By getting upset they only give validity to the tormentors and damage themselves. Teach them to consider racist acts as beneath contempt (also see the advice regarding bullying in Childhood page 206).

- Eating disorders need very special handling. It is often the case that the last person to suspect that a child or teenager is anorexic or bulimic is the parent. A major feature of eating disorders is that the person is extremely clever about concealing the problem. These are conditions where the need to be in control is an overwhelming feature and certainly control over what others see of the problem is a large part of it. It is not quite clear why there has been such a huge increase in those with eating disorders and fashion, confused health messages and stress are routinely blamed and probably all have a part to play. But certainly one can add to this self-esteem problem, and any parent needs to be aware that constantly criticizing their child, particularly about their appearance, will not help. It is common for those with eating disorders to have unrealistically high expectations of themselves – only seeing total success or total failure and nothing in between. Not every teenager who follows a food fad, turns vegetarian or goes on a diet will become anorexic or bulimic, but be aware of the possibility. With anorexia there will be weight loss, or lack of weight gain at a time of expected growth. This is easily disguised with baggy clothing for quite a long time. Bulimics can disguise the amount of food they eat and the purging (usually vomiting, but often laxatives) expertly. You cannot deal with the problem of eating disorders on your own but need to seek expert help. See Disordered Eating (page 88) and contact the Eating Disorders Association 01603 621 414 (adults) 01603 765 050 (youths) or www.edauk.com Incidentally, boys can be affected as well as girls.

- Learning how to handle alcohol is a hard lesson to learn with more than a few teenagers voiding the results on their parents' carpet! The temptation to smoke will be overwhelming for many. And solvent abuse is rampant. What can the parent do in the face of these? Being available at all times to discuss the issues surrounding these problems, without preaching, is vital. Some parents choose to introduce their teenagers to alcohol and 'soft' drugs, such as cannabis, themselves in the hope that it will take away the 'naughty' factor and hope to control the situation. Certainly if you do not wish your teenager to smoke or drink heavily then you must not do so yourself and set an example. Solvent abuse is widespread and is very damaging. Information leaflets are available from Re-Solv 01785 817 885 or www.re-solv.org/ or see Addictions page 77.

- There is every chance that a teenager will come into contact with drugs at some time or other. Drug abuse (rather than experimentation) undoubtedly can lead to addiction, crime, prostitution, and the spread of diseases if the circumstances are right. Again the parent needs to be aware of the issues, and to a degree pre-empt the situation by educating their child on the issues. Do not alienate them if it turns out that they have tried drugs, but always keep the channels of communication open. Be aware that money is often diverted into buying drugs and if you are supporting your child financially and find that they are doing this you may have some tough choices to make about withdrawing financial support (in the knowledge that they may go elsewhere). Seek professional help.

■ Teenage pregnancies are something that most parents dread. First of all, if you are the parents of a teenage son, educate him on his responsibilities regarding relationships, sex, the girl's right to say no, contraception and unplanned pregnancies. All the above is also obviously true of girls. If you are avoiding the subject, you and your teenager may have to pay the price. If your daughter finds she is pregnant, you have to hope that she confides in you as early as possible. In order for this to happen you need to ensure that you can have easy and relaxed conversations about a range of topics. Avoid being judgmental or dictatorial, as this will only put distance between you. A strategy for dealing with the pregnancy depends on your family viewpoint and of course on her wishes. Overcoming issues, such as your daughter wanting to keep the baby and you thinking it best to not do so, require soul searching and the ability to deal with the practicalities. It is essential to keep communicating and to offer every support throughout the process of deciding what to do, and after. You may also have to support her through talking to the father of the baby and his family, friends and other members of the family.

LEAVING HOME
Whether leaving home to go onto further education or to share a flat or start a new job, this is a significant phase of life. Cutting that cord can seem very liberating, but also a bit scary.

■ This may be the first time you have had to manage your money from pay packet (or student grant) to paying bills. It is so easy to get into debt and getting to grips with your money is the first and most important thing to do.

■ You may have been aching to break free, but suddenly not having a parent to ask for advice whenever you need it can be daunting. Do not be afraid to call home whenever you need to – it is not a sign of weakness. Many avoid calling home because they do not want to worry their parents, but I can assure you if you had a child who had left home that the chances are high that you would want to know how things were going, good or bad.

■ Going to university is an exciting time with lots of possibilities and new challenges. However, if you are a little shy, it can take time to adapt to your new life and really get into the swing of things. Make full use of the various clubs and societies that will be available to you. You may find it easier to live in halls, rather than in digs, at first so that you can meet people. On the other hand it is all too easy to get sidetracked with all the fun and to forget about studying until the exams loom. Work at finding a balance and pace yourself.

■ Certainly burning the candle at both ends can seem tempting and easy to do. In late-teens and early twenties you may just have the stamina to compensate for getting back in the early hours and then presenting yourself for work or study the next morning. And if it is difficult then you may be tempted to take a little chemical help – some extra strong coffee or other, illegal, stimulants. You can probably get by like this for a while, but the reality is that it will inevitably catch up with you. You might start to feel unwell, your performance will suffer and you may get a nasty shock if you are dismissed because you are not doing as well as you thought you were.

■ In your new job, you may be ready to set the world on fire. And you may do so. But it is often a bit of a come down to realize that there are so many mundane things to do, office politics and departmental budgets to sort out, before you get round to setting the world on fire. Do not let this blunt your ambition but use time management skills (see page 65) and planning (see page 34) to make sense of what needs to be done.

■ Avoid subsisting on sandwiches and take-aways. Because home cooking might no longer be an option it can be tempting to just not bother, but it is much cheaper and you will feel a lot better if you brush up your cooking skills and eat properly.

THIRTY-SOMETHING

So now you are into your stride and the chances are you have an occupation or a career and maybe a young family. This is about the time when you find that you really need to slow down a little unless you want to be hit by fatigue. The demanding reality of mortgage payments, child rearing, and career progression, mean that you need to nurture yourself and look after your health.

Top Tips

■ At about this time the ego of youth is often replaced by angst. The certainties of our twenties are suddenly transformed by doubts. This can be a time for feelings of low self-confidence often caused by the idea that you should have 'done better' by now. Do not measure your achievements against anybody else or think that if you haven't done a thing by a certain age, then you never will. Remind yourself that many people achieve their aims well into middle, and even old age. Make a point of listing all the things at which you feel you have succeeded in your life (even if you don't currently rate them) and use this as a starting point for rekindling your belief in your abilities.

■ Some people find that changing careers can be a significant source of stress at this time. All your training may have been in a particular direction and to date you might have pursued this, but now feel that your career no longer suits you for a variety of reasons. Think if there is another kind of work that appeals to you and set about researching courses and companies concerned with that area. Find out as much as you can about a new career before cutting loose from your former job. It may be that you are simply tired of the ratrace and wish to go part time or freelance. Again, you need to discuss such changes with friends and family, before taking positive suggestions to your boss. (See also Ambition page 43, Goal Setting page 16 and Mindset/Flexibility page 159.)

■ Many people in their thirties are now finding that they have to redefine their expectations of life. Soaring property prices may force them to live at home for longer and delayed marriage and child rearing means can mean that youthful habits last longer. As a result, today many thirty-somethings do not have the financial responsibilities their parents had when they were the same age, but they do have more disposable income and are more inclined to borrow money for what they want or need. It may be difficult, but it is important that you find a balance between partying, work and taking care of yourself.

MID-LIFE

In many ways this may be the best time of all. The kids have left home, you are more confident about who you are and what you do, and you might now have time for other interests. However, for some, low self-esteem can arise when the busy life you once had suddenly changes when the last child leaves home, and this can be a cause of depression. Or you may find that your grown-up children still depend on you for everything from listening to their problems to babysitting.

Top Tips

■ For some women in their forties and fifties proceeding through the time leading up to and following menopause can be a stressful time, with symptoms ranging from hot flushes and lower libido to depression and fatigue. For those whose hormones plague them with psychological symptoms such as mood swings or depression during the menopause there is a choice of approaches, both conventional and complementary. You may choose HRT or opt for natural hormone balancing herbal treatments such as agnus castus, black cohosh or dong quai. For detailed information on treatments using diet and herbs to treat both the short- and long-term effects of the menopause, (including increased risk of heart disease and cancer) read *Natural Alternative to HRT* by Marilyn Glenville (Kyle Cathie). The Women's Nutritional Advisory Centre on 01273 487 366 or www.wnas.org.uk is also a good source of advice. You may also want to find out about natural progesterone by reading *What Your Doctor May Not Tell You About Menopause* by Dr John Lee (Warner Books).

■ If you are the partner of a women going through the menopause, take time to find out what she is going through by reading some of the leaflets or books available.

■ *Meno-Herbs* combine phytoestrogens from red clover, dong quai, black cohosh, wild yam, raspberry leaf, squaw vine and nettles and is available from **Victoria Health** 0800 413 596. Also use *Woman*, one of the range of homeopathic **Australian Bush Essences** (see Useful Resources page 234).

■ The andropause is believed to be the male equivalent of the menopause, when levels of male hormones drop. It is not very well accepted by the medical establishment but if you wish to know more read *The Andropause Mystery* by Robert Tan (Amred Consulting) or *Male Menopause* by Malcolm Carruthers (Thorsons).

■ Men can support themselves against the possibility of prostate problems, which begin to emerge at about this age, by following a diet high in fibrous foods such as pulses and other beans, oily fish, vegetables and fruit. The herb *saw palmetto* is highly effective at preventing prostate enlargement and several brands are available. Take 300mg twice daily to mimic the amounts used in successful trials.

■ Where once we might have not even thought about retiring from our 'real' jobs until our mid-sixties there is a group of people who are taking early retirement because they can afford to. They dream of the day when they can spend endless days on the golf course, take holidays whenever they wish to and concentrate on their other interests. But many realize, to their horror, that they are ill equipped for all this extra time and find that they are bored rigid – which is highly stressful. Many will end up returning to the work place, in a similar industry, often in lesser jobs just to keep from going insane. Life span beyond retirement years is increasing in any event and it makes sense to have some sort of a plan for what you will realistically do with those years. The happiest retirees, of whatever age, are those who are active.

■ If you have no idea of what you want to do with this time there is the airport magazine test. If you were in an airport about to embark on a medium length journey (not long enough to read a book and too long for the paper) what section of the magazine stand would you head for? Taking up a new career in an area that you are enthusiastic, even passionate about, can be rewarding. And having been through one career you may be able to afford to indulge in doing it for the love of it instead of the money.

LATER YEARS

Once upon a time, age was revered, but now we live in a culture obsessed with youth we often do not think about how older people can contribute wisdom and experience. Yet as we ourselves grow older we continue to do many of the same activities that we did when younger. Have you noticed how the older you get, the higher your definition of old-age becomes. When you are ten, twenty seems old. When you are 40 suddenly this is not even middle age. In their 70s people often say they think the same way as they did in their 20s (the only difference is that time has moved on).

■ The idea that people in their seventies are all wearing carpet slippers instead of dancing shoes is quite wrong. Increasing numbers of retirees take up windsurfing, hiking and yoga classes each year. As long as health is reasonably good there is no reason not to. One 87-year-old in my village gets a real kick out of the fact that he takes meals-on-wheels round to the 'youngsters' of 65–70 once a week. Keeping as physically active as you can gives energy and improves health.

■ The romance of a long-term relationship is often rekindled in retirement years as you now have more time to do things together.

■ Sleep problems and depression are often worse in later years. You may be frustrated that you are not sleeping as much as you used to, but remember that the older you are, the less sleep you are likely to need. Check with your doctor that any medication you are taking is not interfering with sleep patterns.

■ Many health problems apart from sleep are exacerbated by multiple medication and if you are taking four or five different potions you probably ought to check these with your doctor. Common side effects include depression, digestive problems, constipation, poor circulation, tinnitus, confusion, balance problems and eye problems.

■ Dependency on others can be a source of stress for some older people whose pride will not allow them to ask for help. For the most part, relatives and neighbours will be willing to help if you ask them, but they can't second-guess your needs.

■ Loneliness can add to depression. Get out and about and develop your interests, such as in hobbies or clubs. This will offer an opportunity to be sociable and may also increase your circle of friends. Remember there will be many people in your neighbourhood in a similar situation. If your children have moved away and you don't have as much chance as you would like to see your grandchildren, you can keep in touch with letters, e-mails and phone calls, or by sending audio or video tapes. You could help out at a nearby playgroup, or children's hospital, or volunteer as a governor for a local school, to be in touch with children of about the same age as your grandchildren, to help you understand the likely stages they are going through.

■ It is important to understand shifts in the 'balance of power' in your relationships as a common feature of being older. For instance the child may now have become, effectively, the parent. Or traditionally the husband may have always dealt with financial issues but with ailing health it is now the wife's responsibility. Don't see such changes in a negative light, whether you now have more or less responsibility, you can still enjoy life.

■ There are many issues to consider when thinking about increasing dependence on family or institutions. It is a good idea to be as well-informed as you can before you find yourself needing, say, a care home. Information, including on financial issues, can be obtained from your local Citizen's Advice Bureau or Help The Aged on 0800 650 065 or www.helptheaged.org.uk or Age Concern on 020 8679 8000 or www.ageconcern.org.uk

TRUTH

We would all agree that truth is fundamental to all successful relationships, but truth is also a slippery concept that means different things to different people. Every time we get upset with someone, it is the case that our idea of truth has been denied. You have a choice to stay upset or to adapt your rules to accommodate the other person. A perceived dishonesty will destroy a relationship faster than anything else, but not everyone can take the truth all the time. Lies can be a major source of stress. What is the truth about truth?

Top Tips
■ Sometimes the truth is painful. This does not mean that it has to be suppressed, but that addressing it has to be done carefully and not in an angry way.

- Even if you suppress the truth, there is no place for lying in a relationship you want to maintain. When (not if) you are caught out the resulting distrust can undermine the foundations of the relationship.

- It might reduce the stress in the short term to tell a lie, but it will only build up major stress in the long run if the lie is compounded or if you are caught out. You need to decide which is easier to deal with.

- People often lie because they want to have their own way and want to avoid the other person's disapproval. In perpetuating this you must acknowledge that the other person will never know the true person that you are because they do not realize what you are really like. You may be ashamed of what you want and so keep it a secret, but the relief that is often felt by sharing the facts can be enormous. And if the other person withdraws from you as a result, they are obviously having trouble dealing with the real you and so you need to re-establish a true relationship.

- Teach your children to tell the truth in two ways. Firstly, never lie to them. Secondly, never punish them for telling the truth. They must feel safe in discussing anything they wish to with you, and that you can remain impartial and non-judgmental when talking about their concerns. In this way they have no reason to lie to you.

- On the other hand, children have a right to hold back (not the same as lying) and as they get older they develop a private side to their personality that they may not wish to share with you all the time. Respecting a child's privacy can be challenging for some parents, but if the child is allowed a private life this means that there is less reason for them to lie.

More Hints

- We all have our own truths. How we perceive things might be absolutely convincing to us, but not to others who have a different truth. Your belief in God might be an absolute truth for you, but others may believe in another God, or no God. Nations fight wars and people have rows to defend their perceived truths. Given that you don't want to be at war or have rows all the time, the only way forward is to acknowledge the other person's truths, while retaining your own view. You can still seek to build bridges and find common ground even if you have different truths.

- Just as often as others lie to us, we lie to ourselves – 'I only smoke 5 a day', 'I do all the work around here', 'I eat enough fruit and veg each day'. You have the power to change this. By being truthful with yourself (not pessimistic or talking down to yourself) you get a real handle on the situation and can do something about it.

- Hypnosis is a useful way to get to a truth you may be suppressing about a particular issue. (See Useful Resources page 234 for more information.)

- Of course there is always a place for some 'white lies'. It is a question of how good your judgement of what an unimportant white lie is, and whether you can make constructive suggestions. For example, if your friend has a new dress and looks a bit of a fright in it but asks what you think, your response might depend on the circumstances. If you meet at a party and there is nothing she can do about changing it, you would be kinder to tell a little white lie and say that the dress looks nice. On the other hand if you meet at her house before going out, you have an opportunity to say you think the blue dress suits her better and you'll wait if she wants to change. If she asks in the shop before buying then you can say outright that it looks frightful and not risk hurting her.

■ When you are embarking on telling someone a 'truth' which is something they may not want to hear, it is important that you communicate it in a considerate manner. Bear in mind that the idea is to achieve a constructive result and if the truth you are telling is perceived as a serious confession or a criticism it may not be well received. Tell it straight by all means, but avoid criticizing and make sure you have the suggestion of a constructive solution up your sleeve.

■ Sometimes it helps to polish up diplomatic skills before telling a truth. The sandwich principle of criticism often works well. Say something nice, then say what you need to say, then finish off with something nice again. This may sound manipulative, but it really can be kinder and people will usually respond favourably if it is done well. For instance, to your partner 'You haven't taken the rubbish out yet' might yield 'Don't nag' or 'So, you take it out'. Instead you could say 'Have you had a tiring day? Because I notice you haven't taken the rubbish out yet. Tell me about your day'. This is empathetic, is unlikely to result in a sarcastic retort – it may or may not get the rubbish taken out, but at least it will be friendly. And if there was not the excuse of a tiring day the chances are that your partner will jump up and take out the rubbish pronto.

Holistic Help

■ Truth and trust are closely linked. If you trust someone you won't mind them telling you uncomfortable truths. Here is an interesting trust exercise. It is best done in unfamiliar territory, and you must only do it with someone you really can believe (and as the roles will be reversed they need to trust you as well). Keeping your eyes closed, or wearing a blindfold, let the other person guide you gently by the arm for between 3–6 minutes around an unfamiliar territory. Progress slowly. No words must be spoken and light non-intrusive touch is used to communicate the territory. For instance you might be steered lightly to the left or right, or a slight upward pressure might indicate going upstairs and downward pressure to go down a step (the signals are not pre-agreed but are worked out in real time). It is absolutely vital that the person doing the steering acts responsibly and treats the other person as the most precious and delicate of objects. As you go down a step, for instance, you need to have it indicated to you that you are about to level off otherwise you might trip. When you have completed the exercise, you change roles. This is a powerful exercise, helping you to learn the significance of complete trust.

URBAN LIVING

You might not wish to change your fast paced, cool, urban life for anything, but if you want to stay sane you might want to think about some of the effects it can have. Urban living has a huge impact on relationships of all kinds and understanding some of the pressures can help to relieve them.

Top Tips

■ We are assaulted on so many fronts in urban centres – traffic, radios, people, road works, visual intrusions such as billboards – so much so that most of us aren't even aware of them anymore. We deal with this onslaught by a process called sensory adaptation. We filter out all that is not immediately necessary and, in essence, become numb to the stimuli. But even if we are not conscious of them on a minute-by-minute basis, our senses are still overloaded and this takes its toll. By taking ourselves 'out' of the situation on a regular basis, using relaxation, visualization, meditation or other means (even a warm, scented, candle-lit bath is healing), we can rejuvenate ourselves and heal the damage of this sensory overload.

■ The sheer volume of people in urban centres means that we behave in particular ways towards our fellow urban dwellers. We don't look people in the eye (it is too challenging and invasive), we rarely acknowledge their presence, we deal with small courtesies (such as holding the door open) with curt acknowledgement in case it is seen as an entry point for communication and we create invisible barriers around ourselves. This lack of human contact is actually quite stressful because it emphasizes our aloneness and distances us from other people's feelings. You can spread a small, but significant, amount of bonhomie by smiling at people and making eye contact with them (no they won't put you away, nor will this be an invitation for every madman – you can still use your judgement). But what you will find is that people smile back at you (mostly) and this will immediately put you in a better mood. Once you have got into the habit of smiling at people you can take a further risk and say good morning to five people on your way to work each day!

■ One of the ways of dealing with the artificiality that urban anonymity engenders is to treat your immediate environment as a village. Get to know your neighbours, your neighbourhood shops and services. If you regularly go into the same shop, acknowledge any familiar faces and you will gradually build a sense of belonging in your community. You can't grow and learn and prosper if you shut out humanity.

■ Get to know your neighbours. Not only will you be able to call on them in emergencies but you will be able to pre-empt any local problems with friendly discussions rather than with antagonism.

More Hints

■ Whereas once upon a time families lived within a short distance of each other, urban living often means that there are large distances between generations or cousins. If you live in a city and want to maintain strong family bonds, you need to work at it a bit harder, and this requires energy and dedication. But the payoff is that when times are tough you can often fall back on your family, and they will often understand you as no one else can.

■ If you are new to the city, you might find that it can be a lonely place. There are a lot of opportunities to meet people but nobody is going to bring them to you on a platter and you will need to go out and find them. Frequenting the same places so that people get to know you, joining clubs and classes and just getting out and about will be the first step.

Holistic Help

■ Maintaining personal space in an urban setting is an important issue. On an empty tube train people will sit as far apart as possible and then new arrivals will slowly fill in the seats between in a pattern until there is no choice but to sit next to someone. Yet during the rush hour we all snuggle up to our neighbours' armpits of necessity while rarely making eye contact. You can do an exercise with some colleagues to test this (you need five or six people of both sexes to make this workable). Pair up and one person in each pair stands still while the other places themselves about six feet away. The person who is six feet away starts to move very slowly towards the person who is standing still. At any time the person who is standing still can say stop and the other person must do so. The idea of the exercise is to find the point at which you feel uncomfortable because that person has got too close and is entering your 'space'. Change partners and repeat it with a different person and observe if the distance is the same or different. Also repeat the exercise while maintaining eye contact. Do you feel more comfortable with people of the same sex, or opposite sex? This will tell you a lot about your reactions to other people, how you relate to them and how comfortable you feel about extending yourself into the 'village' where you live, at work or among friends.

APPENDICES

These appendices have been added as an extra resource for those who wish to explore in greater detail some of the stress-reducing methods referred to in this book. Obviously there are many other disciplines that individuals find helpful for managing stress, and this list does not attempt to be comprehensive. Rather I am highlighting the disciplines that I have found particularly useful and effective for many people, and which are flexible enough to be used in the context of a hectic modern life. Organizations you might wish to contact are listed in Useful Resources (page 234).

COGNITIVE THINKING

Cognitive thinking is a powerful way of reorganizing your emotional responses, replacing destructive thought patterns with a more constructive, and therefore more positive, viewpoint. Re-training yourself out of a tendency towards negative reactions is an empowering experience.

Cognitive therapies were developed to treat depression and are based on the idea that our emotional responses depend on how we think far more than we realize. In a difficult 'emotional' situation we might cry, be angry, feel fear or sadness, depending upon what we think. Becoming 'cognizant' or aware of your thought patterns offers an alternative and, many would argue, faster route to wellbeing than other 'talking cures'. Many find it easier to change their thinking than they do to change their emotional processes. As anyone who has been through any analytical therapy can testify, digging deep can often be a painful and difficult process which might even lead to taking a few emotional steps back before you take a step or two forward.

The cognitive approach concerns itself with the immediate problem. Instead of being asked to delve into the past, clients are encouraged to look at how they perceive their truths, and to discover where such thoughts do not serve them well. The value of exercises used by cognitive therapists is to get you to replace destructive, undermining thoughts with practical alternatives: thought patterns that are more realistic and so have the power to give you back the ability to grow and achieve your goals.

DEPRESSED THINKING

The depressed person will see themselves, variously, as not having choices, being a failure or inadequate and deprived of opportunities. However, from the outside looking in, this same person appears as a fine and capable human being. The depressed person's feelings (thoughts about themselves) probably don't tally with their actual achievements. This understanding – that depression involves disturbed thinking – recognizes that it is the individual's perception of themselves and their environment that are the problem.

You don't have to be clinically depressed to think this way. Most of us are familiar with this type of thinking to various degrees. We will often devalue our achievements, misinterpret other people's meaning and imagine negative outcomes that do not tally with the facts.

Cognitive therapy is extremely useful for handling stressful events. While you cannot always avoid experiencing crisis situations, you can change the way you think about and therefore, react to, these events. The cognitive process further affects the way you then represent bad times to others, improving your ability to communicate your views without descending into bad feelings. One of the great advantages of cognitive therapy is that it has proved extremely successful as a self-help tool, and is used by many counsellors and psychiatrists in a variety of crises.

Below are some examples of the approaches taken. If you would like to investigate the subject further, I highly recommend *Feeling Good, The New Mood Therapy* by David D. Burns MD (Quill, Harper Collins). As the blurb says 'Feeling Good Feels Wonderful!'

RATING HOW YOU FEEL ABOUT SOMETHING

This exercise is so simple to do that it is easy to underestimate its power. It is also useful for when you feel overwhelmed by worry. Simply write down all the anxieties (just transferring worries to paper has a power effect of de-cluttering your mind). Rate each worry on a scale of 1–10 and then you can tackle the most pressing ones first.

If you habitually dread doing things, on the next few occasions rate your sense of dread before you do whatever it is. Then, after you've done it, re-evaluate your feelings, noting any sense of achievement or satisfaction you feel. By rating your feelings, and understanding them better, you can transform the imagined pain of doing something into the tangible pleasure of success and transform the experience.

COGNITIVE DISTORTIONS

It was the Stoic philosophers of ancient Greece who stated, 'Men are disturbed not by things, but by the view which they take of them'. Learning how to monitor our thoughts, then to question our reactions forms a fundamental part of any cognitive therapy. To help you 'think about thinking' I have listed the most common ways in which we distort our realities.

Jumping to conclusions
Assuming a reality that is not necessarily the case: 'Because she did not return my call today she is obviously not interested in what I have to say'.

Mind reading
Imposing your belief system on what the other person might be thinking: 'My boss must think I am disorganized because I got in late today'.

Fortune telling
Deciding in advance what the outcome of a situation will be: 'My parents will be angry with me if I don't do well in the exams'.

Personalization
Assuming responsibility for a negative event even when it is not the case, thinking: 'I must be a bad mother' when your child gets a black mark at school, rather than 'His behaviour was out of order and I can best help by getting him to understand why'.

Mental filter
Picking a single negative from a situation and dwelling on it: 'Because I forgot to tell them about my previous promotion I messed up the whole interview' instead of 'I forgot that detail but the rest went well and I can forward them a note with this information'.

Should statements
'Shoulds', 'Musts' and 'Oughts' are used to whip up action. They feel like punishment and lead to guilt: 'I ought to phone my parents tonight' (when you are feeling tired) instead of 'I will phone them tomorrow when I am feeling fresh and able to have a more rewarding conversation'.

Emotional reasoning
Letting your emotions get the better of your thinking: 'I feel terrible that he didn't particularly enjoy himself, I'm so selfish for insisting we do what I want'.

Overgeneralization
Seeing one or a few instances as being typical: 'Why do I always mess things up?'.

Labelling
Using a definitive term: 'I'm an idiot' or 'I'm a failure' instead of 'I made a mistake'.

All or nothing thinking
Assuming that any less than perfect is not good enough: 'I goofed with the first bit of the presentation so I am a total failure.

Disqualifying positive data
Filtering out the good bits: 'If I am stuck with the kids it will be an exhausting experience',

instead of 'I get tired towards the end of the day but before then we have plenty of good times together'.

AUTOMATIC THOUGHTS AND RATIONAL RESPONSES

We usually have pre-programmed responses to situations, based on some of the information in Cognitive Distortions above. Chit-chat fills our head with negative viewpoints of events. One way to imagine the destructive cycle this sets up is to 'hear' how it would sound if you heard someone say it to another person or, even more powerfully, to a child. So if you are always saying 'You idiot' to yourself, hear yourself say it to a child, in the tone of voice you adopt to yourself, usually condescending and judgmental. Say it out loud. It is usually cringe-making, upsetting and demoralizing.

Working out rational responses requires first that you identify your automatic thoughts. Over a period of a couple of days write down, without fail, all your automatic thoughts. For example: 'I can't do that', 'He looks cheesed off with me', 'Why can't I get anything right', and so on.

At a quiet time, link those thoughts to the list of Cognitive Distortions on page 221 and identify what the typical patterns of your thoughts seem to be. Now write down, next to each automatic thought, what a more rational response might be. Instead of 'My boss is looking miserable which probably means he hates everything about the report'. A more rational response might be 'My boss is looking miserable –it could be that he had a bad morning getting to work, that he's had some bad news or possibly he is concerned about the report'. If you feel that he is not happy with the report then remind yourself that you can work on it. Approach your boss after you've thought the distortions through.

By regularly working through more rational responses, you eventually begin to change your way of thinking. You automatically check your destructive thought patterns and counter them with more positive thinking. To begin with, it may seem strange to counteract all your negative thoughts. But by replacing 'I'm so stupid' with 'I've made a mistake' you will gradually chip away at bad habits of thought.

An advanced level of the exercise is to add in a score from 1 to 10 to evaluate how much you believe the positive statements. At first you might only score a response at 1 or 2, but with practice and persistence your scoring will creep up nearer to the higher numbers. Keep up these sheets for as long as you can because we are always learning. It is also fascinating to take them out a year later, when you are feeling more positive because of all the work you have been doing, and re-reading what your thoughts were and how you view them a year on. It is quite an education!

CREATIVE VISUALIZATION

Visualization is a way to focus your imagination in order to create what you want in your life. It can also be directed towards healing and resolving anxieties and phobias. You will find that visualization is a skill that you are already using in your everyday life, though in an unconscious way. For instance, if you have an appointment with the bank manager tomorrow, and you are a little anxious about this meeting, the chances are that you are playing out the situation in your mind and rehearsing the possible conversation. If you are to play tennis, you might be imagining yourself serving the ball superbly. If you are unwell, you might be imagining being fit.

What you need to learn now is to channel your visualization to a higher level, so that it becomes a tool to use whenever you wish. See that bank manager handing over the overdraft you want, imagine the ace you'll serve and visualize a healthy, pink-cheeked you striding through the countryside. Initially, it is probably easiest to practice creative visualization when relaxed or meditating. Here are some pointers.

- Do not worry if you are unable to see a 'picture' when you practice visualization. Some people see clear images, others feel feelings, perceive a general ambience, or replay conversations or sounds in their mind.

- A simple beginner visualization exercise involves closing your eyes while in a relaxed position, at a comfortable temperature. Imagine a time when you were happy, say on holiday on a warm beach. Feel the warmth of the sunshine, hear the sounds of the waves lapping on the shore and gain that sense of calm and contentment that you felt. It is as simple as that. You can imagine any happy time, such as cradling a baby, eating a delicious meal, walking hand in hand with someone you love, giving or receiving a massage.

- Passive visualization is when you allow thoughts and feelings to come to you as and when they appear. Active visualization involves consciously choosing what you want to imagine. Guided visualization is when another person takes you through a step-by-step using description, for instance: 'You are in warm, sunny weather, on a beach listening to the sound of the waves, feeling relaxed'. The person would then possibly guide you through relaxing the different muscle groups in your body, and finally seeing yourself in a given situation with a beneficial affirmation, or perhaps tapping into your self-healing capabilities.

- You can use any visualization you find helpful while meditating (see page 224).

- If you reach a block in your visualization, this may point to a fear, probably subconscious, that is stopping you from progressing. This can usually be worked through once you are aware of this.

- These are the four steps to creative visualization.

  - Set your goal. Choose goals that are easy to believe in and that are small steps, usually along the way to greater goals.

  - Create a clear idea or picture of what it is that you want. Think of it in a positive form and in the present tense. Do not think of it as an abstract form at some time in the future, or in a negative form.

  - Focus on your visualization frequently, both at dedicated times, but also at other times, whenever you are able, throughout the day.

– Give your visualization positive vibrancy and energy. Make strong positive statements to yourself and about yourself. These are called affirmations.

■ Work through these simple exercises.

– Imagine yourself applying to do a course you have always wanted to do. How does it feel? What do you have to do to apply? How does it feel to start learning something new, something that interests you?

– Imagine yourself in a situation where you are doing something you do not enjoy. Notice what happens to your body – do you tense up anywhere, does your pulse race? Hold on to the thought while consciously relaxing those parts of the body. Visualize the unpleasant experience waning in importance. See yourself coming through the unpleasant experience intact and happy.

– Stand 'at ease' with your legs a shoulder width apart and your arms hanging loosely by your body, and your neck muscles relaxed, feeling balanced, imagining a nourishing white light all around you, feeding your energy centre in your solar plexus (behind your belly button), as you grow tall and strong and confident.

– Imagine yourself playing a sport you enjoy. Visualize yourself actively participating and enjoying what you are doing. Imagine yourself performing better than ever before. If swimming, imagine rhythmic strokes that carry you faster, while each arm extension takes you further. If gymnastics or dance, imagine yourself extending your limbs further and finding strength in your solar plexus. If playing football, imagine being more nimble, running faster and scoring more goals. You will find that your confidence grows and your performance improves.

– Visualize yourself going to a gathering and meeting new people. Imagine yourself energized and interested in the other people. See yourself finding the other people a pleasure to meet and find what is best about them. Imagine it being an enriching experience and that you can learn something positive from every person you meet.

■ Read *Creative Visualisation* by Shakti Gawain (Bantam).

■ Read *The Silva Method* by Jose Silva and Philip Miele (Souvenir Press). Jose Silva is one of the pioneers in the field of creative visualization.

MEDITATION

Meditation has a proven track record for helping to reverse the physical and psychological changes brought about by stress. Blood pressure, breathing rate, heart rate, metabolism and muscle tensions are lowered, calmed or relaxed, while brain waves slip into calming alpha and theta levels. All sorts of conditions can be helped by meditation including irritable bowel syndrome, chronic pain, anxiety, panic attacks and chronic fatigue.

However, many people who might be interested and who would benefit do not investigate meditation further because of some common misconceptions about the practice. Mistakenly seen by some people as a 'tune in and turn on', 'hippy' philosophy from the sixties, meditation is not about switching your mind off in order to achieve some kind of enlightenment.

Meditation may sound like a very specialized discipline. But in reality it is simply a heightened and more focused form of what we naturally do to unwind, whether it be stroking the cat, swimming or knitting. You can think of meditation as achieving a high level of awareness, which is often accompanied by gentle, repetitive actions.

■ The easiest form of meditation is to:
  – sit in a comfortable position in a quiet room
  – close your eyes
  – focus on your breathing and become aware of your in and out breaths. As an alternative chose a word or sound (called a mantra) that is meaningful to you and soothing, and focus your attention on this as you repeat it in a low voice rhythmic voice
  – do this for ten to twenty minutes and repeat daily.

■ A mantra is used to focus your attention, so that your mind can return if you are distracted. The best known mantra is the Sanskrit term Om (I am all of that which is divine). It is pronounced a-a-o-o-u-u-m-m, though you can choose any sound, word or phrase that you find calming.

■ Thoughts coming into your mind are a part of meditation. But instead of allowing them to interfere with the process and struggling to blank your mind, recognize them as simply being 'thoughts', distance yourself from them and retake control. For instance, if you begin to think that you can't cope with something, meditation teaches you to observe yourself thinking this, so that you are not directly affected by the fear of lack of coping skills.

■ You can also use other focuses for your attention: a candle flame, a positive affirmation, a feeling (of kindness, warmth or loving for instance), a visualization (see page 222) or a rhythmic physical movement such as t'ai chi or yoga.

■ A form of meditation called 'mindfulness' is particularly good for relieving symptoms of stress. A recent study showed that guided mindfulness combined with cognitive therapy (see page 217) was more successful than ultraviolet treatment at healing psoriasis (a notoriously difficult skin condition to control). The first stage of developing mindfulness is to devote an hour a day for a couple of months to sitting quietly while concentrating on breathing and meditating. This is to prime your ability to focus. Mindfulness then involves focusing on all actions as specific experiences. So for instance if you are about to eat a tomato, look at it, note its texture and colour and how you feel about eating it. As you bite into it, be aware of the interplay of tastes and sensations, chew and swallow it slowly, all the time being aware of the experience. You then practice mindfulness for, say, thirty minutes daily as a particular exercise. However, it will have a longer lasting effect that this half hour and has the habit of insinuating itself into a person's general life, making them calmer and more focused.

- It helps to go on a meditation course if you are able. However, finding a course that doesn't promote Buddhism or Transcendental Meditation, if these are not disciplines you are interested in pursuing, may be difficult. *The Good Retreat Guide* by Stafford Whiteaker (Rider) lists secular and non-denominational centres as well as those allied to Christian and other faiths.

- Look up www.newawakenings.com for online guided meditations. They offer a free trial, after which a small fee gives access to a number of different meditation choices.

- *How To Meditate* by Lawrence LeShan (Little Brown & Co) or *Meditation For Life* by Martine Batchelor (Frances Lincoln) is a good place to start.

- Contact the School of Meditation 020 7603 6116 or www.schoolofmeditation.org or Transcendental Meditation 020 7486 0141 or www.t-m.org.uk

MIND MAPPING

Mind mapping is a fantastic tool for organizing your thoughts, planning and problem solving. At its simplest, the mind-map replaces lists with a pictorial representation of the subject in hand and all its possible connections. Even for those who firmly believe they don't have a creative bone in their body, mind mapping enables access to our creative flow and intuition. It can also be used as a powerful way of improving memory, organizing projects and studying. Mind mapping allows you to see the whole picture. Of course, the more effective you are at organizing your thoughts, the less stressed you can be as your life gains order and your thoughts are permitted expression.

One of the things I like about mind mapping is that it is easy to understand the basic principles, and you can achieve quick rewards from your first attempts. However, like any discipline, the more you do it and the better you understand how it works, the more you get out of it. Nevertheless, some simple tips will open up all sorts of possibilities – and, because it is an expressive tool, you can use it in any way you wish and really personalize your approach.

- When most of us want to remember or to plan something, we will jot down a list. This is, of course, useful but does not tap into the real power of memory. Lose that list and the chances are that you will not remember some of the items and would not be able to recreate it in the same way if you have another stab at it. The problem with lists is that they are linear and do not allow for associations and relationships between items on the list to be explored. The brain does not really work in straight lines, but rather in patterns of interconnectedness best imagined as a web. The whole point about mind mapping is that it is an approach that uses this interconnectedness. Mind mapping can even be thought of as an extended, but highly focused, doodle – which takes it out of the realm of a difficult technique to learn and into the realm of being quite good fun!

- Take a clean sheet of paper. At the centre of every mind map is a single thought or item. Write in your name, or the word ME.

In this instance we will build a mind map which allows you to access your extended network of people. Use this example to find help when setting up a small business, planning a reunion party or if you just need help with a particular problem. Begin by creating a simple list – you might come up with between 20 and 100 people depending on how extensive your address book is and how well connected you are.

- Radiating out from ME at the centre draw thick lines in such a way that you can write a single word on each one. These words might be: FAMILY, FRIENDS, NEIGHBOURS, LOCAL SERVICES, COLLEAGUES, SCHOOLS, SPORT/LEISURE CLUB, and so on (you may well think of others more relevant to you).
- From each of these main branches you can now add sub-branches.
- You can see that there are links between groups which you might want to highlight with coloured arrows – this is not duplication but a true representation of the connected nature of both our lives and thought processes. These links are a help not a hindrance.
- Remember that each one of these people has their own network, which means that your network can go even further than you first imagined. Persuade just a small percentage of these people (say a brother or sister, a couple of friends, a work colleague or two) to create their own network mind maps of their contacts and you have a huge potential network, perhaps numbering hundreds of people.
- Why not just do this as a list? If you did, the chances are that you would not remember half of your possible contacts. Adding to your list would make it very messy with lots of writing in the margins. Your list would not grow as effectively because your mind works in a pictographic way more suited to the mind-map method.
- Mind maps work best when they are clear and well presented. One of the few 'rules' is to use only one word or thought on each line for clarity. You may even find it easier to use an image (images can be much more powerful than words and are excellent mnemonics for recalling things (particularly for exam revision). You may find that your first mind map, say notes taken at a lecture, is messy but there is nothing to stop you revising it and improving it, to make it a useful tool for revision later.
- Using colour adds to the clarity of your mind map. On your ME map, for instance, you would use a different colour to draw the lines of each of the main categories of people you know. This just helps the eye, and therefore the mind, sort out the information more quickly when you need it. Another possibility is to use colour to sort out the different 'levels' of people you know. So, for instance, you might use red for those in your immediate sphere, blue for those one step removed, and so on. Unless it is all very obvious to you, take a moment to add a small colour-key in a corner of the page.

■ Now you have had the chance to experiment with a simple mind map work on others. Trust your intuition and allow yourself to free-associate. Work as fast as you can, and without judgement or evaluation. You can review and amend it later if you need to.

■ Practice by doing a mind map of your strengths, good points and the support and blessings you have in your life. Focus on what is good in your world. Keep this mind map and frame it, placing it where you can see it every day.

■ This is only the simplest explanation of how to mind-map and I would urge you to explore the subject further as it is so simple and yet so powerful. I use it to plan all of my books and find that it cuts across a lot of dithering about where to place chapters and thoughts. I have used it to sort out my degree project, to organize my time, to take notes at lectures and meetings, to help sort out priorities and make decisions when faced with different options. At low times, I have used it to work out what it is that is contributing to depressing moods and what positive solutions might offer themselves up. I cannot recommend it highly enough as a stress reduction tool with a fast return for little effort.

■ Begin by reading the definitive book on mind mapping, written by Tony Buzan, *The Mind Map Book* (BBC Books).

■ Look up www.mapyourmind.com

NEURO LINGUISTIC PROGRAMMING (NLP)

Neuro Linguistic Programming (NLP) has enjoyed a huge surge of interest in the last few years, because it works so well. NLP is a highly flexible tool – a kind of instruction manual for the brain – that incorporates many approaches, including cognitive thinking and visualization (see pages 219 and 222). NLP is a fantastic yet simple way of reprogramming negative thoughts and habits into more positive ones. It is immensely powerful when used for goal setting (see p16).

NLP is often targeted at particular audiences, such as the business community. But it is also used by those interested in performing or public speaking, and by health management and therapists. There are many books, courses, audio and video tapes on the subject and some of these are listed below. Personally, I have found the audio tapes and courses to be the most effective, though as I have said elsewhere in this book we all respond to learning media in different ways.

Some of the principle tools used in NLP are summarized below. Because there is such a variety of approaches within the discipline, there is not the space to give a comprehensive set of exercises that you can take away with you (as I have done with other therapies). Here, I have concentrated on giving the 'flavour' of what is available.

STRATEGIES FOR SUCCESS

We all have 'strategies for success'. Even the most apparently mundane activities, that we do every day, such as travelling to work, explaining an idea to another person or handling a difficult phone call, can be done more or less successfully. Understanding what your strategies are and transferring those skills to uncharted territory is one of the tools of NLP.

On the other hand, you may feel that you lack a strategy when you upset someone, miss a deadline or give up on a goal. Any one of these might have left you feeling deflated and frustrated. Yet, believe it or not, you did have strategies for handling these events as well – they just didn't work. What can you apply from the previous list of 'success stories' to those events where you wish to achieve a different outcome?

To change your strategies you need to understand your previous strategies. Get into the best mental and emotional state. Visualize yourself succeeding and feel how happy you are as a result. Talk to yourself in a positive and encouraging inner voice. Take action; if you do not achieve your desired results – learn from the outcome. Repeat the cycle until you achieve your desire.

A strategy for success does not focus on the idea of failing or losing. There are only results that are measured against the desired outcome. If you achieve your desire, you achieve the result you wish.

SENSORY INPUT

Some NLP approaches involve understanding your response to sensory input, and the responses of others around you with whom you wish to communicate successfully. This approach holds that because we often speak a different 'language', we frequently don't really understand each other and the resulting miscommunication leads to misunderstanding and diminishes the ability to achieve desired outcomes from conversations. Analyse your own language to find which technique you use most and whether it works for you.

Auditory
You take in information most readily from sound and respond well to audio tapes and soundtracks. You litter your language with expressions such as 'Sounds good to me', 'I hear what you're saying' and 'When I understood the concept it's like a bang went off in my head'.

Visual
You are most likely to respond to pictographic and other visual stimuli. Your language tends to contain expressions such as 'I see what you mean', 'I couldn't see the wood for the trees' and 'A light went on in my head'.

Kinetic
You are more of a touchy-feely person and enjoy experiencing things by participating physically. Your language contains many expressions such as 'I feel that the thing to do is...', 'I've got a gut feeling and I sense that what you are saying is...'

Analytical

As the name implies, you tend to weigh things up and analyse everything. You might say things like 'If I understand what you are saying…' 'On balance I think…' and 'In the final analysis…'

TIME LINE THERAPY

The principle of this NLP approach is to understand how you view your experiences in relation to your 'time line' and then re-aligning them to work more effectively for you rather than against you. Your time line is an imagined line, that mirrors your progress in a given area such as your career. The line might best be visualized as moving in front, behind, or to the side of you. You might find that your career can radiate in various directions, it can spiral up above your head, it could involve large or small steps up or down, it can be scattered all over the place or even dig into you – it can be anything you imagine it to be.

An example of how we might make this image work is when we use an expression such as 'I've put the situation behind me'. If you are fretting about say, a broken relationship, and you are carrying the baggage of your feelings into your next relationship, it is obvious that it will effect you. By putting such feelings behind you, you will be able to free up emotions for a new relationship and progress unhindered. Applying the same principle to other areas of life is highly effective. When frustrated by lack of progress in your career, for instance, you may find that the image of your time-line shows that you have put your career somewhere to the side of you which is compelling you to shuffle sideways in your career, crab-like, instead of striding forwards.

■ For more information contact the Association for Neuro-Linguistic Programming (ANLP). Call 0870 870 4970 and they will send you an booklet or look up www.anlp.org

■ You will find a stack of books about NLP in your bookshop. The most useful I have found are those written by Anthony Robbins (the motivation guru) such as *Unlimited Power* and *Unleash the Giant Within*.

NUTRITION

The basics of improving the nutritional content of your diet has already been covered in Healthy Eating (see page 98), and more tips are summed up in Let's Do Lunch (see page 50) and Disordered Eating (see page 88). You will also see, throughout the book, a number of references to how nutritional supplements and herbal preparations can help with various conditions. More detailed information – about how to implement these changes in your diet and on using nutritional supplements and herbal preparations – is listed here.

MAKING EASY CHANGES

■ Concentrate on adding in healthy habits to your life. Don't sweat, right now, over what you need to be giving up and avoiding. Instead enjoy the satisfaction of making small, but important, positive changes to your diet.

■ Never allow yourself to feel deprived. If and when you do decide to wean yourself off particular foods (junk food, fatty dishes, foods that do not agree with you), take the time to work out what you really enjoy eating, and which foods are most satisfying. If you want to indulge occasionally, let yourself.

■ Get organized. When you come back from work and all you have in the fridge is a bit of mouldy cheese and half a jar of jam, then it is no surprise that the next move is to the phone to call the take-away. Stock up on some basics for your food cupboard:

  – tins of tuna, salmon, anchovies and sardines
  – jars of sun dried tomatoes, olives and gherkins
  – varieties of delicious pastas, cous cous, quinoa, rice and buckwheat grains (kasha)
  – cans of tomatoes and peas
  – pesto sauce, tapenade dips
  – tortilla wraps
  – packets of unsalted nuts and seeds (pine nuts, walnuts, etc).

■ Shop twice a week for fresh fruits and vegetables. Make sure at least one-third of your fridge is fresh produce.

■ Cook at weekends in triple quantities and make use of your freezer. Pack serving size portions you can take out in the morning before your go to work.

■ Make a plan each week. Take a few minutes to see what is missing from your larder. Plan a main meal or two and work out how it can do for left-overs in the next couple of days (say roast chicken, followed by chicken cold cuts with salad, followed by chicken soup). You will find that this approach also saves money.

■ Experiment once a week, or once every second week, with one new recipe or one new ingredient you have not tried before. This way you can broaden your repertoire.

■ If you think you can benefit from a more in-depth approach to managing nutritional changes you could find it helpful to consult a nutritionist. For registers see Useful Resources (page 235).

NUTRITIONAL SUPPLEMENTS

There are many brands of nutritional supplements on the shelves. The consumer is bombarded with so many varieties of multi-vitamins and minerals, or of single nutrients, that a trip to the health food shop can feel overwhelming. In addition to this there are many 'ancillary' nutritional aids available. It is difficult to tell, just by looking at a label, if the contents of the bottle are going to be any good or not. If you are a nutritionist, you can get some basic information from the label such as what form of a particular nutrient is in the formula, and what the balance of quantities is between various nutrients and if there are any complementary (synergistic) compounds. But even for the trained nutritionist there is little to tell you about the quality of the ingredients and how absorbable the ingredients are. And in some cases the contents simply do not match what is put on the label and this can only be uncovered by a testing laboratory.

For all these reasons, I list below supplement companies in whose products I have confidence. These are the ones I have used effectively with my clients, or which I know have stood up to testing procedures. This does not mean that there are not other excellent products which I have not included in this list, and omission does not imply that other products are necessarily not of a suitable quality. By and large, it has to be said, you get what you pay for in nutritional supplements and those that are of a good quality (in other words absorbable) will usually be a little more expensive).

If you prefer to not swallow capsules or pills you can get many supplements in liquid or powder form, though you may need to do a little detective work with different companies. Alternatively you can get a pill crusher from Health Plus (see below).

Be aware that, if you are planning a pregnancy, are pregnant or breast-feeding, you must only take specially formulated ante-natal products. This is to protect you from taking too high a dose of some nutrients, such as vitamin A, or consuming ingredients unsuitable for pregnancy such as many herbs. If you are on medication, you need to consult a qualified nutritionist or doctor to find out if the medicine is known to clash with your supplements, or vice versa.

BIOCARE 0121 433 3727 or www.biocare.co.uk
An excellent range of products from an innovative company, available via mail order direct from the company and from some selected good quality health food shops.

BIOFORCE 01294 277 344 www.bioforce.co.uk
Herbal tinctures and supplements made from freshly prepared organic ingredients.

BLACKMORES 020 8842 3956 www.blackmores.com.au
A full range of herbal supplements.

GNC (General Nutrition Company) 0845 601 3248 or www.gnc.co.uk
A number of stores around the country supplying a full range of products.

HEALTH AND DIET COMPANY 0845 076 5358
A wide range of products at a number of stores throughout the country. FSC supplements are stocked by them and by other companies.

HEALTH PLUS 01323 737 374 www.healthplus.co.uk
A range of useful supplements packaged for particular conditions in one-a-day pouches.

HIGHER NATURE Order line 01435 882 880 www.highernature.co.uk
Nutrition line 01435 882 964 for advice.
A wide range of products including some helpful products brought in from overseas and not generally seen in other ranges. Available by mail order.

LICHTWER PHARMA Info line 01803 528 668 www.lichtwer.co.uk
Herbal preparations under the Lichtwer and Kira brands formulated to give standard doses of active compounds as used in many clinical trials.

NAPIERS HERBALISTS 0131 343 6683
A full range of herbals including some very good condition specific formulations. Available by mail order. They also have a herbal advice line staffed by 4-year qualified herbalists on 0906 802 0117 (this is a chargeable call line).

NATURE'S STORE 01782 794 300 www.naturesstore.co.uk
Suppliers of a wide range of natural products and supplements. Nature's Store Ltd is the UK's largest independent wholesaler and distributor of wholefoods and natural products.

NUTRI CENTRE 020 7436 0422 or www.nutricentre.com
A drop-in centre with an extensive range of high quality products and books, as well as a mail order service.

REVITAL 0800 252 875 or www.revital.com
A comprehensive selection of supplements, books and natural healthcare products.

SOLGAR 01442 890 355 or www.solgar.com
An excellent range of supplements from a reliable company and available widely through independent health food shops.

HERBAL PREPARATIONS

Herbal preparations complement the benefits of a nutritional programme. In particular we use many culinary herbs which have known soothing, stimulating or healing qualities, and which also add delicious variety to meals and make satisfying drinks.

However, it must also be recognized that herbs have the potential to be powerful medicines, and indeed a vast number of modern pharmaceutical medicines are drawn from this natural pharmacopoeia. Because they are 'natural' does not necessarily mean that they are benign. But they can be highly effective if used properly. These are some pointers to watch out for when taking herbs.

■ There are a limited number of herbs which are safe to take during pregnancy and breast-feeding (see my book *Eating for a Perfect Pregnancy* (Simon & Schuster), but apart from these all herbal preparations need to be avoided at this time.

■ If you experience any adverse effects from taking a herbal preparation, stop immediately.

■ Herbal preparations will usually take a bit of time for you to notice an effect. Some are effective within an hour or so, but more commonly you need to take a herbal preparation for a month or two to notice a radical change in symptoms. They usually have a more subtle effect than medications as they have a full spectrum of complementary compounds found within the plant. Even extracts that have a certain amount of the 'active compound' will still have other beneficial synergistic compounds in it.

■ Combinations of herbs are often more effective than single herbs and mean that you can take lesser amounts. For this reason some products are formulated with several synergistic herbs, and herbalists might recommend herbs which support each other.

- Herbs have a medicinal effect and so it is not surprising that there are known interactions with medicines. For example Ginkgo biloba has blood thinning effects and should be used cautiously if on blood thinning medication such as Warfarin (the same is true of vitamin E, garlic capsules and fish oil capsules). Sedative herbs such as valerian and kava kava (see warning below) should be avoided with other sleep medications. St John's wort needs to be avoided if you are taking prescribed antidepressants. It also speeds up the clearance of drugs through the liver and so can reduce the effectiveness of some medication such as migraine medication, the contraceptive pill, asthma, blood thinning (heart) and AIDS medications. It is impossible to give all possible interactions here, so the best advice is, if you are on any medication to check with a medical herbalist.

- Follow dosage guidelines given and do not fall into the trap of thinking that 'if a little is good, then more is better'.

WARNING

At the time of going to press, there has been a voluntary, temporary withdrawal of the herbal supplement Kava kava by manufacturers pending investigations into the reported ill effects in a small number of people. This may be related to high doses or excess length of use. Consult a doctor or medical herbalist before taking.

USEFUL RESOURCES

For information about Suzannah Olivier and her books visit her website www.healthandnutrition.co.uk

The following list gives ideas of where to look further for help, however no responsibility can be taken for any services offered. For other resources see the relevant sections.

COUNSELLING THERAPIES AND MENTAL HEALTH

ASSOCIATION OF CHILD PSYCHOTHERAPISTS
020 8458 1609

BRITISH ASSOCIATION FOR COUNSELLING (BAC)
01788 550 899 or www.bac.co.uk

ASSOCIATION FOR NEURO-LINGUISTIC PROGRAMMING
0870 870 4970 or www.anlp.org

BRITISH ASSOCIATION OF PSYCHOTHERAPISTS
020 8452 9823 or www.bcp.org.uk

BRITISH ASSOCIATION FOR SEXUAL AND MARITAL THERAPY
PO Box 63, Sheffield S10 3TS

BRITISH CONFEDERATION OF PSYCHOTHERAPISTS
020 8830 5173

BRITISH ASSOCIATION FOR BEHAVIOURAL AND COGNITIVE PSYCHOTHERAPIES
01254 875 277 or www.babcp.org.uk

CENTRE FOR STRESS MANAGEMENT
www.managingstress.com

THE COMPASSIONATE FRIEND
For people affected by bereavement 0117 953 9639 or www.tcf.org.uk

DEPRESSION ALLIANCE
www.depressionalliance.org

DIRECTORY OF INTERNET MENTAL HEALTH RESOURCES
www.mentalhealth.com

FAMILIES ANONYMOUS
For families affected by drugs 020 7498 4680 or www.famanon.org.uk

INSTITUTE FOR FAMILY THERAPY
020 7935 1651

INTERNATIONAL STRESS MANAGEMENT ASSOCIATION
07000 780 430 or www.isma.org.uk

MIND
www.mind.org.uk Write enclosing an A4 SAE for information leaflets about mental health to Mind Publications, Granta House, 15-19 Broadway, London E15 4BQ

NATIONAL FAMILY MEDIATION
020 7383 5993 or www.nfm.u-net.com

NATIONAL REGISTER OF HYPNOTHERAPISTS AND PSYCHOTHERAPISTS
01282 716 839 or www.nrhp.co.uk

PSYCHOTHYNSESIS TRUST
020 7403 7814 or www.essential-life.org

RELATE
01788 573 241 or www.relate.org.uk

ROYAL COLLEGE OF PSYCHIATRISTS
020 7235 2351 or www.rcpsych.ac.uk

UK COUNCIL OF PSYCHOTHERAPY
020 7436 3002 or www.psychotherapy.org.uk

NUTRITIONAL AND HERBAL THERAPIES

BRITISH ASSOCIATION OF NUTRITIONAL THERAPISTS (BANT)
0870 606 1284 or www.bant.org.uk

FOOD AND MOOD PROJECT
Founded with a grant from MIND www.foodandmood.org

GENERAL COUNCIL AND REGISTER OF CONSULTANT HERBALISTS
01792 655 886 or www.aromacaring.co.uk/choosing_a_therapist.htm

GENERAL COUNCIL AND REGISTER OF NATUROPATHS
A combined approach using diet, herbs, water therapy and sometimes osteopathy, fasting and supplements to treat the root cause of illness and restore health.
01458 840 072 or www.naturopathy.org.uk

INSTITUTE FOR OPTIMUM NUTRITION
London, 020 8877 9993 or www.ion.ac.uk

NATIONAL INSTITUTE OF MEDICAL HERBALISTS
01392 426 022 or www.btinternet.com/-nimh/

REGISTER OF CHINESE HERBAL MEDICINE
07000 790 332 or www.rchm.co.uk

RELAXATION AND OTHER THERAPIES

AUTOGENIC THERAPY (BAFATT)
A self-help method which brings about profound relaxation and relief from the negative effects of stress. 020 7837 8833 c/o Royal London Homeopathic Hospital, NHS Trust, Great Ormond Street, London WC1N 3HR
Send an SAE for a list of therapists.

BRITISH AUTOGENIC SOCIETY
www.autogenic–therapy.org.uk

BRITISH SOCIETY FOR AUTOGENIC TRAINING
www.interconnections.co.uk

BRITISH WHEEL OF YOGA
01529 306 851 or www.bwy.org.uk

PILATES FOUNDATION
020 8281 5087 or www.pilatesfoundation.com

SCHOOL OF MEDITATION
020 7603 6116 or www.schoolormeditation.org

SOCIETY OF TEACHERS OF ALEXANDER TECHNIQUE
020 7284 3338 or www.stat.org.uk

T'AI CHI (QIGONG)
0161 929 4485 or www.qimagazine.com NATIONAL T'AI CHI CHUAN ASSOCIATION 020 8556 6393 or www.taichifinder.co.uk

TRANSCENDENTAL MEDITATION
020 7486 0141 or www.t-m.org.uk

OTHER USEFUL APPROACHES

AROMATHERAPY ORGANISATIONS COUNCIL
020 8251 7912 or www.oac.uk.net

ASSOCIATION FOR SYSTEMATIC KINESIOLOGY
A system of obtaining bio-feedback by testing and measuring the strength of muscle responses to stimuli, which can include mental, nutritional or physical stressors. 020 8399 3215 or www.kinesiology.co.uk

ACUPUNCTURE AND OSTEOPATHIC ASSOCIATION
020 7834 1012

ASSOCIATION OF REFLEXOLOGISTS
0070 567 3320 or www.aor.org.uk

AUSTRALIAN BUSH FLOWER REMEDIES ANCIENT ROOTS
020 8421 8777 or www.ancient-roots.com

BACH FLOWER REMEDIES
The Bach Centre 01491 834 678 or www.bachcentre.com

BRITISH ACUPUNCTURE COUNCIL
020 8735 0400 or www.acupuncture.org.uk

BRITISH ASSOCIATION FOR APPLIED CHIROPRACTIC
01869 277 111

BRITISH CHIROPRACTIC ASSOCIATION
0118 950 5950 or www.chiropractic-uk.co.uk

BRITISH HOMEOPATHIC ASSOCIATION
020 7566 7800 or www.trusthomeopathy.org

BRITISH MASSAGE THERAPY COUNCIL
www.bmtc.co.uk

COMPLEMENTARY MEDICAL ASSOCIATION
020 8305 9571 www.the-cma.org.uk

GENERAL OSTEOPATHIC COUNCIL
020 7357 6655 or www.osteopathy.org.uk

HEALTH PRACTITIONERS' ASSOCIATION
187a Worlds End Lane, Chelsfield Park, Orpington, Kent BR6 6AU Write enclosing an SAE for information about methods of stress control.

INSTITUTE FOR COMPLEMENTARY MEDICINE
020 7237 5165 or www.icm.co.uk

KINESIOLOGY FEDERATION
08700 113 545 or www.kinesiologyfederation.org

NORDOFF-ROBBINS MUSIC THERAPY CENTRE
020 7267 4496 or www.nordoff-robbins.org.uk

SHIATSU SOCIETY
01788 555 051 or www.shiatsu.org

PUBLICATIONS I HAVE FOUND INSPIRING

FEEL THE FEAR AND DO IT ANYWAY
Susan Jeffers (Rider) 1997

GIANT STEPS
Anthony Robbins (Simon & Schuster) 1994

LIFE WAS NEVER MEANT TO BE A STRUGGLE
Stuart Wilder (Hay House) 1989

MOOD AND FOOD HANDBOOK
Amanda Geary (Harper Collins) 2001

OPTIMUM NUTRITION COOKBOOK
Patrick Holford and Judith Ridgeway (Piatkus) 2000

POSITIVE HEALTH MAGAZINE
A monthly magazine of complementary health solutions, call 0117 983 8851, and well worth visiting their website www.positivehealth.com

WHO MOVED MY CHEESE?
Spencer Johnson (Vermilion) 1999

WHY ZEBRAS DON'T GET ULCERS
Robert Sapolsky (W. H. Freeman) 1998

ALPHABETICAL LIST OF ENTRIES